SOPHIA GOODRIDGE
Courtesy, Aretta H.S. Hansen
Salt Lake City

MARGARET FRINK
Courtesy, California State Library

THE FAMILY OF SARAH DAVIS
Left to right: Sarah, Cleora Adelaide, Elbridge Allen,
and Zeno Philosopher, around 1856.
Courtesy, Nevada County Historical Society

Covered Wagon Women

Diaries & Letters from the
Western Trails
1850

Volume 2

edited & compiled by
KENNETH L. HOLMES

Introduction to the Bison Books Edition
by Lillian Schlissel

University of Nebraska Press
Lincoln and London

♾ The paper in this book meets the minimum requirements of American National Standard for Information Sciences—Permanence of Paper for Printed Library Materials, ANSI Z39.48-1984.

First Bison Books printing: 1996

Library of Congress Cataloging-in-Publication Data
The Library of Congress has cataloged Vol. I as:
Covered wagon women: diaries & letters from the western trails, 1840–1849 / edited and compiled by Kenneth L. Holmes; introduction to the Bison Books edition by Anne M. Butler.
p.   cm.
Originally published: Glendale, Calif.: A. H. Clark Co., 1983.
"Reprinted from volume one . . . of the original eleven-volume edition"— T.p. verso.
"Volume I."
Includes index.
ISBN 0-8032-7277-4 (pa: alk. paper)
1. Women pioneers—West (U.S.)—Biography.   2. West (U.S.)—History.
3. West (U.S.)—Biography.   4. Overland journeys to the Pacific.
5. Frontier and pioneer life—West (U.S.)   I. Holmes, Kenneth L.
F591.C79   1996
978—dc20
95-21200   CIP

Volume 2 introduction by Lillian Schlissel.
ISBN 0-8032-7274-X (pa: alk. paper)

Reprinted from volume two (1983) of the original eleven-volume edition titled *Covered Wagon Women: Diaries and Letters from the Western Trails, 1840–1890*, published by The Arthur H. Clark Company, Glendale, California. The pagination has not been changed and no material has been omitted in this Bison Books edition.

Introduction to the Bison Books Edition
Lillian Schlissel

When Ken Holmes began collecting the journals and diaries of overland women, there were few such writings in print. A quarter of a million men and women moved west between 1845 and 1860 knowing they were part of a historic adventure, and there was an outpouring of narratives, but women's observations were not considered significant to the historical process and their writings were largely overlooked.

A few historians, though, recognized gems of historical evidence when they found them, and Ken Holmes was one. A diary like Margaret Frink's brought the excitement of a great discovery. This diary, he wrote, is "one of the real rarities of historical publication." Holmes loved this project and shared his unabashed pride, telling his readers the thrill he felt when he "held the actual book in [his] hands."

And Frink's 1850 diary is certainly one of the best accounts we have of the westward journey. A clear-eyed woman, Frink wrote that she "hired a seamstress to make up a fully supply of clothing," but though she might have been well-suited, she and her husband "knew nothing of frontier life." She traveled with an "india rubber mattress that could be filled with air or water" and a feather bed and pillows. She was well provided with "plenty of hams and bacon, . . . apples, peaches, . . . rice, coffee, tea, beans, flour, corn-meal, crackers, sea-biscuit, butter, and lard" (61), and her husband shipped enough lumber for a house by flatboat down the Wabash and Ohio rivers, down the Mississippi to New Orleans, round Cape Horn and up the coast of South America and found it waiting for them in Sacramento.

During the peak years of 1850–53, the overland journey was a rare spectacle. Margaret Frink wrote, "I had never seen so many human beings in all my life before. . . . in all manner of vehicles and conveyances, on horseback and on foot, all eagerly driving and hurrying forward, I thought, in my excitement, that if one-tenth of these teams and people got ahead of us, there would be nothing left for us in California worth picking up" (85–86). Like a demonic driver on a freeway, "some careless person . . . drove his team up too close behind, and the pole of his wagon ran into [our] stove, smashing and ruining it" (97).

That crowded road could also turn treacherous—"a safe ford today might be a dangerous one tomorrow," Frink wrote. "Our horses could sometimes be in water no more than a foot deep; then, in a moment, they would go down up to their collars" as quicksand sucked down both drivers and oxen (91–92). Sometimes nature itself seemed in raw opposition to the travellers: "I stood in the sleet and held four horses for two hours, till I thought my feet were frozen" (67).

Indians followed the progression of wagons, sometimes from the safety of distance, sometimes at close hand. Frink was careful to name the tribes whose lands she crossed—the Cheyennes, Blackfeet, Snakes, Arapohoes, Oglallah Sioux, Pawnees, and Crows. In June, her wagon party passed a large encampment of Sioux. They "were quite friendly. The squaws were much pleased to see the 'white squaw' in our party, as they called me. I had brought a supply of needles and thread, some of which I gave them. We also had some small mirrors in gilt frames, . . . with which we could buy fish and fresh buffalo, deer, and antelope meat" (94). Social encounters with Indians are often described in women's diaries. Anna Morris, wife of Major Gouverneur Morris, a lady who traveled with her maid, noted that she too visited an Indian "house" in Kansas. The mistress of the tent "spoke french [and] . . . was making mockasins" (23). A young squaw "took a great fancy to my diamond ring" (30). Sarah Davis, a young wife traveling with an infant, told that "the Indians swarmed a round" her wagon train and that "their was one Indian come to us for his diner" (188). All along the trail, overlanders and Indians negotiated a peaceful commerce. Sophia Goodridge, daughter of a large Mormon family, noted that "Aunt Hattie sent a blanket shawl" for the special purpose of its being bartered with the Indians. En route, travelers watched attentively while 300 Shoshone warriors with about 1,000 horses were preparing to war with the Cheyennes (230).

These casual observations of Margaret Frink, Anna Morris, Sophia Goodridge, Sarah Davis, and dozens of others provide extraordinary evidence of the ways in which the tribes along the overland route participated in the lives of the travelers. Dozens of diarists note that Indians were usually paid fifty cents a wagon for assisting at river crossings and Indians routinely traded salmon and buffalo with travelers whose supplies were dwindling. Sometimes understanding broke down; it seems clear that tribes expected tribute from people moving through their lands—women wrote of Indians who came "begging." Overlanders, for their part, had not the least sense that the land "belonged" to anyone. But it is also clear that women were not afraid and that they bartered with Indians who moved freely among the wagon trains. The daily exchanges were part of the day's routine, and women wrote to relatives back home to include extra shirts and coffee and trinkets for trade when they prepared for the journey. The women's diaries show that, for better or worse, Indians and overlanders came together out of need and out of curiosity, and that they wove an imperfect understanding each of the other.

Lucena Parsons, on her honeymoon, was more horrified by tales of Mormons than she was of Indians. The Mormons, she wrote, were "an unprincipled sect. . . . They live like the brute creation more than like white folks. . . . These demons marry some girls at 10 years of age" (273). In Mormon homes women "have not as much liberty as common slaves in the South" (274). Indians, by comparison, seemed quite civilized: "[A]n Indian chief visited my tent to day. I gave him some dinner & he gave me a knife" (240).

If anything, the tribes were at risk from the overlanders who brought diseases for which Indians held no immunity. Small pox, whooping cough, measles, and cholera wiped out whole tribes along the way. As cholera spread and springs were contaminated, Lucena Parsons noted that "many [overlanders] have lost nearly all their teams by letting them drink the water" (261).

At the South Pass of the Rockies, travelers often stopped for a "grand frolic" with "music from a violin with tin-pan accompaniment." Margaret Frink wrote that someone planted an American flag and it seemed a good omen. By midsummer, however, the Blue Mountains made travel agonizing. The terrain was so rugged that the wagons were lowered down ravines with ropes. Some guidebooks showed that the Great Salt Lake emptied into the Pacific Ocean though travelers were still a thousand miles from California. Tempers flared as the danger of being caught by an early snow made late summer travel risky. Arguments broke out over detours and "cut-offs," and orderly wagon parties splintered and went their separate ways.

Sometimes a road held signs no one could read. Margaret Frink recounted that a group of packers crossed the path of her wagon party. They were traveling east as fast as they could go, not stopping to talk, shouting words over their shoulders as they fled something unspeakable behind them.

And there were unspeakable things on the road. Cholera was an apocalyptic nightmare between 1851 and 1853. Women, who were caretakers of the sick and the dying, meticulously recorded the toll of the disease. Lucena Parsons wrote that they passed graves from morn until night: "Passt 8 graves to day. . . . Passt 13 graves. . . . Passt 18 graves to day. . . .

We have passt some 12 graves & I am told there is a burying ground near here of 300 graves." A man in the next wagon buried his wife and quickly baptized his three children, hoping to ward off the disease. The same dismal records fill the pages of the diary kept by Sarah Davis. "I saw twelve graves to day it semed like a grave yard almost to me. . . . we have past six graves to day we past twe[l]ve more and one grave that they had not put the body in yet. . . . I saw thirten graves to day" (177–78). Travelers who had only laudanum and kitchen remedies such as tabasco to ward off disease sat behind their oxen, covering ten or fifteen miles a day, desperate to outrace cholera as it spread all around them. People who went west dreaming of wealth and prosperity sometimes met death on a lonely landscape.

Reading the diaries is not always a straightforward task, for nineteenth-century women concealed almost as much as they revealed. When Margaret Frink wrote that "there was no other woman" in her wagon party, one needs to hear the anxiety, one needs to recognize that a woman alone in a company of men faced difficulties in matters of privacy and personal hygiene. The simplest regimen of bodily functions entailed tactical provisions, and the bare prairie landscape offered little to accommodate a woman's desire for modesty or shelter.

Information about personal matters is never offered and never volunteered. I wondered for years why overland women persisted in wearing the long, full skirts and petticoats that were heavy with mud and stiff with dust long before the journey ended. In a classroom a student whose grandparents made the journey raised her hand to ask, as if I were a slow-learning child: hadn't I guessed? Two women together could hold out their skirts to raise a curtain for a third. It was a simple stratagem. But a woman alone had to find some other way to outwit her circumstances.

Relations between husbands and wives may have been infrequent, since pregnancy made a woman a less useful working member of the family. When sex did join couples, it was probably far from the wagons, which groaned at every movement. Childbirth made every woman a midwife, and illness made every woman a nurse.

Diaries keep their "deep" meaning hidden, and even statistical data can be misleading. Census records, for example, note only living children and give no idea of failed pregnancies, of the number of infants buried under headstones marked "S. B." for stillborn, or of those who died in infancy. Ken Holmes once sent me a photograph of a ring and a lock of hair he found between the pages of an 1851 diary kept by Mary

Bowers. "Baby dreadful sick all night, had to carry him all night." The infant died two days later. Migration caught women during their childbearing years, and although they rarely wrote about it, labor in a wagon wet with rain, or birth by the side of a road, was precarious. A woman who died in childbirth left an infant likely to die slowly if no other nursing mother could be found, and burial on the trail meant a grave with no marker. The historian who would read women's diaries must "hear" what is not written, and understand what is spoken only by allusion and indirection.

Given the trials of the early years of travel, it is surprising so many emigrants made it through. Margaret Frink and her husband reached Sacramento, rented a house and put up a sign that announced Frink's Hotel, but they abandoned the hotel when cholera emptied the mining camps. The following season, they found the lumber they shipped around Cape Horn waiting for them and they built a new house, bought twelve cows, and operated a dairy. She wrote, "We never had occasion to regret the prolonged hardships of the toilsome journey" (167).

Although there were few women panning for gold in the mining camps, Lucena Parsons was a young woman with a bold heart—"I went out this morning, with my men folks & the rest" (290). And then she went out again. "We again went to the canion to find that bewitching ore that is called gold" (291). Lucena and her husband made sixteen dollars in gold dust, and bought themselves two cows.

Mary Colby was brimming with optimism and assurance. "I think with good health and good economy we shall get along verry well. . . . I have got two of the prettiest children in the whole family. . . . I have got a first rate husband. . . . we have about 140 acres of our land under fence. . . . give my love to all your children and pleas to accept a good share your selfe" (50–53).

The young nation could hardly hope to plant the western territories with better citizens.

Twenty years ago I was writing *Women's Diaries of the Westward Journey* about the same time Ken Holmes was working on *Covered Wagon Women*. It seemed to most of us that the ideology we called the "Cult of Domesticity" defined the attitudes of the women whose histories we were writing. The idea of "True Womanhood" filled the writings of all classes of women, although it sometimes seemed stubbornly wrongheaded to adapt the prescriptions of domestic ideology to life on the frontier. Sophia Goodridge's diary is filled with details of the ways in which overland women imposed a domestic routine on that long, dirty, dusty road. "Did our washing. Did our ironing and picked some goosberries." They rolled out pie dough on buckboard seats, collected buffalo chips, killed rattlesnakes, and made sentimental notes about the "beautiful day."

The Cult of True Womanhood was a powerful impulse in concealing parts of a woman's life. A true lady did not speak of fatigue or the burdens of caring for infants and children. Sarah Davis, who traveled with a year-old infant, only hinted at her relief at the journey's end. "I feel that I [will] never want anything more for now I have a chair and a table and a roof over my head" (206).

As I reread the diaries today, it seems we were perhaps too eager to see that the idea of "separate spheres" or the "cult of domesticity" answered for all the evidence before us. The diaries reveal countless occasions when separate spheres were breached in everyday life. Men in mining camps cooked and washed for themselves and Lucena Parsons knew all about panning for gold: "They take a pan nearly full of sand & stones & shake it & in the meantime pore off the water & the stones till they get it all pored off but the gold; this sinks below. I washed a little & got a little gold. . . . Came home tired to night. . . . It is very hard work to dig & wash sand" (290–91).

Women shared the work of the trail and of the first settlements. They drove the teams of oxen, and cared for the livestock. Moreover, they were surrogates during the extended period when their men left to look for new land or to work in the towns for the winter, or to sell crops. Linda Peavey and Ursula Smith in their book *The Gold Rush Widows of Little Falls* (1990) document the lives of the women in Minnesota who stayed behind while their husbands went off to the Gold Rush. When James Fergus was absent for periods that stretched into years, his wife Pamela raised their four children, managed the small farm, took over the family's failing business, hired and fired men to help her, sold crops, and bought supplies. Men did not expect to sacrifice their stake in the land when they went off to explore new opportunities, and communities recognized women's authority when the men were gone.

Listen to the voices of the women in this volume, to the timbre and the assertiveness of their judgments. Sharp-eyed Sarah Davis noted that "we have past some of the handsomest pine trees I ever saw in my life" and driven through "some pleasant valeys of grass and a handsome creeke runing through the valey plenty of grass to for the catle all a rounde" (202). Margaret Frink was literate, capable, and in her judgments of the journey, she yielded to no man. Domestic ideology was a driving force but it was also only part of the life of women on the frontier, who took up the chores and the authority of their men when need demanded, and then relinquished that authority when, in the cycles of frontier life, their men came home.

Collecting and publishing the women's diaries began as a modest impulse; the idea was simply to add sources that had been lacking. Ken Holmes intended the volumes of *Covered Wagon Women* to document the story "of ordinary people embarked on an extraordinary experience." But the diaries changed the way in which Western history was written. The history of the West had been framed as national myth, the saga of men engaged in nothing less than the conquest of nature; heroes and outlaws became legends. But women did not write of "conquering the wilderness." They wrote about Indians who helped them cross rivers that hid quicksand, they wrote about cholera and death on the open road. Though the women were stalwart and stoical, they had a profound sense of the fragility of life and of the great blessings of survival.

In their simple and unassuming details, women's diaries were revolutionary because they offered a vision different from the one that had prevailed for so long, and they reminded historians of Henry Adams's cautionary word in *The Education*: "Where [one historian] saw sequence, other men saw something quite different, and no one saw the same unit of measure." Historians began to write about Native Americans, and African Americans, Asian Americans, Hispanics and Chicanos, and, of course, Henry Adams was right—"no one saw the same unit of measure." And western history has again been rewritten as the ecological and environmental history of the land. Stories of the Old West have been transformed; the "New" West has become a complex heritage.

Larry McMurtry wrote that "On the rim of the West—and perhaps, in America, only there—one can still know for a moment the frontier emotion, the loneliness and the excitement and the sense of an openness so vast that it still challenges—in Gatsbian phrase—our capacity for wonder" (*In A Narrow Grave*, 108). But we have learned over time, and first from the diaries of women, that our "capacity for wonder" is a prism compounded of the vision of many different eyes, the lives of many different people, the natural history of different sections of this vast land.

Contents

Illustrations

Introduction to Volume II

In the first volume of *Covered Wagon Women: Diaries and Letters from the Western Trails, 1840-1890,* the records of the women overlanders of the 1840s were published. In this, the second volume, the diaries and letters of the female travelers of 1850 will be presented and discussed.

The key word for the 1850 season was "cholera." This dread disease had made its appearance in 1849, and plagued the whole of the United States through 1854, with some let-up in 1851. It then disappeared, only to return after the Civil War. The disease reached the North American continent through three coastal areas: the eastern seaboard, especially New York; the Mississippi-Missouri basin through the Port of New Orleans; and California, where it reached San Francisco via the Pacific in October, 1850. The Pacific Northwest was not affected.[1]

All of the women's diaries in our selection for 1850 mention the disease. Sophia Goodridge, a Mormon, tells how cholera killed five of their wagon train (July 7 entry). Two of our 1850 diarists were "grave counters": Sophia Davis and Lucena Parsons, both headed for California. Davis counted half-heartedly, noting 47 graves between June 13 and 24. Parsons noted over

---

[1] Georgia Willis Read, "Diseases, Drugs, and Doctors on the Oregon-California Trail in the Gold-Rush Years," *Missouri Hist. Rev.,* XXXVIII (1944), 260-76; Charles E. Rosenberg, *The Cholera Years* (Chicago, 1962); John E. Baur, "The Health Factor in the Gold Rush Era," John W. Caughey, ed., *Rushing for Gold* (Berkeley, 1949), pp. 97-108; O. Larsell, *The Doctor in Oregon* (Portland, 1947), "Cholera," pp. 587-90.

300 grave markers between the Missouri Valley and Salt Lake City and told of some seventeen deaths in her own company. One man recorded 963 graves, according to George R. Stewart.[2]

How many overlanders were there in 1850? John D. Unruh, Jr., an authority on this subject, estimates 6,000 for Oregon, 2,500 for Utah, and 44,000 for California, a total of 52,500 travelers, more than the total of all who had moved across the Plains during the 1840s.[3]

The lure of gold in California, added to the already magnetic draw of farmland there and in Oregon, now combined with the planned, promoted and well-organized immigration of Latter-day Saints (Mormons) to Utah, and the result was one of the greatest human pilgrimages of all time. Mary M. Colby, one of the correspondents in this volume, described the scene while in St. Joseph on May 6, 1850:

> I could not begin to tell you how many their [are] in St. Joseph that are going to Oregon and California but thousands of them it is a sight to se the tents and wagons on the banks of the river and through the country they are as thick as camp meeting tents 20 or 30 miles and some say for 50 miles their is 30 or 40 familys in the mess that we intend to get in with.

We have decided to arrange the journals and letters in chronological order, from the date of departure at the Missouri River. This was the starting point in the minds of the immigrants. Lodisa Frizzell, a diarist writing on May 9, 1852, voiced this sentiment: "This is considered the starting point from this river time is reconed, & it matters not how far you

2 *The California Trail,* (New York, 1962), p. 301.
3 *The Plains Across* (Urbana, Ill., 1979), p. 120.

have come, this is the point to which they all refer, for the question is never, when did you leave home? but, when did you leave the Mississouri [sic] river?" [4] The dates that our women of 1850 crossed the Missouri are as follows: Anna Maria Morris, late April; Mary Colby, May 12; Margaret Frink, May 14; Sarah Davis, May 24; Sophia Goodridge, June 7; Lucena Parsons, June 7.

For those readers who have not read our introduction to the series in volume one, a reiteration of a few salient points which guide our editorial hand are in order. It is our purpose to let the diarists and correspondents tell their own story in their own words, with as little scholarly trimming as possible. The intent has been to transcribe each word or phrase as accurately as possible, leaving as written whatever misspellings or grammatical errors are found. The only gestures we have made for the sake of the reader have been as follows:

1. We have added space where phrases or sentences ended and no punctuation was to be found in the original.

2. We have put the daily journals into diary format even though the original may have been written continuously line by line because of the original writer's shortage of paper.

Many geographic references are mentioned over and over again in the various accounts. The final volume in the series will include a gazetteer, in addition to the index and bibliography, to aid the reader.

---

[4] Lodisa Frizzell, "Across the Plains to California in 1852," *Bull. of the New York Pub. Lby.*, XIX, No. 4 (April, 1915), 344.

We have sought out the scarce and the unusual in overland documents. Readily available accounts are not included, but will be referenced in the final volume in the bibliography. If you know of a special account written at the time of the journey, please let us know. Our goal is to add to the knowledge of all regarding this portion of our history – the story of ordinary people embarked on an extraordinary experience.

KENNETH L. HOLMES

Monmouth, Oregon, 1983

The Diaries, Letters and Commentaries

A Military Wife on the Santa Fe Trail
⸦ Anna Maria Morris

INTRODUCTION

No ordinary journal is this of Anna Maria De Camp, wife of Major Gouverneur Morris, United States Army. This was not a middle-class American family going west for freedom or farm or fortune. Husband and wife were representatives of two of New York's great pioneer families from the colonial days. She was traveling as wife of the commander of a military unit, and was consequently given all the attention and care that such a position demanded while she recorded her daily diary observations.

When F. X. Aubry, the Santa Fe trader and entrepreneur, encountered the Morrises while returning eastward along the trail, he wrote the following in his own diary on June 22, 1850: "[I met] Majors Morris and Graham Capt. Easton and several other officers and their families, also 100 recruits for the Third U. S. infantry."[1] Here was a unit of the frontier army traveling on foot, by horseback and wagon train in a follow-up to the Mexican War as they wended their way along the trail to Santa Fe, where they would be stationed for several years.

The key phrase in Aubry's quote is "and their families," for those were the days when commissioned officers were allowed to take wives and children to the forts and garrisons where they would be stationed as part of the defence of the western frontier.

Anna Maria Morris was one of these women. She was

---

[1] Louise Barry, *The Beginning of the West, 1540-1854,* (Topeka, 1972), p. 947.

36 years old, having been born in Morristown, New Jersey, on November 25, 1813.[2] She mentions her birthday each year in her diary but never once gives her age. Anna Maria was the daughter of Surgeon Major Grandin Johnston De Camp of the United States Army and of Nancy (Wood) De Camp.[3] The De Camps were descended from the New Amsterdam family of de Kamp. The fact that they were living in Morristown, New Jersey, at the time of Anna Maria's birth tells us that there had probably been a relationship between the De Camp and the Morris family for many years. The Morris family had included Lewis Morris, a signer of the Declaration of Independence, and Gouverneur Morris, one of the important writers of the United States Constitution. Their grand estate was Morrisania, a sprawling country place just north of the Harlem River in what is now a well-known part of New York City.

In 1670 Captain Richard Morris, a Welshman who had served in Cromwell's army, and his brother, Colonel Lewis Morris, had purchased a property then called Bronxland, five hundred acres in extent, on the north side of the Harlem River. Their lands quickly grew by nearly 2,000 acres. In addition to this Lewis Morris became the proprietor of extensive lands in New Jersey Province. The name is associated in New Jersey with Morris County and the historic city of Morristown.[4]

In his 1866 book *The Hudson From the Wilderness to the Sea,* Benson J. Lossing described the approach to and the locale of the "Morris House":

> A broad, macadamized avenue, called the "Kingsbridge Road," leads from the upper end of York Island to Manhattanville, where it connects with and is continued by the "Bloomingdale

2 Elizabeth Morris Lefferts, comp., *Descendants of Lewis Morris of Morrisania* (New York, 1907), chart E II.

3 Notes accompanying manuscript of the diary, from the Univ. of Virginia Lby., Charlottesville.

4 W. W. Spooner, "The Morris Family of Morrisania," *American Historical Mag.,* I, no. 1, pp. 25-44.

Road," in the direction of the city. The drive over this road is very agreeable. The winding avenue passes through a narrow valley, part of the way between rugged hills, only partially divested of the forest, and ascends to the south-eastern slope of Mount Washington (the highest land on the island), on which stands the village of Carmansville. At the upper end of this village, on the high rocky bank of the Harlem River, is a fine old mansion, known as the "Morris House," . . . The mansion is One Hundred and Sixty-ninth Street. It is surrounded by highly ornamented grounds, and its situation is one of the most desirable on the island.[5]

Gouverneur Morris, Anna Maria's husband, was raised in this aristocratic setting. He was the son of another military man, Lieutenant William Walton Morris (1760-1832) and of Sarah Carpenter.[6] In the same generation as this pair of overlanders were numerous Morrises and De Camps who were associated with the military.

Anna Maria's husband had been born about 1804 at Morrisania, so he was 46-years-old in 1850.[7] His military career is summed up officially as follows in Hamersly's *Army Register:* [8]

MORRIS, GOUVERNEUR. 2nd Lieut. 4th Infantry, 24 May, 1824. 1st Lieut. 31 April, 1831. Captain, 6 September, 1837. Major 3rd Infantry, 31 Jan. 1850. Lieut. Colonel 1st Infantry, 31 May, 1857. Retired 9 Sept. 1861. Died 18 Oct., 1868. *Brevet Rank:* Brevet Major, 9 May, 1845, for gallant and meritorious conduct at Palo Alto and Resaca de la Palma [Mexican War].

So Anna Maria Morris traveled in style across the Plains in 1850 as the commanding officer's wife. She had a maid, Louisa, whose last name is never mentioned. Anna Maria often rode in the unit's ambulance wagon. She never cooked

---

[5] (Troy, New York, 1866), p. 371-73.

[6] Notes accompanying manuscript of the diary, from the Univ. of Virginia Lby., Charlottesville. [7] Lefferts, chart E II.

[8] Thomas H. S. Hamersly, *Complete Regular Army Register of the United States: For One Hundred Years, (1779-1879)* (Washington, D.C., 1880), p. 649.

a meal nor did a wash — there were laundresses for that.[9]
As was stated at the outset, "This was not a middle-class
American family going west for freedom or farm or fortune." Yet, for that very reason the journal is of intense
value as a record of a different type of experience on the
overland journey.

What must the average infantry soldier have felt about
the whole matter of officer's wives and families accompanying them to the far-western frontier forts. Oliver Knight's
fine book titled *Life and Manners in the Frontier Army*,
dealing with the post-Civil War period, goes into the entire subject with great and fascinating detail. What he
says about a later time often held true for the 1850's as
well.[10] The very best quote that we have found showing
the feelings of the enlisted men toward the subject is to
be found in A. Frank Mulford's *Fighting Indians in the
7th U. S. Cavalry*. It was published in 1878.

> Here we find the greatest bother that there was ever in a camp
> with a regiment. General Sturges' two daughters and small son
> have been riding in one of the ambulances all day, and now
> "are so tired they don't know what to do."
>
> It is really too bad to have them get tired. But do you sup-
> pose they ever think men are tired?
>
> I think not, at least they have a special wall tent put up for
> their special benefit, wood and water carried, and their supper
> cooked by the men who are detailed for head quarter fatigue
> (work).
>
> All that there is any need of saying in this case is that woman
> is humbug in a cavalry camp.
>
> May 5th, they, that is the ladies, left us this morning, to
> return to Fort A. Lincoln, and pass the summer in doing noth-
> ing but giving orders to the men.[11]

Anna Maria and Gouverneur Morris remained stationed
in the Santa Fe area from July 11, 1850, till they were

---

[9] Oliver Knight, *Life and Manners in the Frontier Army* (Norman, Okla.,
1978), pp. 68-69.

[10] *Ibid.*   [11] (Corning, N. Y., 1878), pp. 47-48.

sent east in 1853. The return journey began on June 30
of that year. They reached St. Louis overland on July 30
and boarded "the cars" (the train) for New York and
home on August 3. They reached Chicago on the 4th and
Detroit on the 5th. There they boarded ship on Lake Erie
for Buffalo. Then it was by train again to Albany and on
to New York City and the sanctuary of the Morrisania
estate on August 7th. There she continued to keep her
diary, but generally with very short entries until the last
one made on June 1, 1858, Monday. She wrote of visits
with friends, going to church, shopping in New York City,
lives and illnesses and deaths of the family members.

She made a fascinating brief entry on March 1, 1855,
"at half past 4 Ocl: I gave birth to a fine little son   The
Lord be praised ——" She never mentions the baby's name
in the diary, but we know from a family genealogical record that he was Gouverneur Morris, b. 1 March 1855,
d. 2 Feb. 1896, unmarried.[12]

Anna Maria would live on at Morrisania herself until
at age fifty she died on May 6, 1861.[13] Her husband lived
on until his death on October 18, 1868.[14]

The Anna Maria Morris diary is in the Manuscripts
Department of the University of Virginia Library (MSS
#3448), and is published with their permission. We have
been privileged with invariable graciousness by the office
of the Curator of Manuscripts to have the use of a microfilm of this document.

THE DIARY OF ANNA MARIA MORRIS

Camp on the Stranger [River] 13 miles from
Fort Leavenworth   May 2d 1850.
To my dear Father   We left Fort Leavenworth
this morning at 1 Ocl   I should say afternoon for we

---

12 Lefferts, chart E II.   13 *Ibid.*   14 *Ibid.*, also *Hamersly*, p. 649.

left after dinner I started our Spring Wagon with
my Maids and Sargeant Jones as driver & guide. When
we arrived at the Camp the Command was waiting
for Rations to be open and as I thought it would be
[a] more agreeable camp We drove on to Salt Creek
where we halted till the whole command came up, we
then came on to the place where we shall encamp for
the night – Evry body left Ft. L. in good health and
spirits the day delightful and the country perfectly
lovely – As soon as our carriage halted Dr. McDougal [1]
and the other officers were invited to take a social glass
which they appeared to enjoy very much particularly
as we had a good supply of ice which all the others
had forgotten – then Capt. Easton [2] brought me a glass
of Champagne which I feel the better for taking. We
passed any number of California emigrants to day
and altogether I have had a pleasant time *so far* –
Dr. McDougal bought a beautiful carriage just before
leaving Leavenworth which I am to have the use of
and also of his Poney which is perfectly gentle – after
travelling six miles we struck a new road which extends to Council Grove, and cuts off 60 miles of the
route to Santa Fe it was made this spring I am
resting in the wagon while waiting for the baggage
wagons to come up. I see the camp fires already blaz-

---

[1] Maj. Charles McDougall was an Ohioan and West Point's physician
from 1846 to 1848, when he was sent west. Thomas H. S. Hamersly, *Complete
Regular Army Register of the United States for One Hundred Years, (1779-
1879),* (Washington, D.C., 1880), p. 618. Hereafter referred to as *Army
Register;* also Appleton's *Cyclopaedia of American Biography* (New York,
1888), IV, p. 108, hereafter referred to as Appleton, *Biography.*

[2] Capt. Langdon Cheves Easton was in the Quartermaster Department.
His wife, a close friend of Anna Maria Morris, was pregnant during most
of the journey. Easton had a long military career through the Civil War
and afterwards. *Army Register,* p. 421; Leo E. Oliva, *Soldiers on the Santa
Fe Trail* (Norman, Okla., 1967), p. 114.

ing around me. Mr. Ritch[3] & Capt Lovell[4] was out
after dark to say good bye. Mr Ritch desired to be
remembered to you & said I must tell you he came
out to see me in my first encampment. – Dr. McDougals
horse kicked him last night which makes him a little
lame – The Quarter Masters clerk started in a beautiful
carriage, the horses ran off and it was broken *all* to
pieces. He came into camp horseback – these are the
accidents the first day

Wednesday May 22nd. We were off at 6 Ocl a m
had our breakfast of Mr. Henry's[5] Misc Chest which
opens and makes a good table. left the Stranger [River]
at 8½ Ocl and after going about mile we were obliged
to halt till 1 Ocl – as in crossing the creek the wagons
stalled and the whole command were sent ahead to
repair the road & crossing. I was riding with Mr.
McDougal and altho' we were stationary three whole
hours we did not get very much out of patience – The
Dr. had two parlor chairs left in the mud broken all
to pieces – I fear mine will go next – We crossed the
Stranger [River] in safety tho' the banks are very
steep indeed – on arriving at the camping ground
most of the tents were pitched on a most beautiful
Prairie, bordered on one side by low land, presenting
altogether a very pleasing prospect – We have only
advanced two miles to day   I do not think we shall
gain much by coming the new road, the detentions
will make up the distance   one wagon was turned

---

[3] William G. Ritch, a prominent citizen of New Mexico who later became
Territorial Secretary. Robert W. Larson, *New Mexico's Quest for Statehood,
1846-1912* (Albuquerque, 1968), p. 138.

[4] Capt. Charles Swain Lovell, a son of Massachusetts, held rank in the
6th Infantry. Appleton, *Biography*, IV, p. 35; Oliva, *Soldiers*, p. 111.

[5] Mr. Henry and his wife (*see* June 7 entry) are so far unidentified.

up side down in the creek   it belonged to the Quarter
Masters clerk, the unfortunate individual who had
his carriage broken to pieces the first day we left
Ft. Leavenworth –

Thursday [May] 23rd.   We left the Stranger [River]
at 7 Ocl and after a pleasant journey of 20 miles encamped on the bank of the Grasshopper [now the
Delaware River] a beautiful river in which there are
some fish – the young officers went fishing & Dr. Mc
to kill some birds he thought were Golden Plover for
my dinner which Louisa boiled for me & it was very
nice – We had a dinner to day which would have been
called good anywhere – I had a delightful bath in the
water of the Grasshopper every afternoon about 5
Ocl You can all imagine me seated in a tent on a
Buffalo roab making my toilet – I shall be rather
brown when I get there I am afraid to pass for an
"Americano" When we overtook the Herd this morning we discovered that the little heifer Dr. McDougal
gave me was not among them. On questioning the
Herdsman we find he had not brought her from
Leavenworth She got away & he came off without
her. Capt. Easton lost a cow in the same way – Mrs.
Easton & I get along nicely together we exchange
calls every evening we are encamped in a delightful
spot if it could only be as pleasant all the way I
should be glad

Friday 24th We camped the Grasshopper at 7 O'cl
Came 9 miles and encamped at 2 O'cl on Walnut
Creek 13 miles from the Kansas – We find the new
road very bad in places the horses sink very deep
in thick black mud – The new road extends to Council

Grove instead of 40 miles as I at first mentioned --
Maj M.[orris] had no choice about the road but was
ordered by Maj. Sumner [6] to take it – We live so far
first rate have an abundance of milk & cream. The
Dr. (My excellent friend) brought me some nice little
fish for my dinner.

Saturday 25th   We left Walnut Creek at 7 Ocl and
after travelling ten miles crossed the Solain [Saline]
creek – We then arived at Kansas river where we
halted a long time   went into one of the Indian houses
– the woman was pretty & spoke french   She was
making mockasins, plenty of Caw Indians about the
door; a dirty bedaubed set – a man belonging to the
Fort was left dying of Cholera at Walnut creek. we
have since heard of his death – at Kansas we overtook
Lt. Field [7] & his party who had preceded us to repair
the road so our party is on the increase –

Sunday 26th [May]   I & [?] left the Kansas at the
usual hour   went ½ miles & encamped at Camp Walker – I do not know the name of the creek – the Thermometer yesterday at 3 Ocl was 95.

Monday 27th   Left Camp Walker at 7 Ocl travelled 10 miles & encamped at Wacanuske [Wakarusa]
Creek. We came over a trackless Prarie most of the

---

[6] Maj. Edwin Vose Sumner, a Boston-born officer, was Military Commandant of New Mexico and later served as acting Governor. He became a
Brigadier-General early in the Civil War and was highly decorated. He
died of natural causes on March 21, 1863. His biography, written by Thomas
M. Spaulding, was published in the *Dictionary of American Biography* (hereafter referred to as *D. A. B.*), Vol. xviii (New York, 1936), pp. 214-15.

[7] Lt. Charles W. Field, of the 2nd Dragoons, was in charge of 75 1st
Dragoons, recruits. Louise Barry, *The Beginning of the West, Annals of
the Kansas Gateway to the American West, 1540-1854* (Topeka, 1972),
pp. 894-95.

morning & were detained a long time finding out the
way & repairing bad crossings we halted at 2 Ocl
& had to wait a long time for the wagons to come up.

Tuesday [May] 28th   a great change in the weather
it is *very* cold – left Wacanakie [Wakarusa] Creek
at the usual hour and were obliged to leave one of the
men in camp dying with Cholera and four more were
taken soon after we started   in consequence of it we
were obliged to shorten our days march   came 11½
miles to Dragon [Dragoon] Creek – Maj Graham [8]
overtook us this morning

Wednesday 29th   Left Dragoon creek at 7 Ocl &
struck the Santa Fe trail in half an hour   came 21½
miles and encamped on Turtle creek a beautiful stream
& good water   Capt. Campbell [9] Lt Robertson [10] &
Lt. Park Eng [11] & Dr Magruder [12] overtook us this
morning

Thursday 30th   Left Turtle creek at 7 Ocl   arrived
at Council Grove at 2 Ocl – marched 13 miles –

Friday [May] 31st   Passed at Council Grove

Saturday June 1st   Left Council Grove at 12 Ocl

---

[8] Maj. James D. Graham was a Virginian who started his military career
as a 3rd Lt. of Artillery many years before, in July 1817. He transferred to
the Topographical Engineers in 1829, and this was the work he was associated with in New Mexico. He took part in the survey of both southern
and northern boundaries of the United States. *Army Register*, p. 470.

[9] Not identified among the many Campbells.

[10] Lt. Beverly H. Robertson was in the Second Dragoons with the overland party. *Army Register*, p. 725.

[11] Lt. John Grubb Parke had just graduated from West Point, second
in the 1849 class of 43 cadets. He would go on to serve as an engineer and
astronomer in the western surveys. *D. A. B.*, XIV (New York, 1934), 211-12.

[12] Lt. and Asst. Surgeon David L. Magruder, a Marylander, had just
achieved his rank on February 1, 1850. He went on to have a long military
career through the Civil War and beyond. *Army Register*, p. 598.

the delay was caused by our losing our horses – arrived at Diamond Spring at 4 Ocl –

Sunday June 2nd   Left Diamond Spring at 7½ Ocl. arrived at Lost Spring 16 miles at 2 Ocl and encamped on the wide open Prarie without wood except what we brought with us – the water is cold but not good taste – a terrible storm all night –

Monday 3rd.   Left Lost Spring at the usual hour and arrived at the Cotton wood creek at 3 Ocl the stream is too much swolen for us to cross at present

Tuesday June 4th   The creek so that we cannot get over with safety therefore we remain here (Cotton Wood) to day – We had another awful storm last night it is impossible to keep dry in a tent in such storms The Fly protects the top, but the rain beats in at the sides – The Maj received a note from Capt Saunders (who was left at Council Grove with 30 men) early this morning, saying he was very ill with Diarhoea and requested a Medical officer to be sent to him, accordingly the Maj sent Dr. Magruder with two men, & no sooner had he started than Dr Mc-Dougal reported sick, too ill to attend the Command and a man was sent off Post Haste to recall Dr. Magruder thus Capt Saunders will in probability die in the woods with no one to care for him but his soldiers [13] the man said this morning they did not believe he would be alive when they got back to the Grove I believe Dr. McDougal has a bad headache and did not sleep well last night I think he has made up his

[13] Capt. William H. Saunders did not die on this journey. Army records indicate that this Virginia-born officer resigned on June 20, 1851. *Army Register*, p. 742.

mind not to be left without an assistant & I do not
think it would be safe. When Capt. Saunders was left
at the Grove the Dr. said he did not believe he would
ever reach Santa Fe he was too sick to be left & I
wonder he did not report so

Wednesday June 5th Left Cotton Wood at 10 Ocl
crossed without much difficulty and arrived at Little
Turkey Creek 19 miles at 5 Ocl. I rode all day with
Mrs. Easton She has a most comfortable carriage.
We saw Antelope to day for the first time. I saw them
thro a Spy glass – I was a little afraid of Indians last
night but they say we are not on dangerous ground yet
    The roads are very muddy, as it has rained every
day since the month came in – We have water here,
but *no wood* except what we brought with us – Dr.
McDougal is better and Dr. Magruder glad enough
to be recalled he returned in *double quick time* –.

Thursday 6th Left Little Turkey Creek at 7 Ocl
intending to go 26 miles (to the Little Arkansas) but
at 11 Ocl We were brought up all standing at Big
Turkey Creek which it was impossible to cross – We
found a Merchants train waiting its fall. They have
been here three days – the Creek is 12 feet deep &
rising, as it rains every night or during the day. We
have advanced only eight miles to day & are encamped
on the Prairie with *plenty of water* but *no wood or
chips* – The provident ones brought a few brands (left
from the mornings fire along in case of accident – I
was one of that number, just as we were about starting
– the wood was out we *must* go to the Little Arkansas
to day in order to have a good camping place with
wood & water but as I thought something might occur

to detain us on the road, I told Louisa to take some
brands along sufficient to get our suppers & breakfast
– so when most of our Company were lamenting the
want of wood, I told them I had a small stove laid in
– one of the young officers said he reconed I had been
on the Prairie before, I told him no, but I thought it
always well to provide against accident – I sent Mrs
Smith a pan of charcoal to have her supper cooked
with, & just as I had sent it – our Mexican came along
panting for breath, with quite a wood pile on his back
which he had been four miles to procure he threw
it down looking as well pleased and indeed we all
were, as tho he had laid down a greater treasure. I
sent him a good drink of Brandy & he felt well com-
pensated for his trouble

Friday 7th   This is a lost day to us. it is impossible
to cross the Creek – I took a ride on horse back this
morning & intend to ride every day as our horse is
easy & gentle – The Adjutant sent me half a loaf of
bread to day & it was quite a treat – The woman who
cooks for him came over with her yeast & made me
up a loaf for tomorrow. She says I look so much better than when we left Leavenworth that I ought to
stay on the Prairie all the time – the woman came
from Santa Fe with Mrs. Henry and understands
Camp life a soldier private Fisher was drowned this
afternoon

Saturday June 8th   By 9 Ocl this morning the Creek
had fallen sufficiently to allow us to cross after re-
plenishing the wagons the Express from L.[eaven-
worth] arrived this morning by it I now have a letter
from Father and one from Sarah – Mr. Rich also

kindly sent me two papers – In the Republican I regretted to see the death of Col. McKay [14] recorded –

Sunday June 9th   We had a delightful journey to day of 22 miles from the Little Arkansas to Big Cow Creek – the officers chased Buffalo all day & the Maj captured a live calf which he let go at night having no way to support it

Monday June 10th   The express arrived from Santa Fe early this morning   by it I sent my journal home

Tuesday June 11th   We came 22 miles this morning from Walnut Creek to Ash Creek – the weather is delightful – We have seen thousands of Buffalos to day & are kept well supplied with fresh meat   Maj Haynes lost one of his carriage horses last night – he hung himself [15]

Wednesday June 12th   We overtook an ox team this morning & Maj Fitzpatrick [16] with it. by him I sent two pages of my journal home – We are encamped three miles from Pawnee Fork   came 9 miles to day

Thursday June 13th   Left Pawnee fork at the usual hour & are encamped on the Arkansas   came 22 miles no wood pleanty of chips The Prairies are perfectly covered with flowers & beautiful ones too

---

14 Col. Aeneas McKay (or Mackay) was an important officer in the Quartermaster Department who died May 23, 1850. Fort McKay at Cimarron Crossing (later called Fort Atkinson), was established soon after his death. Oliva, *Soldiers,* p. 95.

15 Maj. Haynes is so far unidentified. The assumption in reading this part of the diary would seem to be that *the horse* "hung himself," somehow in a tangled harness situation.

16 This is the noted trapper-guide, Thomas Fitzpatrick, who left the Arkansas Crossing on June 10 and arrived in St. Louis on June 26. Leroy R. Hafen, *Broken Hand, The Life of Thomas Fitzpatrick: Mountain Man, Guide and Indian Agent* (Denver, 1973), p. 277.

Friday June 14th   Our journey to day was 22 miles
& we are again encamped on the banks of the Arkansas – It has been very hot to day but in consequence
of the high wind we have not felt the heat very much

Saturday June 15th   My journal of one day will do
for the next day as long as we are travelling along
the Banks of the Arkansas where we are again encamped after a journey of 22 miles which became very
tiresome towards the last the Thermometer being at
96   it blows a huricane at night. The tents do not
protect one from such winds – We were out of the
range of Buffalo to day, no game of any kind   beyond
the land of flowers too almost except the Cactus which
is just beginning to bloom and is very beautiful – We
met a party of "Arapahoes" to day   they approached
us rather timidly at first   were quite sociable afterwards & had a long talk which they carried on by
signs. Mr Macarty understood them – When we were
ready to start the Drum was beaten unexpectedly – &
Indians and horses took to their heels pretty much
frightened until they found it was only the signal for
our departure

Sunday June 16th   The Thermometer at 98   we have
travelled 20 miles to day & we encamped on the Arkansas for the last time   I hope – We passed Fort
Mann this morning or rather its remains, a few old
logs & mud chimney   the logs we had chopped up
for fire wood & packed in our wagons enough to last
300 miles – We expect to cross the Arkansas tomorrow
– The heat to day is intolerable

Monday June 17th   a delightful morning. We crossed
the Arkansas to day. it was high & we had a good

deal of difficulty getting all over. Mrs. Graham, Mrs.
Smith & I crossed in an Ambulance. they were frightened, but I was not in the least, tho the Doct informed
me after we landed that we came within an ace of
upsetting. We passed our wagon (which the Maj was
driving) in the middle of the river & a little farther
on we passed Capt Eastons (with his family in) the
tongue broken, then we passed the Doct's with a trace
broken, & he on horse back trying to mend it, assistant
was sent to those in the River, and after a while the
carriages were all over – We were then obliged to
wait in the boiling sun several hours for the train
to cross we were perfectly beset with Indians and
amused ourselves with them. One of the young squaws
took a great fancy to my diamond ring & generously
offered me a brass bracelet in exchange which I de-
clined Mr. Macarty & the Express left in this morning they wished the Maj to give them an escort but
he had no men to spare –

Tuesday June 18th We went only four miles to day
to the upper crossing of the Arkansas where we encamped to have our washing and some extra cooking
done – it being the last place where there is plenty of
water. The men enjoyed their rest and bathing very
much. this is a hard march for Infantry Recruits I
had a nice beef gumbo to day which on the plains
is quite a treat We still live very well, but the scorch-
ing heat from 9 Ocl in the morning till 6 Ocl in the
evening is intolerable –

Wednesday June 19th We have travelled 18 miles
to day & are encamped at the first *water hole* after
leaving the Arkansas – it is intensely hot, no wood,

miserable grass, & only hot muddy water for the men
& horses which they drink as tho' it was delightful —
We had an awful wind storm this afternoon accompanied by a little rain, it came up very suddenly. the
first intimation we had of its approach was my port-
folios blowing open & scattering my papers to the
winds all over the Prairie — The Maj & the servants
went in pursuit & I was left alone in the tent. I thought
every moment it would blow down, but it did not quite,
however had to be repitched   Several of the tents blew
down   the Dr's among them. he took refuge with Col
Chandler [17]   After the storm had abated. I saw two
water spouts   the sky was perfectly beautiful sublimely
beautiful and I quietly enjoyed it

Thursday June 20th   We left Water hole at 7 Ocl in
the morning and marched 34 miles to Sand Creek
the day was a very favorable one for the long march
    We passed an old encampment where a Mr. Brown
passed last winter in his wagons. after all his animals
had perished in the snow — The same man was captured by the Indians some time since and taken out to
be killed. when he selected his prettiest mule (a little
white one) and presented it to the Chiefs wife she
became interested in him from that and saved his life.
the Indians then gave him a pass a mule & a few provisions and allowed him to go — the squaw who saved
his life was the one who took a fancy to my ring; she
was pretty & neat looking   she had the white mule
with her. Mr. Smith wished to buy it

Friday June 21st   The men & animals being so much

---

[17] Daniel T. Chandler had been made a Brevet Lt. Col. in 1846 for
"gallant and meritorious conduct" at Monterey. *Army Register*, p. 353.

fatigued from the long march of yesterday we did not leave camp till 8 Ocl. and after a hard march of only ten miles encamped at the lower Cimarrone Spring water brackish –

Saturday June 22 – Left Cimarrone Spring at 6 Ocl marched 20 miles & encamped on the bed of the Cimarrone where we dug for water & attained some pretty good & very clear – Near sun down Mr Aubry's[18] train arrived from Santa Fe & encamped near us – by it I sent my journal home

Sunday June 23rd   We left Camp on the Cimarrone at 6 Ocl and marched 20 miles and encamped near Miracle spring of the Cimarrone – To day we noticed the first appearance of Volcanic rock   the day has been pretty warm to those exposed to the sun but to me it has been pleasant & now while I am writing in the Ambulance there is a pleasant breeze   We have passed numerous dog towns and have seen the dogs & their neighbor owls sitting at the hole of their habitation into which they run on our approach

Monday June 24th   Two days since I sent you six pages of my journal by Mr. Aubry's train in route to the States. We left Miracle Spring on the Cimarrone at 6 Ocl   Marched 13 miles and are encamped on the Cimarrone still, awful water. I am told   I have not tasted it and do not intend to   The roads are heavy & sandy   the mules by degrees failing

---

18 This was the noted Frenchman out of Quebec, François X. Aubry, who was dubbed by his biographer Donald Chaput, "the busiest, most effective merchant on the Saint Louis-Santa Fe-Chihuahua-California routes." *François X. Aubry, Trader, Trailmaker and Voyageur in the Southwest, 1846-1854* (Glendale, Calif., 1975), p. 11.

Tuesday 25th   We have marched 15 miles to day
this sand, heat, & flies   to the last Crossing of the Cim-
errone – We encamped about 2 Ocl   the heat *intense*
– We passed a large pile of Mule sculls to day. it is
said 180 perished there last winter in the snow – a
party of Merchants overtook us this morning   they
have joined us for their protection thro the dangerous
defiles – I feel less afraid now than when we first
started being more accustomed to this savage life –

Wednesday 26th   We are encamped at Cold spring
this evening after a pleasant march of 18 miles   I
enjoy my ambulance more & more each day particularly as Mrs. Graham shares it with me a few hours
each day. We took a grand sleep together this morning and when we got up we enjoyed our lunch – it
is the most sociable pleasant time we have during the
day, we have good water this evening, plenty of wood.
Miserable grass at the sight of our Camp. there is a
high hill before which the Guard tents are pitched
and the guard marching back & forth gives it quite
a picturesque appearance – We are approaching the
little mountains & I rejoice in them and breeze

Thursday 27th   We passed the day at Cold Spring
the heat intense–

Friday 28th   Left Cold Spring with renewed strength
and spirits – after our rest yesterday   marched 16
miles, are encamped at Cedar Spring pretty good
water now. poor grass   the day as usual extremely
hot   the nights are always cool and so it is in the
morning early. every day is alike and nothing to make
a journal interesting. one of the men killed an antelope

Saturday 29th   Left Cold Spring at 4 Ocl this morning having a long march of 24 miles before us   the
Maj and the Doct. thought an early march advisable
tho' there is generally great diversity of opinion as to
the best time for starting. The Dragoons prefer a late
start on account of their horses, and in this they are
Seconded by the Quarter Master who thinks of his
mules. The Infantry like an early start to avoid the
heat of the day   *I can* stump for an early start particularly now that I have a most comfortable bed made
up on the back of my Ambulance where I can sleep
to my hearts content – I have taken two walks to day
but I do not think I shall attempt it again   the roads
are too sandy and the whole earth in this county is
covered with Cacti and a kind of palmetto as to render
a walk anything but agreeable – We have passed thro
a hilly mountainous country to day much more interesting than the dead level over which we have lately
travelled – We passed McNees Creek to day called
after a man by that name who was murdered there [19]
his grave is near the Creek –

One of our cows has become lame from the long
journey and the Maj is having shoes put on her this
morning   I think it cannot be a pleasant undertaking
for the men who are shoeing her as every now & then
she gives a most vigorous kick at them – I am in
hopes we shall get our cows thro' safely as I wish
to make our own butter   Our encampment is near
Rabbit ear

---

[19] Two young men, McNees and Monroe, had been killed at this place by
Indians in the autumn of 1828. The story is best told by Stanley Vestal, *The
Old Santa Fe Trail* (Boston, 1939), pp. 190-91.

Sunday June 30th   We started at 6 Ocl this morning
and have travelled 28½ miles   encamped at Rock
Creek   fine water, no wood, and poor grass – the day
has been cool & pleasant – our tents are just pitched
and the fire made. it is near sun down   the teams are
nearly worn out – We have the Raton mountains constantly before us now and farther off the Spanish peak
covered with snow – I never thought I should be as
near the Rocky mountains as I am *but here I am* seeing
their distant grandeur

Monday July 1st 1850   Started from Rock spring at
7 Ocl and marched 8 miles to Whetstone Creek where
we encamped at 11 Ocl   the heat as usual intense for
a few hours – a party of Dragoons are sent a short
distance ahead to day to reconnoitre the Indian[s] in
this vicinity but no Indians were discovered – We
are within five days travel of Las Vegas

Tuesday July 2nd   Left Whetstone Creek at 6 Ocl
marched 20 miles to Water pool   very poor water &
scarcely sufficient for the animals – We have water in
our packs for our own use, some of our neighbors have
none   We are encamped now 2 Ocl three miles beyond Point of Rocks scene of the White tragedy [20]
which we passed this morning   We did not see the
sculls of the murdered party so conspicuously displayed
in the sand as I expected to from what I had been

---

[20] James M. White was an Independence merchant who with his wife,
Ann (Dunn) White, their daughter Virginia, employees and fellow travelers, suffered attack by the Apaches at Point of Rocks on October 23, 1849.
White and several men were killed, and mother and daughter and black
maid were taken captive. In November 1849, when a military search party
caught up with the Indians, the three women were also killed. *Beginning
of the West*, p. 885.

told – The Maj however found a scull with a beautiful
set of teeth – farther on we saw holes dug for the
defence of a party of Mexicans who accompanied
White and who were likewise killed – the party seven
in number was three days ahead of their company
when they were surprised by the Indians – The place
seems the most favorable for an ambuscade that we
have seen on the journey –

Wednesday July 3rd We started this morning at 6
Ocl marched 21½ miles to Ocatí Creek five miles
from Red river, at the river we filled our Casks with
water as that in the Ocatí is salt, grass poor and a
scanty supply of pine used the first we have been
able to obtain since leaving the Arkansas In Maj
Kendricks [21] notes he maintains this as a desirable
place for a Settlement I think differently

Thursday July 4th Left Ocatí at 6 Ocl marched
20 miles & encamped at 2 Ocl at Wagon mount Santa
Clara spring. delightful water plenty of grass. *no wood*
– soon after our tents were pitched we had quite a
severe hail storm The Doct is the only one who has
had a merry making in honor of the day he made
egg nog for all of us – he has kept very quiet about
those eggs he had been saving up for this occasion–
It has cleared off delightfully and we shall encounter
less dust tomorrow in consequence of the storm – At
this place the Express mail men eleven in number were
murdered about a month since – The Spring here is
called Santa Clara, it is the best water we have had

---

[21] Maj. Henry L. Kendrick had taken two artillery companies over the
trail to Santa Fe the year before in the summer of 1849. He published a
table of marches for the route. *Beginning of the West*, pp. 869-70.

on the route, grass pretty good, no wood – Maj Grear [22]
reconnoitering about 15 miles from this place

Friday July 5th Left Wagon mount at 6 Ocl
marched 22 miles to a small creek three miles from
Mora – a short time after we started this morning we
passed the place where the eleven men were murdered
& buried many things were found on the spot that
gave evidence of the terrible conflict broken arms,
arrow heads, bones, pieces of clothing, scraps of paper
&c – The Maj found a copper coin Marked "The
free state of Chuhuahua" value about three cts and a
quarter – on the other side there is an Indian represented with a bow in one hand & an arrow in the
other –

Saturday July 6th Left the Creek near Mora at 6
Ocl crossed the Mora river in an hour. I saw the
first adobe house soon after crossing and some men
making adobes to finish it. there were two women
standing at the door, and some Peons watching the
flocks – I suppose we are now fairly in New Mexico
and I confess I am a *little* disappointed in the first
Mexican Settlement We marched 22 miles to day
and are encamped on the hill in front of the town of
Las Vegas – the town looks very much like a brick
yard tho' I am told those that have [?] are very comfortable inside The first acquaintance I met was Lt
Barton [23] whom I saw last at Poremas [?] Island --

---

[22] Maj. William Nicholson Grier graduated from the Military Academy
in 1835, had participated in the War with Mexico, and was then serving
in New Mexico. Appleton, *Biography,* II, p. 763.

[23] 2nd Lt. Seth M. Barton was a Virginian, at this time serving in the
First Infantry. *Army Register,* p. 285.

Col Alexander [24] very kindly invited all the families
to his house – Mrs. Graham and Smith accepted the
invitation. We remained in Camp

They are building an adobe church here   the whole
town are obliged to turn out every Saturday and work
on it or pay a fine of $2.00   the grave yard is near
our encampment surrounded by a stone wall – I am
told it is very healthy here   the winter very cold,
they had snow in June – Col & Mrs Alexander called
on us in the evening –

Sunday July 7th   Col and Mrs A. called in their carriage this morning for me to go home with them and
pass the day which I did very pleasantly   Mrs Smith
also went – their house has a cool comfortable look
all in a plain way   I know now exactly how to fix a
Mexican house, a wealth of paper or canvas is indis-
pensible around the wall and the little fire places in
the corner I particularly admire   The wood is put
in endwise   Las Vegas is the most lonesome looking
place I ever saw and has fewer attractions – there is
nothing pleasant to cast the eye on for a moment not
a tree a shrub or a flower, nothing but black [?]
mud walls – They have a hotel at the place called the
American –

Monday July 8th   Left Las Vegas at 7 Ocl   rode
thro the town then I stopped to say good bye to the
Alexanders   We are now finally over the plains, as
we were soon in the pine woods after starting – We
marhed 11 miles to Tacalote, had a delightful ride
and enjoyed the scenery very much. I think some of

---

24 Col. Edmund B. Alexander, a Virginian, was the Commandant of Las
Vegas. His wife is so far unidentified. Oliva, *op. cit.,* p. 105.

the Passes almost equal to Harpers ferry which boasts
the most grand & beautiful scenery in our Country –
when we arrived at Tucalote [Tecolote] we drove
to the town and were kindly invited to the house of
an American, a Mr. McClure who is postage Master
– he told me he was acquainted with you Father and
desired to be remembered to you   We passed the day
with them   so did Mrs. Graham and we were kindly
and hospitably entertained and I assure you we enjoyed the comforts of a house once more. Mr McClure
married a pretty American girl in Santa Fe   her
Father had moved there a year before and is now in
California   her Mother and sister are with her – I
gave Mrs McClure my sun bonnet as she fancied it --
Mr. McClure has the carriage Mrs White was in when
captured   Lt Field lost three horses at Las Vegas
two private & one public – Our Mexican had $70
stolen from his trunk – he was taking it to his daughter in Santa Fe

Tuesday July 9th   Left Tucolate at 7 Ocl   marched
to San Miguel and halted an hour at Pecos river then
proceeded four miles farther to San Jose where we
encamped – the day being very warm and oppressive
we (together with Mrs. Graham & her son) were glad
to avail ourselves of the grateful shade of the Mexican
adobe – the most uninteresting place from the out side
I am sure – We entered a low door way and found
ourselves in as cool a house as we were in before –
lounges and beds all around the room, no chairs, the
mud floor was covered with buffalo robes & other
skins – The walls hung with Images, pictures of
Saints, Crosses, looking glasses and rosetts made of

paper – the whole arrangement was neat & orderly –
We were received by a good looking Mexican woman,
who seated herself on the floor and busied herself
making cigaretes & smoking them – She took little
pieces of shucks from under the skins on the floor &
filled them with tobacco from a paunch on her side
her daughter a fine looking girl of fifteen always
brought her fire to light her Cigaretes and altogether
they were the most indolent looking set I have ever
seen – I sent up to our tent for some sugar which I
gave the woman and with "Muchos gracias" bade her
good bye – I find the mountain air much more agreeable than that of the plains and the grateful shade
of the pine & cedar trees make our marches less warm
tho' every one looks a little fagged & anxious to get
thro' – at Santa Fe we all separate

Wednesday July 10th   Left San Jose at 6 Ocl
marched 23 miles and encamped at Cotton wood the
most pleasant camp we have had on the entire route
water good and cold – We stopped at Pecos springs
to water the animals, and then rode on (about three
hundred yds.) to view the ruins of the Church of
Pecos. as it is very well described in Col. Emory's
Report I shall not attempt it – except to say the walls
are still standing and the church is built in form of
a cross. the carving about it is mad but altogether
it must have been quite an imposing looking church
in its day – Three months to day since I left home.
We are now 20 miles from Santa Fe –

Thursday July 11th   Left Cotton wood at 6 Ocl
encamped at 1 Ocl ½ mile from Santa Fe to the left
of the town – I remained in my ambulance in camp

till the Maj rode in town to see Col Munroe [25] and find out our quarters – The first acquaintance I saw was Capt Sykes [26] he rode up to the ambulance to see me but I did not recognise him at first–he is much stoughter than when I saw him last – We are quartered in the house of the Prefect Anton Ortiz [27] one of the wealthiest men of the town – the room that I occupy has a mud floor partly carpeted   one window Mexican fashion   the room is cool & comfortable and has nineteen looking glasses in it, to say nothing of my two – Segnior Ortiz called on the Maj last evening and embraced him very affectionately – The Dr. came in a few moments after and received a like embrace

Friday July 12th   I am not at all disappointed in the appearance of Santa Fe   it is the most miserable squalid looking place I ever beheld except the Plaza there is nothing decent about it – Tho' all I have seen as yet was in riding thro' the town to reach our habitation which is located in the suburbs – The houses are mud, the fences are mud, the churches & courts are mud, in fact it is *all* mud –

---

[25] Col. John Munroe was by birth a Scot. He had been General Zachary Taylor's Chief of Cavalry in the War with Mexico. He was Military and Civil Governor of New Mexico from October, 1848, to July, 1851. Appleton, *Biography,* IV, p. 461.

[26] Capt. George Sykes had been active in the Mexican War. He served for several years later in the Southwest. His wife was Elizabeth (Goldsborough) Sykes of Cambridge, Maryland. *D. A. B.,* XVIII (New York, 1936), 255.

[27] James J. Webb, in his *Journal of a Santa Fe Trader,* wrote of the Ortiz family that they "were considered *ricos,* and those most respected as leaders in society and political influence; but idleness, gambling, and the Indians had made such inroads upon their means and influence that there was but little left except the reputation of honorable descent from a wealthy and distinguished ancestry"; Ralph P. Bieber, *Southwest Historical Series,* I (Glendale, California, 1931), pp. 91-92.

There are more corn fields & gardens almost than
I expected to see and some pretty trees Capt. Sykes
called to see me this morning   he leaves for the States
on the 15th together with several other officers & Mrs.
Capt. Reynolds [28] – We are to remain here for the
present as Col. Munroe intends putting the Maj on
a Court Martial I am glad of the opportunity to
rest myself for a march of 52 days is enough to try
out any one –

Col MCall Maj Kendrick & Lt. Peck [29] called to
see me this evening   they are all waiting in durance
vile to be relieved & all agree in despising the country
& everything in it I believe –

Saturday July 13th Doct Edwards [30] called to see
me he is relieved by Dr. McD. and leaves on the
15th he is a personable gentlemanly man – I had
a delightful Serenade last night from the 3rd Inf band
– Capt & Mrs. Reynolds called. Mrs. R. is going to
the States if she does not change her mind as she has
done several times before – Lt & Mrs. Thomas [31]
called he is an agreeable man is rich & lives hand-
somely I am told he has been married about two
months – his wife is very young and retiring

---

[28] Capt. Alexander Welch Reynolds was in charge of the quartermaster's
program for convoying units from Santa Fe to various frontier localities.
Later in life, he resigned his commission and fought for the Confederacy
throughout the Civil War. *D. A. B.*, xv (New York, 1935), p. 516.

[29] Lt. John J. Peck, an artilleryman, had been active in the War with
Mexico. He would leave Santa Fe very shortly and be reported in Missouri
by mid-October. *Beginning of the West*, p. 971.

[30] Dr. Lewis A. Edwards was a military doctor. He served during both
the War with Mexico and the Civil War, from 1846 to 1876. *Army Register*,
p. 424.

[31] Lt. Francis J. Thomas, a Virginian, served a short four-year career
in the Artillery. He had joined on July 1, 1844, and would resign on June
30, 1852. *Army Register*, p. 804.

Sunday July 14th   One of the teamsters was shot by a sentinal last night   he did not answer when hailed

Monday July 15th   Capt Sykes called to bid me good by   it made me quite homesick to see him going to the States and direct to my dear home – Mrs Easton had a daughter born this morning – An artillery Soldier shot himself last night being as he said weary of life.

Tuesday 16th   I was sick & low spirited.   took a short walk in the evening –

Wednesday 17th   I went in town to see Mrs Thomas & Mrs Graham – I was surprised to hear Mrs Smith had left without even calling to say goodbye   I sent my letters to the office this evening   the mail leaves early in the morning

"We Live in a Log Cabbin"

∮ Mary M. Colby

INTRODUCTION

Millions of persons would never dream that two of their private letters, written in utmost confidence to close relatives, would be published and thus made part of their country's history. With the following documents, a very quiet personal experience is revealed in public print a century and a third after being written.

Mary M. Colby wrote the first letter on May 6, 1850, from St. Joseph, Missouri, as she, her husband and two children passed through the city on their way west. It was written to her brother and sister in Ohio. She wrote the second letter nearly two years later on February 8, 1852, from the new western land where they were living. The home address was "Lebenon," Oregon, a new little town in Marion County a few miles east of Salem, the capital. That Lebanon lasted only a few years. The area where it lay is now rolling farm land.[1]

Mary Colby was 44 years old when she crossed the plains in 1850.[2] She grew up in New England, as she was born in Gilmanton, New Hampshire, and lived most of her early life in Haverhill, Massachusetts. She was born Mary M. Edwards to John and Betsey Holden Edwards.[3] She and

---

[1] This is not the same Lebanon as the one in Linn County, Oreg., today.

[2] We have so far found no record of Mary Colby's birth date. This age figure was worked out by studying the Federal Census figures for 1860, 1870, and 1880.

[3] Letter from Haverhill Public Library, Howard W. Curtis, director, May 19, 1982.

Elias Colby were married on June 6, 1841, in Bristol, New Hampshire, after which they made the long trek to Uhrichsville, Ohio, where they farmed.

At the time of the 1850 covered wagon journey to Oregon, there were two Colby children: Frances Ann, age 8, and Allen James, age 6. The little boy lived only a few years after their arrival on the West Coast. The *Oregon Statesman* newspaper of Salem reported on April 1, 1856, that Allen J. Colby had died on March 24, "aged about 12 years."

Elias lived an active public life in the Colby's new Willamette Valley home. The Oregon archives are replete with references to his political activities, but with a bare reference to Mary in a census return. Elias was a Democrat [5] and was made postmaster of Lebanon for a short time.[6] He represented Marion County in the Oregon House of Representatives from 1853 to 1857 and in the State Senate for a term following that.

Their daughter, Frances, was married in her parents' home on April 3, 1862, to a prominent political figure, Blair Forward.[7] He had been United States Marshal and at the time of the wedding was the Marion County Surveyor.[8]

The Marion County probate files reveal that Elias F. Colby died on April 29, 1884, leaving to his widow an estate of $12,243.15, "said widow" being "aged and in feeble health." Mary M. Colby herself died at her home on November 24, 1889, exactly 39 years after their arrival in Oregon in 1850.[9]

---

[4] Place of marriage from Land Claim Record, Claim No. 541, Marion County Oreg. Arch. Date of marriage from above cited letter from the Haverhill Public Library.

[5] Salem, *Oregon Statesman,* April 17, 1860.

[6] *Ibid.,* Nov. 14, 1854.   [7] *Ibid.,* April 7, 1862.

[8] Many references to Blair Forward in the Oreg. Arch.

[9] Probate File No. 1185, Marion County Courthouse, Salem, Oreg.

The two letters reproduced here are located in the collection of the Haverhill Public Library, through the courtesy of whose director, Howard W. Curtis, we have been
given permission to publish them. We learned of the cor-
respondence on reading a quote from Mary Colby in Lilian
Schlissel, *Women's Diaries of the Westward Journey*
(New York, 1982), pages 155-57.

LETTER I

St. Joseph [Missouri]   May 6, 1850
Dear Brother and Sister   I suppose you would be
glad to no how we are getting along on our journey
well we left our home in ohio the first day of April
we went 27 miles in a 2 horse wagon then we took
the cars and went to Cincinatta   from their to this
place on a steam boat   we were on the boat 2 weeks
had a safte sail   nothing of any account happened
on the boat save one man was drounded but he was
not a pasenger   we rented a room not much better
than a hog pen for about ten days which we had to
pay 4 dols a week for then we went out onto the paraie
and campt out for a weeke then we moved our camp
3 miles father in to the country where we now are in
an old log cabbin where we go to bed on the flour   at
night the big norway rats run and caper over you so
you can not sleep   the first night we was here one was
verry glad to se me   he just came up and took me by
the hand but not so hard as to hurt much   when we
came down the ohio river about the 6 of april the
peach trees were in bloom but here they just begin to
blosom   I used to think ohio was a handsom country

but Dan I tell you what it is   this is the prettiest
country I ever did se   you can look for miles all
around   you se nothing but the handsomest parraie
and fields of wheat that ever one did se   it would
do your soul good just to se the fields of wheat some
of them so large that you cannot se from one end or
side to the other   I wish in my heart you and your
family were with us   you would enjoy your self first
rate   I do for one but should feel better if I was rid
of a bad cold and cough which I have had for this
2 months but still I feel pleased with our trip so
far   shall feel better I hope when we get on the road
a gain   I want to be on our way but cannot till the
grass grows for our cattle which I hope will be in a
week or ten days   you would laugh if you could se
us camping out   we have a splendid table made of
a goods box   our dining dishes are tin plates knives
and forks   our tea table set with same and tin dippers
for cups   a six quart pan to serve our meat up in   the
bread laid on the table and so on with appatites like
the hungry hogs and a plenty to eat   when we can not
get a house to s[l]eepe in we sleepe in our wagons   we
have 2 wagons and 4 yoke of oxen and 3 yoke of cows
and shall have another yoke of cows if we can get
them   jus call in you and Mr Pettys folks some evening and se how folks live [in] Missourie   I could
not begin to tell you how many their [are] in St Joseph
that are going to Oregon and California but thousands
of them   it is a sight to se the tents and wagons on the
banks of the river and through the country   they are
as thick as camp meeting tents 20 or 30 miles and some
say for 50 miles   their is 30 or 40 familys in the mess
that we intend to get in with   some of them we have

see and got acquainted with one lady we found here
that lived in Urichsvill [Uhrichsville] the first place
we lived in in Ohio she is married and moving to
Oregon Citty we have not got any letter from you if
you wrote we did not stop at Indeppendance [May]
12 tomorrow we move our camp a gain go to St Jo
lay in our provisions and cross the river to the indian
territory then move on towards Oregon which will
take us some 5 months if we have good luck to get
through since I commenced this the St Jo paper
states that 20 thousand has started from their to Calli-
fornia this spring if I am only well and the Indians
do not trouble us I shall enjoy the trip first rate but
I [have] the horridest cough that ever one did have
but hope it will get well some time if ever it does
Allen has a bad cold and the ear ache for a day or
two the rest are tolerable well I do not think of
much more to write at this time so good by

M M Colby

LETTER II

Lebanon   Oregon Territory
Marion County   Feb 8 1852

Dear Brother and Sister

It is a long time since we have seen each other but
I have not forgotten you altho many miles of land and
water separate us   yet I often wish I could se you and
your family and many dear friends in Haverhill   I
supose you would like to here how we like this country and how we prosper in the first of our living here
I did not like [it] verry well but after we had taken
our claim and become settled once more I began to

like much better and the longer I live here the better
I like [it] the summer is beautiful not but a very
little rain tho it is not so warm in the summer here
as it is in the States the nights cool and comfortable
and I can sleepe like a roack. the winters is rather
rainy but is not cold and so bad getting about as it
is in the States here the grass is fresh and green the
year round and our cattle are all fat enough now for
beef their is not a month in the year but I can pick
wild fllowers I saw strawberry blosoms yesterday
to d[a]y I saw leaves on some bushes as large as a
rose leaf as to our prosperity we are getting along
as well as one could expect we have a section of land
one mile square in the best part of Oregon it is prairie
all except a strip of timber on two sides of it with a
stream of water runing through each piece of timber
our stock concists of seven cows one yoke of oxen
six calves fifteen hogs and 24 hens; hens here are one
dollar a piece eggs are only one dol per dozen I
sold a lot yesterday for that price butter is from fifty
cents to one dol per pound I think with good health
and good economy we shall get along verry well I
cannot say that I wish to go back to the States to live
at present if ever I know when one gets comfortably
fixed here they can live as well as they can any where
else and with one half of the labour that you do in
the States you can rais all you want to live on and have
a good lot to sell you are not obliged to sow your
wheat every year when once sowed you can get three
crops of verry good wheat we have put in 20 acres
this fall and winter and shall put in more yet wheat
is from one dol to one fifty per bushell vegitables
grow verry large here turnips as large as a half bushell

and beats as large round as my waist   are not them
bumpers   it is a fact for I saw the beats when growing   I intend to go in for a garden this year and for
raising chickins and making butter and cheese   cows
are worth 50 dollars a piece   the gold mines still continue to be good   the reports from their last week say
they are making from 20 to 40 dols a day   I do not
wish to brag but I think we shall ere long be as well
of for property as some of the rest of the family think
they are and if I do not get what honestly belongs to
me   Our health is good and has been for the most of
the time since we have been here   the children are
healthier than when in Ohio   well Ruth I have got
two of the prettiest children in the whole family
Frances Ann looks like her father and she you no
must be pretty for Sabrina said he was   Allen James
looks as Brother John used to   [February] the 11
yesterday I was visiting at Esq Dunbars[1]   had fresh
readishes from his garden for diner and cabbage in
blosom   everry thing now looks as it doese in may in
the states   prices of goods here are not much higher
here than in Mass   I bought home a mirror the other
day that I can se my whole body in for 15 eggs   we
are in the best neigborhood I ever lived in   all it
wants to make it right is to have some of my friends
here   I supos by this time your children are all maried
if so write me who they maried and all about them
and how your health is and how you prosper and where

---

[1] "Rice Dunbar, with his family, crossed the plains to the Willamette
Valley in 1845. . . The Dunbars lived on their claim in the Waldo Hills,
from the fall of 1845 until 1863, when they moved to Salem." Fred Lockley,
"Impressions," *Oregon Daily Journal* (Portland), Dec. 2, 1945, sec. 2, p. 2B.
See also Robert Horace Down, *A History of the Silverton Country* (Port-
land, 1926), p. 37. Rice Dunbar was originally from Ohio, according to
Down.

abouts you live   I want you to write soon   write all
the news you can think of   I wrote to you the first
winter after I was maried but never received an answer
so I thought I would try it once more   Sabrina you
must write me a long letter too   tell me all about my
old friends in H[averhill] and Newtown   is Mrs
Crowell alive   if so give my love to her   ask her if
she has forgot when she and I sat up with Old maid
Greenough   my love to Mrs Sweet and all old friends
that may inquire after me tell them I am the same
that I was when I used to be with them some 20 years
ago   I have got a first rate husband   all the fault I
find with him he is not lively enough   he is verry
still   that you no is very diferent from me but you no
a close mouth maketh a wise heart and I believe it
we have about 140 acres of our land under fence   40
of it is improved   I supose he would not sell it now
for four thousand   that is a small price to what some
value their claims   when our fruit trees begin to bear
it seem[s] more like home we have apples pear peaches
and plum trees   we can get a plenty of dried fruit
here but not much green apples   green are 8 and 10
dols   a basket peaches still higher   Onions from 3 to
6 dols a bushel or 75 cents a pound   we live in a log
cabbin   it has two rooms and is verry comfortable   is
as good as the rest of our neighbors have so I am content with it till we can have a better one   I had rather
live in a log cabbin and have enough to eat drink and
wear than have a large house and fine furniture and
know that it is bought with money that I had cheated
out of my poor brother and sisters   thank God I have
no such things to think of nor mean to have   well Sis
I must soon close this scrawl   now I wish you to write

soon as you receive this   give my love to all your children and pleas to except a good share your selfe

Pleas excuse Mr Colby for not writing this time as he is verry busy at work   his best respects and wishes attend you write soon   direct your letters to Elias F Colby   Lebenon

yours   Mary M. Colby

Pleas send us a paper now and then

Adventures of a Party of Gold-seekers
∮ Margaret A. Frink

INTRODUCTION

"There are but few women; among these thousands of men,
we have not seen more than ten or twelve." *Margaret Frink,
Tuesday, August 20, 1850.*

One of the classics of western history, and a very rare
volume indeed, is this book published in 1897, with the
lengthy title typical for the period: "JOURNAL / Of the
Adventures of a Party of / California Gold-Seekers /
Under the Guidance of / MR. LEDYARD FRINK / During
a journey across the plains from Martinsville, / Indiana,
to Sacramento, California, from March / 30, 1850, to
September 7, 1850. / From the Original Diary of the
trip / kept by / MRS. MARGARET A. FRINK."

The death of this lady in Oakland on January 16, 1893,
was reported in the Oakland (Calif.) *Tribune* [1] and it was
four years later that her husband, Ledyard Frink, thought
it appropriate to publish his wife's daily journal, "owing
to many requests made by relatives and friends."

Today the book is found in just a few libraries, and is
one of the real rarities of western historical publication.
We have been given permission of the Beinecke Rare Book
and Manuscript Library of Yale University to transcribe
their microfilmed copy here. We held the actual book in our
hands and studied it at the California State Library in
Sacramento, and from them received permission to use
her portrait.

Much of the family background is given in the opening

---

[1] January 16, 1893, p. 2, col. .3.

section of the diary, undoubtedly edited with the addition of these facts later, by either Mr. or Mrs. Frink.

She was born on April 25, 1818, in Frederick City, Maryland, as Margaret Ann Alsip, daughter of Joseph and Mary Alsip.[2] She was married to Ledyard Frink in Kentucky on April 17, 1839. There were no children born to them. The Frinks lived in several eastern states before their decision in late 1849 to follow the gold trail to California in the spring of 1850. Their first city of residence in California was Sacramento, where Mrs. Frink became one of the charter members of the First Baptist Church, helping to found that institution with the Baptist frontier pastor, Rev. O. C. Wheeler, and several others. The couple later lived in other parts of California, spending the late years of their lives in Oakland. There Margaret Frink died at the age of 74. Ledyard lived on until March 6, 1900.

There is a memorandum written by hand by the Frink's nephew, L. A. Winchell, in the California State Library[3] in Sacramento saying that Margaret often rode horseback sidesaddle on the overland journey, and that he had given the saddle to the Sutter's Fort Museum in Sacramento. Winchell also reminisced that with the Frinks on the overland journey was "a young lad about 12 years old, named Robert Parker, and a protege of Mr. and Mrs. Frink." Robert is mentioned in Margaret Frink's journal.

Another of L. A. Winchell's remembrances was published in the *Grizzly Bear* for December, 1927, telling of the prefabricated house that the Frinks had sent around the Horn by ship to be set up by them in Sacramento:[4]

In the spring of 1850 my mother's older sister [Margaret Frink], with her husband and her brother, A. B. Alsip, started

---

[2] Much of the information that follows was taken from the "Pioneer Record" card in the files of the Calif. State Lby., Sacramento, and here used with their permission.

[3] "Pioneer Letters: Frink, Mr. & Mrs. Ledyard (Margaret Alsip)," no date.

[4] P. 28. The house stood at the corner of M and Eighth streets.

from Martinsville, Douglas County, Indiana, for the goldfields of the West. My uncles were merchants in Martinsville and men of ample means. Before leaving for California, having learned from newspaper accounts that lumber was selling here for $400 a thousand feet, while it was only worth $3 a thousand feet at Martinsville, they decided to have materials for the home provided. Employing several carpenters, lumber of all necessary sizes was measured, cut and fashioned ready to assemble in a short time.

When the spring freshets came, the materials were loaded upon a raft and floated down the White River to the Wabash, to the Ohio, to the Mississippi and on to New Orleans, thence by ship around the Horn to Sacramento, California, arriving there in March, 1851, just a year on the voyage.

The Margaret Frink Journal is, of course, a treasure of American history. It is printed here in the same style as in the 1897 original, chapter by chapter. We have also included the "Addenda," which tells "What Became of our Traveling Companions," written by Ledyard Frink.

Margaret Frink touches upon a subject that was absolutely crucial to all those traveling the western trails: the danger of scurvy. On March 31st her entry tells of a warning from a man, the landlord of a hotel east of Terre Haute, Indiana, and a former sea captain, "in regard to preparing to defend ourselves against the scurvy." They reached Terre Haute the next day and "laid in a supply of acid to take the place of vegetables." Several other times she mentioned acid, and on August 2 she tells of "pickles and acid." According to Irene D. Paden, it was customary to take along sour pickles or vinegar as antedotes to the disease.[5]

One further introductory note: Margaret Frink mentions in her *Journal* entry for Monday, May 20, 1850, "We had with us some guidebooks (Fremont's and Palm-

---

[5] *Prairie Schooner Detours* (New York, 1949), p. 231. *See also* Thomas B. Hall, *Medicine on the Santa Fe Trail* (Dayton, Ohio, 1971), *passim*.

er's). . ." The first of these by John C. Fremont was printed in 1845, *The Report of the Exploring Expedition to the Rocky Mountains in the Year 1842, and to Oregon and North Califonia in the Years 1843-44.*

The second book was by Joel Palmer: *Journal of Travels over the Rocky Mountains to the Mouth of the Columbia River made during the years 1845 and 1846 containing minute descriptions of the valleys of the Willamette, Umpqua, and Clamet; a general description of Oregon Territory, its inhabitants, climate, soil, productions, etc. etc., a list of necessary outfits for emigrants; and a table of distances from camp to camp on the route* (Cincinnati, 1847). It was re-published in 1906 by the Arthur H. Clark Company as Volume XXX of Reuben G. Thwaites, *Early Western Travels.* There is a helpful article on this subject by Helen B. Kroll, called "The Books that Enlightened the Emigrants," in the *Oregon Historical Quarterly,* XLV, Number 2 (June, 1944), pp. 103-23.

THE JOURNAL OF MARGARET A. FRINK

PREFACE.

Owing to the many requests made by relatives and friends for a history of our journey across the plains to California, made in the summer of 1850, the minutes of which were kept by Mrs. Frink, I have concluded, even at this late day, to issue this book.

Although there may be some errors, it is practically a correct history.

L. Frink

Oakland, California, 1897

CHAPTER I.

Ledyard Frink was born and raised in the western

part of New York. I, Margaret Ann Alsip, his wife, was born in Maryland, though partly raised in Virginia, on the banks of the Potomac River. From there we moved to Kentucky, where Mr. Frink and myself were married on the seventeenth day of April, 1839. We spent that summer in Cincinnati; and in October moved to make ourselves a home at Cheviot, six miles west of that city, where we continued to live very pleasantly till 1844, when we made up our minds to try our fortunes farther west. We situated ourselves one hundred and twenty-five miles from Cheviot, in the town of Martinsville, the county seat of Morgan County, Indiana. Here Mr. Frink engaged in merchandising, in which he succeeded very well. We continued to live here nearly six years during which time we built a pleasant and convenient residence, having large grounds about it. But we were not yet satisfied. The exciting news coming back from California of the delightful climate and abundance of gold, caused us to resolve, about December, 1849, that we would commence preparing to cross the plains by the spring of 1850.

The first thing on Mr. Frink's part was to have a suitable wagon made for the trip while I hired a seamstress to make up a full supply of clothing. In addition to our finished articles of dress, I packed a trunk full of dress goods not yet made up. We proceeded in the spring to get our outfit completed. There was no one from our part of the country, so far as we knew, that intended to cross the plains that season, and we were obliged to make such preparations as our best judgment led us to do, without advice or assistance from others. We knew nothing of frontier life, nor how to prepare for it. And besides, we were met with all the discouragements and obstructions that our neighbors and the people of our county could invent or imagine, to induce us not to attempt such a perilous journey. But, nothing daunted, we kept at work in our preparations for the trip, thinking all the time that we should have to make the long journey by ourselves, as no one in all that part of the country was offering or expecting to go to California that season.

But it appeared as if there was a Providence planning for us. First, we had a boy that we had taken into our family to live with us when he was seven years of age, and now he was eleven. He was much attached to us and could not be reconciled to be left with his own friends and relatives. The child being so determined to cling to us, Mr. Frink consented to take him if his uncle and guardian, Mr. W. Wilson, would give his consent. This he very readily did, though with all his family opposed to the plan. The consent was given about four days before we started.

The wagon was packed and we were all ready to start on the twenty-seventh day of March. The wagon was designed expressly for the trip, it being built light, with everything planned for convenience. It was so arranged that when closed up, it could be used as our bedroom. The bottom was divided off into little compartments or cupboards. After putting in our provisions, and other baggage, a floor was constructed over all, on which our mattress was laid. We had an India-rubber mattress that could be filled with either air or water, making a very comfortable bed. During the day we could empty the air out, so that it took up but little room. We also had a feather bed and feather pillows. However, until we had crossed the Missouri River, we stopped at hotels and farmhouses every night, and did not use our own bedding. After that, there being no more hotels nor houses, we used it continually all the way to California.

The wagon was lined with green cloth, to make it pleasant and soft for the eye, with three or four large pockets on each side, to hold many little conveniences, – looking-glasses, combs, brushes, and so on. Mr. Frink bought, in Cincinnati, a small sheet-iron cooking-stove, which was lashed on behind the wagon. To prepare for crossing the deserts, we also had two India-rubber bottles holding five gallons each, for carrying water.

Our outfit for provisions was plenty of hams and bacon, covered with care from the dust, apples, peaches, and preserved fruits of different kinds, rice, coffee, tea, beans, flour, corn-meal, crackers, sea-biscuit, butter, and lard. The canning of fruits had not been invented yet – at least not in the west, so far as we knew.

Learning by letters published in the newspapers, that lumber was worth $400.00 per thousand in California, while it was worth only $3.00 in Indiana, Mr. Frink concluded to send the material for a small cottage by the way of Cape Horn. The lumber was purchased and several carpenters were put to work. In six days the whole material was prepared, ready for putting it together. It was then placed on board a flatboat lying in White River, to be ready for the spring rise – as boats could not pass out except at high water. The route was down White River to the Wabash, to the Ohio, to the Mississippi, to New Orleans; thence by sail vessel around Cape Horn to Sacramento, where it arrived the following March, having been just one year on the voyage.

Our team consisted of five horses and two mules. We had two saddles for the riding-horses, one for Mr. Frink and one for myself.

I believe we were all ready to start on the morning of the 27th of March. On the evening before, the whole family, including my mother, were gathered together in the parlor, looking as if we were all going to our graves the next morning, instead of our starting on a trip of pleasure, as we had drawn the picture in our imagination. There we sat in such gloom that I could not endure it any longer, and I arose and announced that we would retire for the night, and that we would not start to-morrow morning, nor until everybody could feel more cheerful. I could not bear to start with so many gloomy faces to think of. So we all retired, but I think no one slept very much that night.

I believe Mr. Frink, more than myself, began to fully realize the great undertaking we were about to embark in, almost alone. Our conversation finally turned on the likelihood that a young man of our acquaintance, named Aaron Rose, might wish to go with us. Some remark he had made led us to think he might like to join us. But Mr. Frink was of the opinion that his father and mother would never let him go, as they were already wealthy people and had but two children with them. Besides, Mr. Rose had been a confidential clerk in Frink & Alsip's store in Martinsville, during the past three years, and could not be spared from the business, as my brother, Mr. A. B. Alsip, was to remain in Martinsville and carry on the merchandising as before. But, after discussing all these objections, Mr. Frink left the house early the next morning and went to Mr. Rose's residence, where he met the young man's father, and inquired of him if he had ever heard his son say anything about wishing to go to California. "Yes," said the old gentleman, "and he has thought quite hard of you that you have never spoken to him on the subject. But he says he is determined to go when he is twenty-one years old." Then the mother came in weeping, saying, "If he ever does go, I want him to go with Mr. and Mrs. Frink, for I know he will have a father and mother in them." And it was decided on, by six o'clock that morning, that we should wait a few days longer, until the young man could be fitted out for the journey. I think all the young ladies in town offered to help, as he was a general favorite. And for the next three days there was a very busy time among his young acquaintances, in making him ready for the California journey. During the meantime, we were practising the driving of our four-horse wagon, with lines in hand, and gradually educating ourselves to bear the final separation from our relatives and friends. We were all ready to leave our home on Saturday, the thirtieth day of March.

We bade farewell to all our relatives, friends, neighbors, and acquaintances. Mr. Frink and myself, having each a horse to ride, rode out of town on horseback, and with the four-horse wagon, went seven miles before stopping for lunch. It was a beautiful spring day. Our faces were not at last set westward. We arrived on the west bank of the Eel River about sundown. We were quite tired, and there being a large brick house near by, we inquired there for quarters for the night. It appeared that the landlady was, for the moment, in

the stable, and, hearing our inquiry, she thrust her
head out of the stable window and answered rather
impatiently that she had no time to give to strangers;
that she had a cow in the stable that she was going to
break if it took her all night to do it; that we had
better go on about three miles, where we might be
accommodated with lodgings. This looked like a poor
chance for us; but Mr. Frink was not to be discour-
aged in this manner. He went to the stable and gave
the milkman such instructions as enabled him in a
short time to bring the unruly cow under subjection,
so that the old lady came out highly pleased, and
allowed us to stay in the house all night.

Sunday, March 31.   We continued our journey to-day
and struck the national road at Manhattan, where we
had dinner. We lost our road, however, and had to
retrace about three miles. We stopped at night about
twenty miles east of Terre Haute, and were very pleasantly entertained. The landlord of the hotel had been
a sea-captain, and volunteered some advice that afterwards proved very beneficial to us, in regard to preparing to defend ourselves against the scurvy, from which
so many California emigrants had suffered in 1849.

Monday, April 1.   We started again in good spirits,
every one at the hotel, strangers and all, wishing us
good luck on our long journey. On this great "national
road" the towns are near together; and whenever we
stopped, even to water the horses, there would be
squads of people standing about, full of curiosity, and
making comments upon ourselves and our outfit, thinking we were certainly emigrants bound for California.
But some would remark, "There's a lady in the party;
and surely there's no man going to take a woman on

such a journey as that, across the plains." Then some
of them would venture to approach the wagon and
cautiously peep in; then, seeing a lady, they would
respectfully take off their hats, with a polite saluta-
tion; and we felt that, if there was anything in having
good wishes expressed for us, we should certainly
have a successful and pleasant trip. We stopped to
dine four miles east of Terre Haute. Here we heard a
great many comments upon the hardihood of a woman
attempting to make such a difficult journey.

We reached Terre Haute at two o'clock in the afternoon, and made some additions to our outfit. We laid
in a supply of acid to take the place of vegetables after
we should get out on the great plains. This is a beautiful town, situated on the east side of the Wabash
River. Our outfit attracted much attention and was
greatly admired, particularly our fine horses. The
first California emigrants we had seen passed us here,
they having been fitted out in this neighborhood. We
passed them in the afternoon. We stopped at night
nine miles west of Terre Haute. The accommodations
were very poor. However, we were fully prepared to
board ourselves whenever the people refused to accommodate us. Here we ate our supper from our tin plates
and drank coffee from our tin cups for the first time.
Mr. Frink expressed regret that we had omitted to
bring our tea cups, and suggested that he would buy
some when we came to the next town. But for my
part, I was satisfied to do as other immigrants did, and
if it was the fashion to drink out of tin, I was quite
content to do so. The landlady was cross and snap-
pish, thinking, I suppose, that we were not quite
worthy of her valuable attention, though I tried to

adapt myself, as far as possible, to her notions. However, she gave us a nice bed, and by the time we were ready to take our leave the next morning, she seemed to have concluded that we were tolerably respectable people.

Tuesday, April 2. We had a rather late start this morning, having some fixing up to do. We reached Paris, Illinois, in time for dinner, and found it quite a pretty place. It is something smaller than Martinsville, yet quite a tastefully built town, and has a large seminary for young ladies. Here again the inhabitants had many comments to make upon the propriety of a lady undertaking a journey of two thousand miles, across deserts and mountains infested with hostile savages. But they would finally wind up and conclude by saying that I was "certainly a soldier to attempt it;" and, putting their heads inside the wagon, they would wish us all possible success in the undertaking.

Wednesday, April 3. We staid last night on Grand Prairie. Our hostess and her husband were German people, and made us very comfortable. We traveled all day on the prairie. The distance was twelve miles between houses, and no timber in sight at many times, though occasionally we passed some beautifully timbered spots. We staid all night at a house on the west side of the prairie.

Thursday, April 4. We launched out on the fourteen-mile prairie this morning, and such a time as we had, – storming, snowing, and sleeting, – and we with no place of shelter. Before we had gone far, we came to a bad-looking, muddy place, to avoid which he turned off the beaten track upon the grass, which looked firm and solid. To our astonishment, the horses broke through the sod, and, being unable to pull their feet out, they were all soon flat on the ground, and could not be gotten out until they were unhitched from the wagon. I stood in the sleet and held four horses for two hours, till I thought my feet were frozen. My cloak was frozen stiff, and I was chilled through and through.

While we were in this predicament, there came up a team with five men from Ohio, who stopped and helped us. They spaded the wagon out of the mud, and then hitched their horses to the hind axle, and we were pulled out safe; and we learned not to leave the beaten track again. I concluded after that, to ride my pony in preference to riding in the wagon. We came at last, to a half-way house of one room. They had a fire, and it was a real luxury to get warm once more. But it was a forlorn-looking set that had gathered there for shelter and a little rest. There was no woman in the company but myself. As soon as we were thawed out, we started to make the remaining seven miles of our day's journey. It was a hard day, and we did not get through till after dark. Then we found good accommodations in a large backwoods cabin. There were two large rooms with great, wide fireplaces and huge, blazing logs piled on. That great, glowing fire I shall never forget, nor the bountiful supper table, with its good, warm coffee, and, best of all, the cheerful faces that welcomed us.

Friday, April 5. We had tolerably good roads to-day, through prairies. At night we stopped at the last house before entering another lonely prairie. This was thirty miles east of Springfield, Illinois. The landlord and landlady appeared somewhat independent and a little indifferent as to whether they would accommodate travelers or not; but they finally consented, and we passed the night under their roof very comfortably.

Saturday, April 6. I felt quite unwell this morning; but we traveled steadily all day, and reached Springfield, the state capital, at nine o'clock at night. The roads were very muddy and bad, but we could not get accommodations till we reached the city; and, it being late and very dark, we came to rather a poor hotel. But we were so tired we were glad to put up with even poor accommodations. We found considerable excitement prevailing over the report that a California emigrant had been murdered that day some ten miles west of the city, on the road we were to travel the next day. I then began to feel that we had undertaken a risky journey, even long before we came to the Indian country. We got out the Colt's revolver that night to see that it was in good order, and made ready to defend ourselves against attack; but happily we were not molested in any way. We concluded, however, that it would be prudent hereafter to answer all inquiries with the reply that we were "on a trip to the far west," and not, if we could avoid it, make it known that we had started for California.

Sunday, April 7. We traveled only fifteen miles to-day. We found good accommodations for ourselves, but our poor horses had to stand out-of-doors, though the night air was damp and chilly. For the first time, we found that horse feed was scarce, and the neighborhood had to be ransacked to get a sufficient supply.

Monday, April 8. We traveled through a beautiful

country to-day, between Springfield and Jacksonville, and stopped at night five miles west of Jacksonville.

Tuesday, April 9. We traveled twenty-one miles to-day, crossing the Illinois River at Naples, which is quite a business-like place, on the east side of the river. A railroad runs from Naples to Quincy.

Wednesday, April 10. We traveled nineteen miles to-day, and stopped at a farmer's house, where we found very pleasant and agreeable folks. To-morrow we expect to cross the Mississippi River. We are now two hundred and seventy-seven miles from home.

CHAPTER II.

Thursday, April 11. To-day we crossed the Mississippi River at Hannibal, Missouri, and traveled four miles west of the city. We got the privilege of stopping at a private farmhouse, it being then dark, where they consented to furnish us with supper and breakfast. After we had entered the house, the gentleman inquired of us what state we were from, to which we replied, "From Indiana." The gentleman and his wife then stepped aside a little, and appeared to be considering the propriety of furnishing accommodations to people from a "free state," for we were now in a "slave state," where negro slaves were everywhere to be seen. The gentleman then very politely informed us that he did not think they could accommodate us with supper and breakfast. He asked, "Have you not a supply of provisions with you?" We replied, "Yes sir, plenty of it." "Then, madam," said he, "we will furnish you with a room, with everything you may need, and a servant to wait on you." We were conducted into their parlor, where there was a large fireplace, with table and chairs, and a bed in one corner – all very good and comfortable. But some other parts of the house were not so nice as the kitchen we left in our Martinsville home.

They gave me a small negro girl to wait on me, and we had a very pleasant time all by ourselves, for we were provided with everything that the country afforded, in the way of provisions, both substantials and delicacies, so as to be prepared for all emergencies. But our prudent host and hostess did not see proper to show themselves to us any more that night. In the morning, however, as we were making our preparations for departure, the whole family made their appearance in numbers. I had put our room in good order, when the two young ladies came in, evidently curious to see a lady emigrant for California. When we were ready to get in our wagons and drive away, they all gathered around, admiring our nice outfit and our nice-looking horses.

"Dear me," said the younger lady, "and are you really going across the plains to California?" "Yes, my dear," I answered. "Are you not afraid of being burned black by the sun and wind on the plains?" "Oh, no; and if I am, I can stay in the house until I am bleached out again!" "But there are no houses in California." "Well, we have already sent our house on ahead." "How did you send your house to California?" Then I told them: "We sent it on a flatboat down the west fork of White River to the Wabash, down the Wabash to the Ohio, down the Ohio to the Mississippi, and down the Mississippi to New Orleans.

There it will be put on a sailing vessel, and go through the Gulf of Mexico into the Atlantic Ocean, and around past Cape Horn into the Pacific Ocean. Then it will go up the western coast to the 'Golden Gate,' into the Bay of San Francisco, and up the Sacramento River to the city of Sacramento, where it will meet us when we get there."

When I had told them this, the interest and excitement were such that, by the time I was seated in the wagon, the whole family, black and white, had gathered about us. We afterwards learned that our landlord had been a member of the state Legislature the preceding winter. This was our first night in Missouri.

Friday, April 12. This was a very cold day. We traveled seventeen miles and were obliged to stop at a place with but few accommodations.

Saturday, April 13. We stopped for our noon lunch at Clinton, in Monroe County, where we overtook the Ohio train that had helped us out of the mud. We reached Paris, the county seat, at night, and stopped at the Paris Hotel, in company with the Ohio emigrants.

Sunday, April 14. The snow was two inches deep. We left about eleven o'clock and traveled seventeen miles over miserable roads. We got stuck in the mud again, and had to be pulled out by ox teams.

Monday, April 15. We traveled all day and reached a place four miles west of Huntsville, the county seat of Randolph County. It rained most of the day and the roads were very bad.

Tuesday, April 16. We remained in camp all day on account of the rain and the deep, muddy roads.

Wednesday, April 17. We had an unusual experience to-day. We traveled twenty-three miles, and as night approached, we found it almost impossible to get accommodations at the private farmhouses along the road, and there were no hotels except in the towns, and they were far apart. Near sundown, Mr. Frink, being on horseback, rode on ahead of the wagon to procure, if possible, shelter for the night, at a place said to be the last house for six miles. But, for some unknown reason, the people, when we reached there, refused to let us stay.

I felt very indignant at such treatment. It was now almost dark, and we knew not what to do. At last we heard of a hospitable lady, a Mrs. Barker, living several miles ahead, who would probably receive us. So Mr. Frink went forward alone in the darkness, while I was left to report to the wagons, which were still behind with the Ohio Company. When they arrived, we all followed the road which Mr. Frink had taken.

It was a moonlight night, which was very much in our favor. We soon came to a fork in the road. We were now in a dilemma, not knowing which road to take. In desperation, we took the left, and traveled on and on. I remained on horseback in preference to riding in the wagon, though the night was damp and chilly, one of the company being with me.

Among the company from Ohio were two brothers named Swift. By and by we heard talking in the distance, but could see no person and no house. We began to think of all kinds of dangers. Perhaps we were going to be trapped and robbed. Finally, I determined to follow up the sound of the voices, for I thought Mr. Frink might have been waylaid and perhaps murdered. At last we came to where several negroes were sitting on a fence. I inquired the way to Mrs. Barker's house. "Why, the Lord bless you, you done come the wrong road. You got to go back three miles and take the right-hand road to get to Mrs. Barker's house." We turned back sorrowfully, and had not gone far before our wagons were caught in a bad place; but soon Mr. Frink appeared with a lantern and a guide, and, though the moon was down and the night was dark, we reached Mrs. Barker's at nine o'clock. She received us very kindly, though we were entire strangers. She had a good warm supper awaiting us, with a great rousing fire in the parlor, and plenty of darkies to wait on us and do our bidding. The explanation of her warm-hearted hospitality was this: Mrs. Barker's husband had crossed the plains to California in 1849, and she felt so much sympathy with the travelers to the land of gold, she was determined that all who stopped at her house should be well taken care of.

Thursday, April 18. We came at night to the house of a Mr. McKinney, called "Squire McKinney," and were very hospitably welcomed. Mrs. McKinney had a nephew who went to California in 1849, and she told me of the wonderful tales of the abundance of gold that she had heard; "that they kept flour-scoops to scoop the gold out of the barrels that they kept it in, and that you could soon get all that you needed for the rest of your life. And as for a woman, if she could cook at all, she could get $16.00 per week for each man that she cooked for, and the only cooking required to be done was just to boil meat and potatoes and serve them on a big chip of wood, instead of a plate, and the boarder furnished the provisions." I began at once to figure up in my mind how many men I could cook for, if there should be no better way of making money.

Friday, April 19. The next "squire" we fell in with was "Squire Barnes." We reached his place at nightfall and stayed all night. During the day one of the Ohio company, a Mr. Terrell, met with a serious accident, putting his shoulder out of joint. This detained us and prevented us from making a usual day's travel. We had to send eighteen miles for a doctor to reduce the dislocation.

Saturday, April 20. We traveled twenty-one miles to-day over desperate roads. We halted before sundown, and were entertained by some very nice people.

Sunday, April 21. We traveled twenty-two miles to-day and staid all night at Plattsburg. Here we heard more wonderful tales of California and the gold mines.

Monday, April 22. We came to-day within nine miles of St. Joseph, which is situated on high bluffs, on the east side of the Missouri River.

Tuesday, April 23. We got into St. Joseph at 10 o'clock this morning. The whole country around the town is filled with encampments of California emigrants. This is the head of the emigration at the present time. They have gathered here from the far east and south, to fit out and make final preparations for launching out on the great plains, on the other side of the Missouri River.

Every house of entertainment in the city is crowded to its full capacity. This has been a backward spring season, and thousands are patiently waiting for the grass to grow, as that will be the only feed for their stock, after crossing to the west side and getting into the Indian country.

We drove out of town two miles northward, on the road to Savannah; and, finding a comfortable log cabin, we rented it from the owner, Mr. Compton, who had built a new cabin which he had just moved into. The cabin was quite well furnished and had good beds. There was also a large fireplace, with plenty of wood close at hand. We here settled ourselves for house-keeping, until the grass should grow on the Kansas and Nebraska prairies, and remained for the next fifteen days.

We still lacked something to complete our stock of supplies; for we had neither pickles, potatoes, nor vinegar. The army of emigration was so numerous that the demand for these and many other articles could only with difficulty be fully supplied. Mr. Frink traveled sixteen miles through the farming country searching for pickled cucumbers.

He was fortunate enough to find a bushel still in the salt, which he bought and brought back with him. This, with some horseradish and one peck of potatoes, was all he could find in the way of vegetables. I prepared these very carefully, and put them up in kegs with apple vinegar; these were to be our principal defense against that dreadful disease, the scurvy, from which the overland emigrants of 1849 had suffered so severely – not only while on the journey, but long after reaching California.

We had some old friends living near Cincinnati, our former home, who came by steamer down the Ohio and up the Missouri to St. Joseph, with their outfit, horses and wagons. Among them were two brothers of the name of Carson, who were raised within six miles of Cincinnati, and twin brothers by the name of McMeans, and a Mr. Miles – making five persons in their company. There was also Mr. Silver's company from the same city. They all came and camped near our cabin, waiting, like ourselves, for the grass to grow, and making the last preparations for the final start. It gave our camping ground the appearance of a village in beautiful woods. The country surrounding St. Joseph is a delightful region. Mr. Frink and myself admired it very much; and we thought that if we were not bound for California, we should like to settle here.

Not many days had passed before we began to hear frightful tales of Indian depredations on the plains, which had a tendency, at first, to shake the resolution of some members of the party. However, we finally concluded that our arrangements were so complete that we were certain to get through safely if any one could; and so the Indian stories ceased to give us any uneasiness or anxiety.

Mr. Frink met here one day a man named Avery, who had come from the same country we had started from, without any team or company, hoping that he could find at St. Joseph some one who would be willing to take him to California. So we agreed to take him in our company – the more readily as we had begun to feel that we were hardly strong-handed enough to be perfectly safe in the Indian country. For, besides Mr. Frink and myself, the only persons in our immediate party were Mr. Aaron Rose, the confidential clerk, and a boy eleven years old, Robert Parker. This new arrangement required us now to buy another wagon, and a supply of provisions for our new associate.

Wednesday, May 8. At last we were all rigged out for the journey. We had two wagons, one drawn by four horses, a lighter one drawn by two horses, besides two saddle-horses for Mr. Frink and myself. We were ready to start to-day, and decided that we would travel up along the east side of the Missouri River before attempting to cross over to the west side. During our very first day's journey something about one of the wagons was broken, so we only went as far as Savannah, where we stopped overnight to have the wagon repaired. Here we found some Indiana emigrants, who called on us, and had us stay in their company that night. Here we again heard alarming and discouraging accounts of deeds of violence and bloodshed that had recently been committed on the plains, along the route that we were very soon to travel over.

Thursday, May 9. We remained all day in camp at Savannah, waiting for our wagon to be repaired.

Friday, May 10. Our wagon having been put in good order and all made ready, we left Savannah this morning and drove twenty-three miles up the east bank of the Missouri River.

Saturday, May 11. Starting early, we drove twenty-eight miles to-day, and stopped one mile from the stream called Big Tarchio.

Sunday, May 12. We drove twenty miles to-day, and staid two miles north of Linden, at a miserable place. The boys for the first time slept in the wagon.

Monday, May 13. This day brought us to the crossing of the Missouri River, ten miles below old Fort Kearney, which stands at the mouth of the Platte River. Here we found a number of wagons and the Carson boys waiting to be crossed over in an old fashioned ferry-boat. Mr. Bullard and Mr. Bray were here with a train of wagons, loaded with merchandise for Salt Lake City. We learned that they were old Santa Fe traders. They were registered to cross first at the ferry, and so they went ahead, as each party must take its regular turn as registered on the ferry-book. This was known as Bullard's Ferry.

This was our first night in a camp. Thus far we had staid in a house every night since we left home. We enjoyed the change very much, and really thought we had lost a great deal of comfort in putting up with the miserable accommodations that we so often had met with; for here, on the banks of this majestic river, surrounded with the freshness of the budding spring, it was a delightful change.

We are now six hundred and thirteen miles from home. The elevation of this place is nine hundred and fifty feet above the Gulf of Mexico and about four hundred feet above our old home. So we have already begun to climb.

CHAPTER III.

Tuesday, May 14. We were safely across the wide

and muddy-colored stream by eleven o'clock this morning. Now that we are over, and the wide expanse of the great plains is before us, we feel like mere specks on the face of the earth.

I think none of us have realized until now the perils of this undertaking. During the past week not much has been discussed but the Indians and their doings. Printed circulars have been distributed informing the emigrants of many Indian depredations. Now I begin to think that three men, one woman, and one eleven-year old boy, only armed with one gun and one Colt's revolver, are but a small force to defend themselves against many hostile Indian tribes, along a journey of two thousand miles.

The Carson company of five men were crossed over at the same time that we were. They confidently talked as if they had studied everything pertaining to Indians and their tactics, and had nothing to fear from them. I had a very strong feeling at the same time, that these men would have felt more at ease if there had not been a woman in the party, to be taken care of in case of danger. However, each company was wholly independent of the others, and our wagons became separated from the other trains. During the day I began to feel, and so expressed myself to the rest of the company, that for greater safety it would be well if we could fall in with some strong company and unite with them for mutual protection; but when camping time came, late in the afternoon, and night was drawing nigh, our little party was all alone. We picked out a camping-ground on a rolling knoll, so that we could the better defend ourselves in case we were attacked during the night. But no one except myself expressed any fear of the savages; it was all nonsense to think they would attack us. But the first thing I did after we halted, was to get out the field telescope which we carried, to see if I could find any Indians; and sure enough I soon espied a party of them riding on an elevated ridge a long way off.

I announced my discovery to the camp. Other glasses were got out and leveled in that direction. All agreed that I was right. Then every one went quickly to work to put our camp in the best condition for defense.

A few minutes later, to our great delight, a company of five fine-looking men from Michigan drove up and asked the privilege of camping with us that night. We were more than glad to have our force increased by the addition of a party of such resolute-looking men, and readily gave our consent. We informed them of our discovery of Indians scouting at a distance. The wagons were then placed in position to form a corral, or circular inclosure, and picket-pins or stakes were driven down in the center, to tie our horses to after they had done grazing. All our ropes and lariats were made ready for the same purpose. After our supper was over and it was fairly dark, all the horses were brought in from their grazing ground and tied and doubly tied to the picket-pins and stakes inside the corral. The wagons were then securely fastened together, to form a solid barrier against a stampede, and every precaution was adopted that would increase our safety. The next thing was to see that our firearms were in good order. Then the guards for the night were appointed for the different watches. Finally the camp-fires were extinguished and the little circular village on the knoll was left in darkness. But no one was inclined to sleep, and I do not think any one retired but Mr. Frink. He evidently thought that the others were pretty badly scared, and therefore there would be enough to watch, so he could sleep undisturbed. For my part, I did not change my clothing during the entire night, neither shoes nor bonnet.

I sat up all night in the wagon to see that the guards kept awake, though it was too dark to see any distance. Once in a while, however, one of the guards would step up to the wagon and cautiously whisper that "no Indians had been seen yet." This, in a measure, would relieve my apprehensions; but still I was in such a state of anxiety and suspense that when I thought Mr. Frink was sleeping too soundly and breathing too heavily, I would arouse him; I could not understand how he could sleep soundly when there was so much danger. In this manner passed our first night on those vast, uninhabited plains. But by the time the day dawned and the guards came in, I was out and had a fire made and breakfast under way.

Wednesday, May 15. When we drove out from our fortified camp on the elevated knoll, and reached the main traveled road again, we met a large train of wagons from Ohio and Michigan. We kept in company with them during the day and encamped with them at night. Our party was now increased to fifty or more. We all traveled together for the next week.

Thursday, May 16. It was about half past six when we started this morning, but we traveled nearly twenty-five miles before night.

The Ohio and Michigan trains who were with us were fitted out with hardy Canadian ponies, small but tough, and capable of enduring greater hardships than ordinary horses. But the drivers were in too great a hurry to get to California before all the gold was dug out, and traveled too fast. Many of our party being young, inexperienced men, thought it necessary for us to pass all the ox teams and loose cattle on the road, fearing there would be no feed left for our own stock. They would whip up furiously and try to pass every train they overtook.

This did not accord with Mr. Frink's best judgment. Our own horses, like most of the western horses, were large and had been accustomed all their lives to be fed on corn. And now, to get nothing to eat but the scanty new grass of the plains, they could not endure what the sturdy Canadians could, and so after the first week had passed we traveled more slowly.

We encamped at night on Salt Creek, which runs northeast into the Platte River. Here Mr. Avery, the man who had joined our party at the camp below Savannah, caught a fine lot of catfish, which we enjoyed very much for supper.

Friday, May 17. This morning we started again at half past six, following, in a westerly direction, the well-traveled road which had been used for many years by teams hauling supplies to the frontier forts. Fort Kearney, at the head of Grand Island, is two hundred miles from the Missouri River. Fort Laramie, at the foot of the Black Hills, is about three hundred and fifty miles further; and Fort Hall, once an English trading post, is about five hundred and thirty miles still beyond. The road along here was in good condition, all the bad streams being bridged.

Saturday, May 18. To-day we traveled about twenty miles, descending the steep bluffs from the high plains, over which we have been marching ever since we crossed the Missouri River, to the low bottom of the Platte River, and coming for the first time to its south bank. Here we encamped for the night, finding grass and fire-wood very scarce.

This river differs from all those we have been accustomed to. A shallow groove, or flat, low valley, from ten to twenty miles wide, has been scooped out of the sandy plains for four hundred miles from the "Black Hills" to the Missouri. Along each side are bold, sandy bluffs, one hundred and fifty feet high. In the bottom of this valley the Platte River has cut out for itself a winding channel from six to ten feet deep and from one to two miles wide.

The valley, as well as the extensive plains on each side, is totally devoid of timber or undergrowth of any kind, except where a few straggling cottonwoods and willow thickets, long distances apart, stand close to the water's edge. In four hundred miles the descent of the stream is twenty-four hundred feet, or six feet to the mile, producing a swift current that plows out deep pools in its bed, and piles up high bars of quicksand, so that the volume of water is constantly changing from one to six feet in depth.

Our road from this point follows the south bank of the main stream and of its northern branch for four hundred and fifty miles. Fifty miles beyond it meets the Sweetwater, which leads two hundred miles further, to the South Pass.

Sunday, May 19. We are resting to-day, remaining in camp by the river. Near us are a few cottonwoods. There are no groves or forests in sight. We left all forests behind us at the Missouri River. Here the whole earth, as far as the eye can reach, is naked and bare except that a thin growth of grass partly hides the sandy ground.

During the day we thought it prudent to organize our forces for protection against the Indians, and to insure the safety of our stock at night. Something like a military system was adopted, with proper officers. In case of an attack by Indians, each man was expected to be at his appointed post. Mr. Frink was elected captain. Four men were to be detailed every night to stand guard over the horses, and bring them in the next morning. As there were now nearly fifty men in the party, no one person would have to stand guard oftener than once in ten or twelve days.

We had passed through the lands of the Pottawattamies, but without seeing any, and without molestation. The Kickapoos and Nemahas were sixty miles south, on the Blue Rivers. But ahead of us were many oher tribes, – the Pawnees, Sioux, Cheyennes, Blackfeet, and others, not supposed to be very friendly. We therefore thought it best to be fully prepared for them.

Monday, May 20. It was about six o'clock when we started this morning. We had with us some guidebooks (Fremont's and Palmer's), from which we learned that to-day we would pass the village of the Pawnee Indians, who had the name of being very warlike. In anticipation, every gun and pistol was put in good order, and regular military tactics were observed. At ten o'clock we came to the village, which was situated on a ridge extending nearly to the river. But instead of a bloody fight, which some expected, we took the village without firing a gun. From appearances, the place had not been occupied for years. There was nothing to indicate a village, except some tent-poles and a quantity of buffalo bones and those of other animals, that may have been killed for food. Our military prowess all disappeared in a twinkling. Up to this time we had seen but a single Indian, and he was a long way off. We learned afterwards that the tribe had removed about one hundred miles to the northward, to the Loup Fork of the Platte, where their chief village is, and where they raise considerable corn, during the times when they are not hunting or fighting.

In the afternoon we came to the junction of the emigrant road from St. Joseph with our road, about twenty-five miles below New Fort Kearney. That road ran westward from St. Joseph to the Blue Rivers, and up the Little Blue to its head, where it turned to the northward across the high plains to the Platte. Here the two roads met. Both roads were thickly crowded with emigrants. It was a grand spectacle when we came, for the first time, in view of the vast emigration, slowly winding its way westward over the broad plain.

The country was so level that we could see the long trains of white-topped wagons for many miles. Finally, when the two roads came together, and the army which had crossed the Missouri River at St. Joseph joined our army, which had crossed the river above Savannah, it appeared to me that none of the population had been left behind. It seemed to me that I had never seen so many human beings in all my life before. And, when we drew nearer to the vast multitude, and saw them in all manner of vehicles and conveyances, on horseback and on foot, all eagerly driving and hurrying forward, I thought, in my excitement, that if one-tenth of these teams and these people got ahead of us, there would be nothing left for us in California worth picking up.

Mr. Frink was not with our wagons just at this moment; he had either ridden ahead to look for grass, or was with some one behind. So I took the responsibility, and gave orders to the drivers to whip up, to drive fast and get ahead of that countless throng of wagons. But in a little while Mr. Frink appeared, and wanted to know of the drivers what they had got in such a hurry about. Already the horses were showing signs of being fretted; and Mr. Frink at once instructed the drivers that it would not do to attempt to travel at that rate of speed if we expected ever to reach California. But I was half frantic over the idea that every blade of grass for miles on each side of the road would be eaten off by the hundreds and thousands of horses, mules, and oxen ahead of us. And, worse than all, there would only be a few barrels of gold left for us when we got to California.

Mrs. McKinney, at whose house in Missouri we stopped on the night of the 18th of April, was responsible for my belief that it would be an easy thing to collect barrels of gold. And when, looking forward or backward at this place on the Platte, it seemed as if a number of cities had gathered here with all their people, on the same errand of seeking for gold, I was impatient at our slow progress, but we gradually toned down. In a few days the crowd strung out more evenly along the road, and was not gathered in such great masses.

There were all conceivable kinds of conveyances. There was a cart drawn by two cows, a cart drawn by one ox, and a man on horseback drove along an ox packed with his provisions and blankets. There was a man with a hand cart, another with a wheelbarrow loaded with supplies. And we were not yet two hundred miles from the Missouri River. The journey was only fairly commenced.

Tuesday, May 21. Leaving our camp in the Platte bottom at the usual hour, we traveled all day up the broad valley. With the exception of a muddy creek, or slough, now and then, the road was very good. During the day we passed New Fort Kearney, a small United States military station near the bank of the river, the walls of which were constructed largely of sods cut out in large blocks, and laid up as adobes are laid in California. This is the first human habitation we have seen since crossing the Missouri, two hundred miles distant. From that point we have been steadily climbing up hill, the altitude here being twenty-one hundred and fifty feet, which is twelve hundred feet higher than Bullard's Ferry. We camped to-night on the bank of the river.

Wednesday, May 22. After we had started this morning, there was great excitement over a buffalo chase, opposite the head of Grand Island in Platte River. Some of our men partook of the excitement. As far as we could see, every one that was on horseback went flying in the direction of the buffalo. Our men gave the saddle-horses a fatiguing run, but not without a reprimand from Mr. Frink when they returned. He informed them very distinctly that he had not started for California to hunt Buffalo. But I really could not blame the men very much, though the chase was bad for the horses. The animation and excitement of the moment beat anything I ever saw, and I would not, for a good deal, have missed the sight of that great chase over that grand plain. Some one brought us a piece of buffalo steak, so that we were not without a share of the prize.

The road to-day continued level and good, with exception of some muddy places and small gullies, which gave us no trouble. Fire-wood is scarce, there being none except along the river bank. Every stray piece we find we pick up and carry with us. The camp to-night presented the appearance of a village of tents and white-topped wagons.

Thursday, May 23. We are now in the midst of the buffalo country; but to our disappointment, we have seen only the small herd that came in sight yesterday. There are hundreds of thousands of them on these plains; but the emigration has frightened them to the right and to the left, away from the road, so that they are seldom seen. We often pass the bones and skulls in great numbers, where they have been killed by the Indians.

Friday, May 24. We left camp at the usual hour. The road often leaves the river to cross a large bend, and does not reach it again at camping-time. In such cases, the only resource for water is by digging wells a few feet deep. But the well water is usually muddy and warm. The soil is a kind of sandy loam, through which the river water makes its way, under the entire bottom.

Our chief inconvenience here is the want of fire-wood. There being no timber except the few cotton-woods and willows along the river, it often happens that we find hardly enough to cook our meals. But Mr. Frink adopted the plan of gathering up all the fragments we found and hauling them until time of need.

To-day the line of white wagons reaches out to the front and to the rear farther than we can see. Among such an army, we have little fear of trouble from Indians.

Saturday, May 25. Still traveling up the Platte. The road is a little monotonous. The scenery does not change much. The river has a winding course, and contains many islands. Some are little more than sand bars, others are covered with low willows. The road is at times along the river bank, and again near the bluffs on our left. The bluffs are getting higher. The face is gullied with deep ravines, in which cedar shrubs are growing, the first we have seen.

From our guide-books we learn that in a few days we shall reach the South Fork of the Platte, beyond which the face of the country changes.

Sunday, May 26. This is the day of rest, but there is not much rest crossing the plains. If our camp is at a place where there is neither grass nor water, we are compelled to travel on until we find them. And in camp there is no end of necessary work. Wagons, harness, and clothing have to be mended, washing to be done, animals to be changed on the pasture and guarded, innumerable small things to be looked after.

There is no time for reading, and there are neither newspapers nor letters to read. We have not heard from home since we left, nearly two months ago, and do not expect to until we arrive at Sutter's Fort, three months hence.

Monday, May 27. To-morrow will bring us to the South Fork, which we are told we must ford. From what we have seen of the river so far, it looks rather dangerous to cross, and we have some apprehensions of difficulty. But it may not so bad when we come to it. If we get safely over, we expect to reach a more interesting country to travel through.

The South Fork heads in a southwest direction from here, among the highest peaks of the Rocky Mountains. Our road will lead us up the North Fork of the Platte, and up its main branch, the Sweetwater, to the South Pass.

Our military organization has fallen to pieces. Those who were in so much of a hurry have driven ahead, reducing our number to about twenty-five. Mr. Frink thought the only sure way to get to California with our animals was to drive slowly. We have found, too, that it is best to travel in small parties, on account of the scarcity, in many places, of grass and water. Many camping places that would afford enough for a small train, would not supply a large company.

Tuesday, May 28. We left our camp near the river about half past six, and in a few miles came to the South Fork, a short distance above the junction, where we were to cross. A great crowd of emigrants was encamped here, making all preparations, though a great many of them were undecided what was best to do. We heard all kinds of reports as to the best route to take, for every one was ignorant. Some thought they would follow up the valley of the South Platte, on the south side; but the majority decided to ford the river at this point. On the whole long journey to California there were neither ferries nor bridges, except a ferry at North Platte and one at Green River, and the small bridges back near Salt River, and a little one in Carson Cañon.

The stream we had now reached was fearful to look at, – rushing and boiling and yellow with mud, a mile wide, and in many places of unknown depth. The bed was of quicksand – this was the worst difficulty. But there was no way to do but to ford it. So we started down the bank and into the raging water.

From a guide-book we had with us, we learned that the proper way to cross the stream was to take a diagonal course, – first down the stream, then up again. Accordingly, after driving into the water, we turned down at an angle of forty-five degrees till we had reached the middle of the river; then, turning up stream at the same angle, we arrived safely at the northern bank, nearly opposite our point of entrance.

Of all the excitements that I ever experienced or thought of, the crossing of that river was the greatest. A great many other wagons and people were crossing at the same time – mule teams, horse teams, ox teams, men on horseback, men wading and struggling against the quicksands and current, many of them with long poles in their hands, feeling their way. Sometimes they would be in shallow water only up to their knees; then, all at once, some unlucky one would plunge in where it was three or four feet deep.

The deafening noise and halloing that this army of people kept up, made the alarm in the river more intense. The quicksand and the uncertainty of depth of water kept all in a state of anxiety. Our horses would sometimes be in water no more than a foot deep; then, in a moment, they would go down up to their collars. On one occasion I was considerably alarmed. Several other wagons, in their haste, had crowded in ahead of us on both sides, and we were compelled to stop for several minutes. Our wagon at once began to settle in the quicksand, and it required the assistance of three or four men lifting at the wheels, to enable the horses to pull out.

Where we crossed, the river was a mile wide, and we were just three-quarters of an hour in getting over. I here date one of the happiest and most thankful moments of my life to have been when we landed safe on the north side. The danger in the crossing consisted in the continual shifting of the sandy bed, so that a safe ford to-day might be a dangerous one to-morrow.

We were now nine-hundred and thirteen miles from home.

The next excitement we met with was some day after, when the rumor came back from the front that the grass ahead was all burned off. What was to become of us, with nothing for our horses to eat, and we unable to go either forward or backward?

But we out-traveled this rumor in a day. We were journeying, of course, in the dark all the time, and never knew what was in store for us ahead.

The elevation of this point is two thousand seven hundred and ninety feet above the Gulf of Mexico.

CHAPTER IV.

Wednesday, May 29. At broad mass of high, rugged mountains filled most of the space between the two forks of the Platte. The point comes down opposite the ford. Many of the emigrants turned to the left, up the South Fork for six miles, then crossed over the hills to the North Fork valley. Our party bore to the right at the ford, and in half an hour came to the low point of the great promontory. This was the outermost spur of the Rocky Mountain chain, and here, for the first time, our wheels and horses' hoofs struck its solid granite ledges. We crossed without difficulty, and drove up the valley of the North Fork for several miles, before going into camp. The valley here is about five miles wide, level, but more sandy than below. High, rocky ridges border it on both sides. There is some undergrowth in the side cañons, but generally timber is scarce. Sometimes we find no firewood, and have to draw from our stock in the wagon.

Thursday, May 30. The road continues up the valley, along the south side of the river. Occasionally it leaves the river, to pass over and around the bluffs. In the cañons the heat is oppressive. This valley is claimed by the Sioux Indians, a large tribe once hostile to the whites. We are now getting near the sagebrush region, that we have heard so much about. The roads continue heavy and very dusty.

Friday, May 31. We expect to reach in a few days some great natural curiosities. One is a large rock in shape like a court-house, or a church without a steeple. The other is a tall, square tower or chimney, which can be seen for a long distance. We are also on the lookout for Indians, though they are thought to be friendly. Our large company is reduced to but a few persons, and our horses are strictly guarded every night.

Saturday, June 1. To-day the bluffs came to the river and cut off our passage along the bank. We had to climb a long hill to go around. We descended to the river again through a deep ravine called Ash Hollow, where Colonel Harney, with a detachment of United States Regulars, had a severe fight with the Sioux, several years ago.

The heavy sand and hard climbing begin to tell on the strength of our horses. Feed is often scarce and they suffer in consequence.

Sunday, June 2. We remained in camp all day, repairing our small wagon. The hind axle was broken. Mr. Frink had seen a wagon abandoned, near the road at Ash Hollow. He went back with a man to-day, and took out the bolts and brought the hind axle and wheels to camp. It was then fitted to the small wagon in place of he old axle, and did very well.

Monday, June 3. We traveled ten miles to-day and stopped on good grass. In the afternoon we passed an Indian encampment numbering seventy tents. They belonged to the Sioux tribe, but were quite friendly. The squaws were much pleased to see the "white squaw" in our party, as they called me. I had brought a supply of needles and thread, some of which I gave them. We also had some small mirrors in gilt frames, and a number of other trinkets, with which we could buy fish and fresh buffalo, deer, and antelope meat. But money they would not look at.

A heavy storm of wind and rain came up afterwards, which we prepared ourselves for by picketing down the wagons with ropes fastened to stakes, and tying the horses securely.

Tuesday, June 4. In the morning it was raining some and Mr. Frink got breakfast. We had been closely on the lookout, and at three o'clock we came in sight of the famous "Court-house Rock," eighteen miles distant, and many miles south of the road. It presented a very imposing appearance. "Chimney Rock" also came in sight, about thirty miles further on. Our camp at night was made nearly opposite the Court-house Rock, and six miles distant; but the atmosphere was so clear that it did not seem to be more than a mile away. Many persons, thinking they could walk to the rock in a few minutes, would start out on foot to examine it more closely; but after walking for an hour, finding it to be as far off as ever, apparently, would give up the attempt.

Wednesday, June 5. The weather to-day was quite hot and oppressive. We had to cross a long stretch without water. The road we took led us close to the base of Chimney Rock, where we stopped for some time to satisfy our curiosity. The base is shaped like a large cone, from the top of which rises a tall tower or chimney, resembling the chimney of a manufacturing establishment. According to Fremont, it was once five hundred feet high, but has been worn down by the winds and rains until it is no more than two hundred and fifty feet in height. It is composed of marl and soft sandstone, which is easily worn away. Mr. Frink carved our names upon the chimney, where are hundreds of others.

Thursday, June 6. We came to Scott's Bluffs to-day. When we reached there, we found water in a deep gully on the left side of the road, where a great many thirsty people were waiting for water. There was a very small weeping spring, where we caught the water in a cup, as it wept out from under the rocks.

Friday, June 7. To-day we crossed over the bluffs, and encamped near the Platte River, not far from Horse Creek.

Saturday, June 8. The mail-carriers passed us on a trot this morning, going to the summit of the Rocky Mountains, where a post-office for the accommodation of the emigrants was established. When we came to the Laramie River, the water was very high, and ran into our wagon. This is a dangerous ford, where a number of persons have been drowned.

At four o'clock we arrived at the place we have so long been anxious to reach, – Fort Laramie. This outpost formerly belonged to the American Fur Company, who built it as a protection against the savages, then very numerous and hostile. After the United States Government bought it, they sent regular troops to protect the emigration.

The fort is one hundred and eighty feet square, having adobe walls fifteen feet high, on the inside of which are rooms built against the walls all around, of the same material. The parade-ground in the center is one hundred and thirty feet square. On top of the wall are wooden palisades. Over the front gateway is a square tower with loopholes for rifles.

As it is not our intention to go by Salt Lake, this is the last human habitation we shall see until we reach Fort Hall, five hundred and thirty miles further on.

The altitude of Fort Laramie is four thousand four hundred and seventy feet. This is almost four thousand feet higher than our starting-point. But we are not yet half way up to the highest point of our road, and have traveled not half its length. Our camp last night was on the forty-second parallel of north latitude, – two and a half degrees north of that of Martinsville.

We should have been glad to stop here and rest a while, before starting out on the next stretch of our long, mountainous journey. But it was necessary to find a good camping-place for the night, and we tarried but a short time. Three miles beyond, we found good feed and there made our camp.

Sunday, June 9. We remained in this camp all day, resting as much as is possible on such a journey and under such circumstances. But it was a very different Sunday from those we had been always accustomed to at home.

Monday, June 10. It was at this camp that we had to leave our cooking stove, which we had found so useful ever since crossing the Missouri. It being light, we had always carried it lashed on the hind end of the wagon. Some careless person, in a hurry, drove his team up too close behind, and the pole of his wagon ran into the stove, smashing and ruining it. After that, we had to cook in the open air. We adopted a plan which was very fashionable on the plains. We would excavate a narrow trench in the ground, a foot deep and three feet long, in which we built the fire. The cooking vessels were set over this, and upon trial we found it a very good substitute for a stove.

We started at twelve o'clock to-day, traveled fifteen miles, and went into camp at five o'clock. The road was among and over the spurs of the Black Hills, and very rough. I rode horseback the most of the day.

Many wagons are being abandoned. Every day we pass good wagons that have been left for any one that might want them.

The Black Hills are so named from the fact that they are covered with pine, hemlock, spruce, cedar, and other evergreen trees, which give them, at a distance, a dark and gloomy appearance.

Tuesday, June 11. Our road keeps on westward up the valley of the North Fork – the river on our right, the Black Hills on our left, bordering the valley. They appear to be about seven or eight miles distant. Among them we can see Laramie Peak, twenty-five miles to the south. It is six thousand five hundred feet high.

In six miles we came to Poplar Creek, which is well timbered with poplars. The bottom is rich and produces good grass, but it is now nearly all eaten off. Seventeen miles further we came to Horseshoe Creek, which runs from the Black Hills to the river. This is a fine stream, having groves of poplars along its banks. It is next to the largest creek between Fort Laramie and the crossing of the North Fork. Seven miles beyond here we came again to the bank of the Platte, where we found the feed to be very scarce. This region is said to produce clouds of grasshoppers in dry seasons.

Wednesday, June 12. The road sometimes follows near the river, then goes over the bluffs, then across deep sand. The hills and bottoms are mostly covered with sage-brush. It grows in dense, tangled thickets, and to break a road through it is hard work for the heaviest and strongest teams. It is about four feet high, with stems two inches thick at the ground, and often matted close together. It is of a dull gray color and gives the country a gloomy appearance. Very little grass grows among it. And yet it is said the soil is rich, and would produce well if cleared and cultivated.

Thursday, June 13. To-day we passed near where an old fort was built by some hunters or trappers, to protect themselves from Indians, who were very troublesome some years ago. The remains of the fort have nearly disappeared. We are coming into the range of the Arapahoes, who are reputed to be fighting Indians, but we have not seen any of them. They are supposed to be on the trail of the buffaloes, that have been frightened away by the crowds of emigration. The buffaloes are the chief means of subsistence of the Indian tribes over hundreds of thousands of square miles of this region.

To-morrow we expect to reach Deer Creek, and hope to find plenty of feed for our horses, who have a hard time of it over the rough and sandy roads, with only a scanty supply of food.

Friday, June 14. In six miles we came to Wood Creek. The grass, abundant in the spring, was now mostly eaten off. A fine growth of poplars lined the banks of the stream, and we were told that when feed is scarce the Indians chop down the young saplings and feed their horses on the leaves and tender branches.

It was three o'clock in the afternoon when we reached Deer Creek, thirteen miles beyond Wood Creek. This is the largest of the many streams running into the Platte, above the Laramie Fork. Along the bottom is considerable timber. With Robert's assistance, I did the washing this afternoon. During the night a heavy storm of wind came up, but passed over without doing any serious damage.

Saturday, June 15. This morning we started at eight o'clock. Our friends, the Carson boys from Cincinnati, came up with us here. We made a long drive to-day of twenty-six miles and camped within three miles of the crossing of the North Platte. For several days past we have been traveling among extensive thickets of sage-brush, or artemisia. It has the odor of turpentine mixed with camphor, which fills the air.

Sunday, June 16. We remained in camp at this place all day. A great many emigrants are gathered here and above, preparatory to crossing the river. The water is too deep to ford and the ferry charges are very high. Some are making ferry-boats of their wagon bodies taken off the wheels, and launched in the water, with long ropes to haul them back and forth across the river. In some cases, empty casks are tied to the four corners of the wagon body, to keep it from sinking. This plan is very dangerous in the swift current, and we hear of many persons who have lost their lives in these attempts.

Monday, June 17. A great crowd was waiting to cross the ferry. But by starting early, we were not delayed, and got over by six o'clock. This ferry was established by Kit Carson, the famous hunter and trapper, one of Fremont's guides. There were several ferry-boats. The water was deep and swift. The boats were attached to strong ropes stretched across the river, and were driven quickly from shore to shore by the strong current. We paid $5.00 each for our two wagons, and $1.00 each for our seven horses.

The Platte River at this place comes out of the mountains from the southward, making a sharp bend at the above. Our road here leaves the Platte, which we have followed for four hundred and fifty miles, and strikes across to the Sweetwater, fifty miles further west. The space between the rivers is mostly a desert, covered with sage-brush, and producing but little grass. There are pools of alkali water and beds of dried-up ponds, crusted with soda or salt, several inches thick. The wheels and horses' hoofs break through the crust as if it were ice.

We started early to cross this long, bad stretch. On our left were some high, red cliffs called the "Red Bluffs." After traveling twenty-two miles without water, we stopped all night by the only good spring. This is called Willow Springs; it lies in a deep, narrow gully, where the water is dipped by the cupful to fill the kegs and water vessels. At dark, while I was cooking supper, a heavy storm of wind and snow came up. There was no shelter, and we ate our supper while it was snowing and blowing. During the night, the men took turns guarding the horses in the snow, Mr. Frink being with them part of the time.

Tuesday, June 18. This was a bright June morning. We snowballed each other till ten o'clock, when the sun got too warm for the snow to remain. We traveled twenty-two miles, and came to the Sweetwater River, up which our road follows for one hundred and thirty miles, to the South Pass.

Wednesday, June 19. We traveled ten miles and came to "Independence Rock," a famous landmark in the Sweetwater Valley. The road runs close to it. It received its name from a party of emigrants on their way to Oregon, several years ago, who celebrated the anniversary of the Declaration of Independence at this point, on the Fourth of July. This singular rock is a granite boulder, about nineteen hundred feet long, two hundred feet wide, and one hundred and twenty feet high, standing on a level plain, entirely detached from the mountains near by. The sides and front, to the height of six or eight feet, contain hundreds of names painted with black paint made of gunpowder and bacon grease.

Thursday, June 20.   Five miles above "Independence Rock" we came to the "Devil's Gate," where the river breaks through a spur of the mountains. The gap is nine hundred feet long, four hundred feet high, and one hundred and five feet wide. The road passes through another break a few hundred yards to the left. This opens into another beautiful valley about five miles wide, hemmed in by mountains that rise abruptly from the plain to a height of fifteen hundred or two thousand feet. There are scattering lines of pine timber on the tops, among which we could see patches of snow.

The valley is nearly level, and mostly covered with sage-brush. On the south side of some sand hillocks there are clums of sage six feet high, with stems six inches in diameter. Along the river are narrow borders of good grass. The elevation of this valley is six thousand forty feet.

We only traveled fifteen miles to-day. Our Cincinnati friends, the Carsons, who have been with us for some days, left us this morning and drove ahead, being in a hurry to get to the end of the journey.

We had the novelty of camping alone for the first time.

Friday, June 21. Our fellow-passenger, Mr. Avery, also left us this morning, concluding he could walk to California sooner than we could get there, at the rate we were traveling. We gave him all the provisions he could carry, and he started, with blankets, clothing, and provisions strapped on his back, to walk fifteen hundred miles to California.

Six miles from our camp we came to the cañon of the Sweetwater, and crossed the river by the difficult fords three times in less than a mile. Eight miles beyond the cañon we encamped on the Sweetwater by ourselves again.

Saturday, June 22. This morning we crossed ford number four of the Sweetwater, and then crossed a desert of sixteen miles without water. About midway was an extensive marsh, said to be underlaid with ice, but to what depth was not known. It is supposed that the marsh is frozen to great depth in winter, and that only a thin surface is thawed in summer.

During the forenoon we ascended a long, sloping hill, at the top of which, looking across a wide stretch of rough country covered with sage-brush, we got our first sight of the Wind River range of the Rocky Mountains. They were covered with snow, and appeared to be about fifty miles distant. We now realize that we are getting near the South Pass, which lies at the left of the snowy chain, where the mountains are broken away.

A few miles further we came to Sweetwater ford number five. The great number of fords on this stream are made necessary by the crooked course of the river, and the rough nature of the country. At this place we fell in with a company from Independence, Missouri, among whom were several emigrants from Kentucky and Indiana. A young Kentuckian, Mr. Thomas Wand, had ridden on ahead that day, and found a good camping place. He invited us to join them and to place our horses and mules with theirs on the pasture, which offer we readily accepted. One of the party, Mr. Johnson, proved to be from our own county.

Sunday, June 23. To-day we traveled twenty-three miles, crossing Sweetwater three times. We then left the river and went around the mountains. After crossing a small rivulet, we came to the Strawberry branch, and a few miles beyond reached what was known as the Quaking Asp branch of the Sweetwater, where we encamped for the night. The days are warm and pleasant, but after sunset the air cools rapidly, and heavy frosts whiten the ground in the morning.

Monday, June 24. This was a day long to be remembered. At five o'clock we drove out of camp, and, in two miles, crossed the east branch of the Sweetwater. Five miles further we came to the main and last branch of the stream, which we had no difficulty in crossing. On the mountains near the road there were deep banks of snow in the gulches.

We then traveled up a long, gradual slope, or plain, free of rocks, trees, or gullies, and came at half past eleven o'clock to the summit of the South Pass of the Rocky Mountains. We could hardly realize that we were crossing the great backbone of the North American Continent at an altitude of seven thousand four hundred and ninety feet. The ascent was so smooth and gentle, and the level ground at the summit so much like a prairie region, that it was not easy to tell when we had reached the exact line of the divide. But it is here that after every shower the little rivulets separate, some to flow into the Atlantic, the others into the Pacific.

It was a beautiful, warm, hazy day. Near the summit, on each side of the road, was an encampment, at one of which the American flag was flying, to mark the private post-office or express office established by Gen. James Estelle, for the accommodation of emigrants wishing to send letters to friends at home. The last post-office on our way was at St. Joseph, on the Missouri River. West of that stream were neither states, counties, cities, towns, villages, nor white men's habitations. The two mud forts we had passed were the only signs of civilization. The entire region between the Missouri River and the Rocky Mountains was then called by the official name of the Indian Territory; and as it was only a hunting-ground for the tribes we had passed, and for the Cheyennes, Blackfeet, Snakes, Arapahoes, Oglallahs, and Crows, its name was appropriate.

To see the old flag once more strongly reminded use of home. There was a hail-storm at noon, but that did not prevent the assembled company from having an off-hand celebration of our arrival at the summit. Music from a violin with tin-pan accompaniment, contributed to the general merriment of a grand frolic. In the afternoon we spent some time in writing letters to our friends, to be sent back by the express. On each letter we paid as express charges

$1.00. The returning messengers delivered the letters
to the postmaster at St. Joseph, and in due time they
reached their destination, one thousand four hundred
thirty-eight miles distant.

Then we set out to begin the long descent to the
Pacific Ocean, bidding farewell to everything on the
Atlantic side. We drove down a ravine for eight
miles and encamped for the night at Pacific Springs.
There being no grass here, the animals were taken
into the hills two miles to the north, where the men
guarded them all night. In the morning Mr. Frink
found a field of bunch grass, not far from the camp,
which he estimated would yield two tons per acre.

CHAPTER V.

Tuesday, June 25. We are now on the borders of the
desert region. Between here and Green River extends
a barren plain seventy miles wide, with only two
streams and but scanty grass. We remained in camp
until half past five o'clock in the afternoon. We then
started across the first stretch of twenty-one miles, prepared to travel in the night to avoid the heat and
lessen the thirst of our animals. The road was level
and good. In ten miles we reached the dry bed of a
small creek called "Dry Sandy." The moon shone
bright as day, and our party was in good spirits. The
violinist played while others sang, and the long night
passed off very pleasantly. We reached the first water,
at Little Sandy, at two o'clock in the morning, pretty
well fatigued. Here we halted, put our horses out to
feed, and staid till morning.

Wednesday, June 26. All around is a plain thinly
covered with sage-brush and grease-wood. A few miles

to our right commence the foot-hills of the Wind River chain, and beyond them the Snowy Mountains rise abrupty to great height. They extend in a north-west direction farther than we can see. About fifty miles north is Fremont's Peak, thirteen thousand five hundred seventy feet high, the loftiest of the Rocky Mountains. Fremont planted the American flag on the summit in August, 1842, being probably the first human being to scale the mountain.

At fifteen minutes before ten o'clock in the morning, we started again, and after traveling six miles came to the Big Sandy, where we remained until half past six in the afternoon. We passed, on the way, the forks of the road, the left hand of which runs southwest to Salt Lake City, two hundred miles distant. We took the right-hand road, which is supposed to be shorter, and is known as Sublette's Cut-off.

Having now a forty-mile desert to cross without water, we filled our water-bottles, containing five gallons each. Starting a little before sunset, we traveled during the night twenty miles and stopped at four o'clock in the morning at a place where we found feed for the animals.

Thursday, June 27. From this camp Fremont's Peak can be distinctly seen, rising above all others. A few miles west of its base, in the valley, are the ruins of an old fort built by Captain Bonneville, of the U.S. Army, who explored this region in 1832.

There was no water on the desert, but our bottles supplied us with all that we needed. At six o'clock we started on, being anxious to get to Green River as soon as possible. After traveling twelve miles, we halted for our noon lunch, but as soon as this was over, we hastened forward. Fifteen miles brought us to the bluffs on the western edge of the desert, about four o'clock. From here we could see the bright waters of the river, several miles away. The bluffs were high, steep, and rocky, and we had to let the wagons down cautiously with ropes. The narrow gorges through which we passed down, were filled with clouds of blinding dust. At the foot of the bluffs the dust was from twelve to twenty inches deep. The river bottom was a plain of dust, crowded with wagons and animals, and thickly populated with emigrants waiting their regular turn to be ferried over. Each of the two ferries had a small flatboat rowed with oars.

Many of the animals had already been swum across; but the water was high, deep, swift, blue, and cold as ice, heading in the ice mountains on our right. The poor horses were reluctant to venture in. One of our animals utterly refused to swim. The ferryman was loath to take him on the boat but at last consented. By leading one or two of our horses behind the boat, the others were induced to follow. Mr. Rose crossed at the same time and took the animals seven miles further to pasture.

Mr. Frink had been taken sick during the day, and when he got to the foot of the bluffs, he was no longer able to walk, and with difficulty climbed into the wagon. As our wagons could not be taken over that night, we had to stop in that miserable desert of dust until late the next day, waiting our turn to cross. Our boy, Robert, remained with us; but, excepting him, Mr. Frink and I were entirely alone. The situation was a serious one. I was frightened at feeling we were almost helpless, a thousand miles from civilization.

Friday, June 28. This morning we heard that a gentleman by the name of Redwine, who had crossed the plains the year previous, was encamped near us with his family. At Mr. Frink's suggestion I called at their camp to learn, if possible, something of the road ahead of us; for our guide-books did not cover this part of the route. Mr. Redwine's reply was that he knew no more about the road than if he had never traveled it; that everything seemed new to him, but he thought it was yet a thousand miles to California. He could give us no information of any value.

Fortunately, Mr. Frink improved so much that he was enabled to cross the river with us in the afternoon.

Green River runs southward to the Colorado, which empties into the Gulf of California. The Spaniards, long ago, named it the "Rio Verde." The Crow Indians call it "Prairie Chicken River," from the quantities of grouse to be found on its upper branches.

Saturday, June 29. Mr. Rose was now taken sick with mountain fever. Mr. Frink was still confined to his bed. The outlook for the future became, for a time, quite dark and discouraging. But at this critical moment Mr. Thomas Wand, whom we had met on the Sweetwater, volunteered to take charge of our horses and to pasture and guard them for us. This was a great relief, for which I felt very thankful. But we had no way of showing our gratitude except by sending to him a present of a few delicacies from our stock on hand. This was the darkest period of our whole journey, and the assistance he gave us was highly appreciated.

Sunday, June 30. This is our third day in this dis-

mal camp on the west bank of Green River. But Mr.
Frink and Mr. Rose are both improving, and matters
look more hopeful. There were frost and ice in camp
last night, though to-day, at ten o'clock, the thermometer shows eighty degrees in the shade.

Monday, July 1. Mr. Wand and his company have
left their wagons here and made pack-saddles, intending to pack their clothing, blankets, provisions, and
cooking utensils on their animals, in order to travel
faster. They stopped here two days for that purpose,
and are now ready to start. Mr. Johnson, of Morgan
County, Indiana, had been with Mr. Wand's party up
to this time, but preferring not to pack through, made
arrangements with Mr. Frink to travel with us. His
horse, a good animal, was harnessed to our wagon and
proved quite useful.

This morning some packers overtook us and brought
the alarming tidings that cholera had appeared on the
Platte River, behind us. This was the first that we had
heard of its being on the road.

Mr. Frink and Mr. Rose are much improved. At
twelve o'clock we started and traveled twelve miles.
We hope in a few days to reach Bear River, where grass
is said to be abundant.

Tuesday, June 2. Our sick people are still improving. We traveled to-day twenty miles over hills and
valleys, and encamped alone by a mountain brook.

Wednesday, June 3. This morning Mr. Rose was not
quite so well. In the afternoon he grew much worse,
having a severe attack of mountain fever. At two
o'clock a company from Illinois overtook us. I rode
on horseback most of the day. We traveled thirteen

miles and encamped on Ham's Fork, which runs south-ward into Green River. This is a beautiful stream of clear water, in a narrow, grassy valley.

Thursday, July 4. At six o'clock we started and after going a short distance down the stream, turned to the right and climbed up a long, narrow spur, to the top of a high mountain. We continued to ascend one after another, until we had reached a great height. This was the Bear River Range of the Rock Mountains. On the summit the road wound through a dense grove of tall young aspens and pines. We were delighted to be among trees once more, but they were soon passed by. This ridge is eight thousand two hundred thirty feet high, being seven hundred forty feet higher than the South Pass.

From this high point the road ran rapidly down, through a long, dusty, rocky ravine, or cañon, to a small valley within three miles of Bear River, where we encamped for the night, after a very hard day's drive. Mr. Rose was very sick all day. At one time his condition was alarming, but about sunset, to our great relief, there was a change for the better.

Notwithstanding our anxiety and fatigue, our dinner, in honor of the national anniversary, was the best we could provide. The last of our potatoes, which had long been saved for the occasion, made it a rare feast.

Since crossing the high ridge, we had descended, in less than half a day, one thousand eight hundred thirty feet, the elevation of this Fourth-of-July camp being six thousand four hundred feet.

Friday, July 5. We started at six o'clock and trav-

eled northward, down the valley of Bear River – the
mountains on our right, the river on our left. About
three miles from the camp, we came to a rapid stream
called Smith's Fork, issuing from the high mountains on our right, and divided into four separate
creeks that ran across our road to the river. The
second one being very narrow and deep, with perpendicular banks, had been bridged in a novel manner.
A log had been split in the center and laid across with
the flat sides up, at the proper distance to fit the wagon
wheels; so that, by using a little care, the wagons could
be safely crossed.

From here we drove on to the bank of Bear River,
some distance to the left, and took our noon lunch.
Then we traveled on to Thomas Fork, which is a
fine stream, coming from the northeast, where we
encamped for the night. Here we found good grass.
Mr. Rose was some better during the day. The thermometer at noon showed eighty degrees.

Saturday, July 6. We started at six o'clock, forded
Thomas Fork, and, turning to the west, came to a high,
steep spur that extends to the river. Over this high spur
we were compelled to climb. The distance is seven
miles, and we were five hours in crossing. Part of the
way I rode on horseback, the rest I walked. The descent was very long and steep. All the wheels of the
wagon were tied fast, and it slid along the ground.
At one place the men held it back with ropes and let
it down slowly.

After coming to the valley, we drove to the river and
rested some time for dinner. In the afternoon we went
seven miles further, down the valley, and encamped
at sundown on a beautiful stream lined with shrubs,

running from the mountains to the river. Here we intend to stay over Sunday.

Sunday, July 7. We are remaining in camp to-day, resting from the severe labors and anxieties of the past week, as far as the pressing duties of camp life on the plains permit us to do so.

Monday, July 8. It rained considerably during the night. Mr. Frink was on guard until two o'clock, when he returned to camp bringing the startling news that, from some unknown cause, the horses had stampeded. We had no means of knowing whether it was the work of Indians or not, but it was useless to hunt for them in the darkness, Mr. Frink lay down and slept till daylight. Then a search was commenced, which resulted in the animals being soon found, not for from camp, very much to our relief.

When we arose, we found the range of mountains covered with new-fallen snow. This is a beautiful valley, and when under settlement and cultivation, will be a delightful region. Wild flax is growing in many places, as thickly as if sowed by the hand of man.

At half past ten we passed a village of Snake River Indians. Soon after, we crossed six beautiful mountain streams. Mr. Rose was much improved to-day, and able to drive the small wagon part of the time.

I visited a lady to-day at a train which had halted not far from ours – an unusual incident on this journey. We traveled ten miles and encamped on the bank of the river.

Tuesday, July 9. At half past five we set out, and in two hours and a half reached the far-famed Soda

Springs and Steamboat Spring, at the big bend of Bear River. At this point the stream – along which for five days we have been traveling northward – suddenly bends to the left around a high, steep mountain, and, reversing its course, runs directly southward for one hundred twenty-five miles, to lose itself in the Great Salt Lake.

The Soda Springs are on the right of the road and boil up from the ground in many places, forming mounds of earth with a little cup or hollow on the top. Some of the mounds are several feet in height, the water bubbling over the top on all sides. By some they are called Beer Springs, from their peculiar taste.

About a mile further on is the Steamboat Spring, on the left of the road near the river. It derives its name from the ebullition of the water at regular intervals of about thirty seconds, which produces a sound similar to that of a steamboat. About three feet from the spring is a constant discharge of steam through a small crevice in the rock.

This region abounds in rare curiosities. I have never visited a place where there was so much of an interesting character to be seen. The whole country seems to have been curiously formed. I left this spot very reluctantly. Everything I saw was full of interest. But a party of Michigan men, who were at this time traveling with us, claimed that they could neither see nor feel an interest in anything this side of the gold of California.

There was an Indian village here of considerable size. The Indians seemed to be well-disposed. Our boy, Robert Parker, made a trade with them, exchanging his worn shoes for a pair of new moccasins.

The emigration was very thin on this part of the route, the heaviest portion of it having gone by way of the Salt Lake road, that turned off a few miles east of the Little Sandy.

Driving on a mile from the Steamboat Spring, we came to the forks of the road, the left-hand one, called Myer's Cut-off, going westerly over the plains and hills to Raft River, the right-hand one taking a northwest direction, and crossing the northern rim of the Great Salt Lake Basin, to Fort Hall, on the Snake River, or Lewis Fork of the Columbia.

We have now traveled sixteen hundred twenty-two miles from home. The elevation of this place is five thousand eight hundred forty feet, indicating that we have descended only one hundred sixty feet in our journey of seventy miles down the Bear River Valley.

CHAPTER VI.

Tuesday, July 9, Continued. When we came to the forks of the road, we decided to take the right-hand one, leading to Fort Hall, because of the advice and illustration given us by an old Indian at the Soda Springs. He raised up the bail of a bucket to signify a high mountain, and passing his hand over the top, said, "This is Myer's Cut-off." Then, laying the bail down and passing his hand around it, said, "This is the Fort Hall road." We were told afterwards that this was correct.

The whole plain, fifteen miles wide, west and northwest of the forks, seemed to have once been the mouth or interior of an immense volcanic crater. It was a level floor of hardened lava, seamed with chasms of great depth.

We soon came to a soda pool, on top of a mound five feet high. We drove by the side of it and I dipped a cupful without leaving my seat in the wagon. Its taste was that of ordinary soda water. I learned afterwards from those who had used it that it made very light biscuit. We had no chance to give it a trial in this way.

In the afternoon we traveled twelve miles, passing many curious objects and crossing one small stream. During the night it rained.

Wednesday, July 10. Five of our horses were missing this morning, but after a short search they were found and brought into camp. After breakfast, we traveled northward for ten miles, crossing to the west side of a stream of water, where we halted for dinner. While there, a party of Snake Indians came into the camp, begging flour, coffee, and bread, of each of which we gave them a little.

About half past twelve we started to ascend the mountain chain which separates the Great Salt Lake basin from the valley of the Columbia. The road was very rough, but we had crossed the main ridge by four o'clock, and soon after came to a small spring branch flowing northward into Snake River, where we made our encampment for the night, in view of banks of snow from five to ten feet deep.

This is the road that was followed by Peter Lassen, one of the earliest pioneers of California, long before the gold was discovered. It is now the main road followed by emigrants to Oregon.

Thursday, July 11. The road to-day was very hilly and rough. At night we encamped within one mile of Fort Hall. Mosquitoes were as thick as flakes in a snow-storm. The poor horses whinnied all night, from their bites, and in the morning the blood was streaming down their sides. At our noon camp we found a thicket of wild currant bushes, from which we gathered currants enough to furnish pies for the next two or three days. They were a great luxury to people who had been without fruit of any kind for three months.

In the afternoon we came to a creek that appeared to be deep and bad to cross. Just as we were beginning to examine for a safe place to ford it, three Indians on horseback came toward us. They rode across the creek before us, apparently to show us the best way. We crossed without difficulty, and they afterwards accompanied us to where we encamped for the night. One of them, much older than the others, informed us that he had traveled as far east as St. Louis; and in order to make us understand, he imitated with his mouth the puffing of a steamboat. He rode onwards after we had reached camp; but the other two turned their horses loose, and stayed near us all night. They told us that this was the Indian's country.

Friday, July 12. We left our camp at half past five in the morning, and at seven o'clock reached a former trading-post of the Hudson's Bay Company, established many years ago, when the English people made claim to all this part of our territory. It was in charge of Captain Grant, a Canadian, who had been here for nine years, and had entertained Colonel Fremont and his party, in September, 1843, while on their way to the mouth of the Columbia River.

We stopped here for a short time, and were hospitably received by Captain Grant, who treated us in a very gentlemanly manner, and formally introduced us to his wife, an Indian woman, of middle age, quite good-looking, and dressed in true American syle.

Before we left, he very kindly presented us with a supply of fresh lettuce and onions, expressing regret that because of the lateness of the season, he had no other varieties to offer us. We thankfully accepted them as a very unusual luxury.

We did not visit the United States Government post, Fort Hall, as it was a mile off the road, though it was in full view on our right as we passed along.

We have now reached the most northerly point of our wearisome journey. The latitude of Fort Hall is forty-three degrees one minute and thirty seconds north, according to Colonel Fremont's calculation. This is three and a half degrees north of Martinsville. The altitude of Fort Hall is four thousand five hundred feet.

We are now to turn to the left at a right angle, and travel the rest of the way in a nearly southwest direction, until we reach Sutter's Fort, which is still seven hundred miles distant; and from all accounts, the worst part of the road is yet to be passed over.

During our halt at the fort, our company had gone on; so we set forward alone. In two miles we came to a stream, which, though deep, we crossed without much trouble. But three miles beyond, a considerable stream running to our right was found to be much deeper. Here, in crossing, we got our things wet, for the first time on the journey. We could not ford in the usual way, but had to draw the wagons across by ropes stretched to the other bank. The next slough was also deep, but we got over safe.

After traveling about ten miles further, we came to Snake River, which here runs in a southwest direction, and encamped for the night on the southeast bank.

Saturday, July 13. We started at five o'clock this morning, and soon came to the American Falls of Snake River. This stream, which is nine hundred feet wide, is inclosed between high walls of black, volcanic rock, and has a perpendicular fall of fifty feet. Beyond it is a wide plain of black lava, so broken and split with deep chasms that it can hardly be crossed by a man on foot. Fifty miles distant, northwest, the "Three Buttes" rise high and bold out of the lava-plain, and can be seen for a long distance. Our first view of them was from the high ridge south of Fort Hall.

We halted for dinner in sight of the falls, and were visited by a party of five Crow Indians, who brought some fine fish into camp, for which we traded. Soon after dinner, we came to a beautiful creek – a long succession of dashing falls. The rock over which it ran had something of the appearance of the soda formations near the Steamboat Spring.

We traveled all the afternoon down Snake River, and encamped at night on Beaver Creek, which comes from the south.

Sunday, July 14. If we could have had our own way, this would have been a day of rest in reality, as well as in name; but such it was not to be. Not only the customary duties of camp life, but the weekly laundry, had to be attended to, although the day was excessively warm, the mercury marking one hundred and twenty degrees inside our wagon. The dryness of the air, and the high altitude, made the heat more endurable than it would have been in a moist climate, at a low elevation.

Monday, July 15.   We left Beaver Creek at six o'clock, still traveling down Snake River, and in eight miles came to Raft River, a small stream that flowed from mountains on our left. Here the roads fork again, the right-hand one turning off northwesterly towards Oregon, while we took the left-hand one, going southwesterly towards California, leaving Snake River, and traveling up Raft River. We crossed it three times during the day, and at dark drove into camp on a branch of this stream, not far from the junction of the Myer's Cut-off, which we had passed near the Steamboat Spring. We are now coming again into a hilly country.

Tuesday, July 16.   It was half past five when we left our camp. The company we were with drove too fast for us to-day, and when we halted at noon, we found ourselves alone. But Mr. Cole and his party came up with us just as we were starting after dinner, traveled with us during the afternoon, and when we stopped at a beautiful nook in the mountains for our night camp, they remained in our company until morning.

Wednesday, July 17.   This morning we started early, at half past five o'clock, and nearly all day traveled over rough roads. During the forenoon we passed through a stone village composed of huge, isolated rocks of various and singular shapes, some resembling cottages, others steeples and domes. It is called the

"City of Rocks," but I think the name "Pyramid City" more suitable. It is a sublime, strange, and wonderful scene – one of nature's most interesting works. The Salt Lake road, which turned off between Dry Sandy and Little Sandy, and which we passed on the twenty-sixth day of June, rejoins our road at this point.

The altitude of Pyramid City is five thousand nine hundred seventy-five feet, being the highest point between the top of the Bear River Range and where the emigrant road crosses the Sierra Nevada.

Eight miles from Pyramid City we recrossed, going southwest, the forty-second parallel of latitude, which we had crossed, going north, on the eighth day of June, near Fort Laramie.

At noon we halted for lunch in company with Mr. Cole's party. But they were quite anxious to travel on and started out before us. During the afternoon the road was very rough – a continual succession of mountains. We only traveled seven miles. The Goose Creek Indians are said to be warlike and troublesome, but we have not found them so up to this time. Our horses, however, are closely guarded every night. We reached the little valley of Goose Creek this afternoon, and encamped near the bank of the stream about sunset, in company with some ox teams.

Thursday, July 18. We traveled up Goose Creek in a southwesterly direction all day. We fell in company with a train that had come by way of the Salt Lake road, and encamped with them at night. This was a cloudy day, with slight indications of rain.

Friday, July 19. We started at half past six in the morning, and continued to travel up Goose Creek.

The road was very rough. The face of the country presents volcanic appearances. At the last crossing of Goose Creek we broke our small wagon, which detained us an hour and a half. It was fourteen miles from this place to the next water. We reached it at five o'clock, at the entrance to Thousand Spring Valley. The spring was a beautiful one, flowing out from beneath a large rock. Four miles beyond this rock we encamped for the night. Here we traded some gunpowder for an antelope ham, with some friendly Indians of the Snake tribe. To-day, like yesterday, has been cloudy, with some sprinkling of rain.

The Thousand Spring Valley, which we have just come into, takes its name from the great number of springs, both hot and cold, to be found in it. If all the tales we hear about it are true, it is an interesting place. At the farther end we expect to reach the head of the Humboldt River, which we have been told extends nearly to the California mountains.

When we encamped in the evening, there being no grass near, the horses were taken some distance to the mountains, where good feed had been found.

Saturday, July 20. It was seven o'clock when we started this morning. We traveled down the Thousand Spring Valley for twenty miles. A party of Indians encamped with us at noon, but gave no signs of being unfriendly. The ox teams that stayed with us last night, came up and camped with us again. It is seldom that we are without company on this part of the journey.

Sunday, July 21. This morning we started at eight o'clock, and soon came to springs that were boiling hot. Only five feet from them was another as cold as ice. Here were men engaged in washing their clothing. Their position was such that, after washing a garment in the boiling springs, they could take it by the waistband and fling it across into the cold spring, and *vice versa,* with perfect ease. There were said to be creeks of running water too hot to bathe in, but we did not have leisure to visit them.

We continued to travel down the valley, in a southwest direction, until three o'clock, when we stopped for the night – this time by ourselves – near the western end of the valley.

Monday, July 22. We started over a ridge, or bluff, at half past six o'clock, still traveling in a southwesterly direction. During the day we reached Cañon Creek, one of the small tributaries of the Humboldt, and encamped on the bottom, where we found abundant grass.

Tuesday, July 23. This day brought us to the farfamed Humboldt River. We had left camp at five o'clock, and after traveling five hours, came to the stream which many said reached nearly to California. Others said that it ran into the ground at the edge of a great desert which the emigrants had to cross; and after that, they would have to cross the highest mountains on the route, covered with snow and ice. Rumors of all kinds passed up and down the line, for very few knew anything about the country ahead of us.

Near this place we met a party of men with packmules returning to the Atlantic states. It was a rare thing to see any one going that way. The emigrants were anxious for information. They asked hundreds

of questions of the packers. Had they stopped to
answer, they would have been kept all summer. They
kept their mules going at a rapid gait, and shouted
back their answers as long as they could be heard.

At noon we stopped for lunch on the bank of the
river, but had to swim the horses across to find pas-
turage. In the afternoon we traveled ten miles and
encamped again on the river, in company with a Missouri train.

We have now traveled eighteen hundred thirty-five
miles. The altitude here is five thousand six hundred
twenty-eight feet.

CHAPTER VII.

Wednesday, July 24. At six o'clock we started and
crossed over some bluffs. We stopped for dinner near
Dr. Miller's company. The river passed through a
cañon near by. This upper portion of the Humboldt
Valley produced fine grass in great quantity. The great
herds of the emigration have already consumed a
large portion of it. The water is bright and clear,
cool and refreshing. At night we encamped with
a party from Cincinnati, some of them being of
McFarland's company.

Thursday, July 25. This morning we were on the
road by six o'clock, and soon fell in company with
Mrs. Foshee. We saw our friend Miss Cole to-day.
Near the crossing of the Humboldt we stopped for the
night. The river was too high and we could not cross.
In the early part of the day we had taken what is
called the "Greenhorn Cut-off," which required fifteen
miles' travel to gain six miles on our journey. What
is called a "cut-off" is a shorter road across a bend.

A "greenhorn cut-off" is a road which a stranger or new traveler takes believing it to be shorter, but which turns out to be longer than the regular road. There were many such on the plains.

Mr. Cole's party caught up with us as we were all starting out of camp at half past four the next morning.

Friday, July 26. After traveling about five miles this morning, we came to the mountains. We had a long drive over them. I walked seven miles during the morning. Mr. Clarke's company and Mr. Cole's was fifteen miles, all the way without water.

Saturday, July 27. Traveled down the river four miles, then came to the mountains, the roughest road we have gone over thus far – a seventeen-mile stretch without water.

Mrs. Foshee rode with us to-day until noon, and took dinner with us, their team not coming up. Our boy Robert took up a horse near the road, it having the appearance of being lost, and by so doing got separated from us. During the afternoon we became quite anxious about him, but reconciled ourselves with the thought that we should find him at the river. But when we reached the river, Robert was not there, and it was getting late. Every one, being tired, wished to get to where we could camp. I was almost frantic for fear the Indians had caught him, and to increase my agony, a company of packers came along, just starting out to travel all night, who informed us that there were some five hundred Indians encamped very near us. I suffered the agony almost of death in a few minutes. I besought them to turn back and help us look for our lost boy, but they had not time, and were, besides, on short rations. But Aaron Rose had unhitched the best horse, and started back over the hills. Never can I forget those minutes. The thought of leaving the boy, never to hear of him again! But just at dark, Aaron came in sight, having the lost boy with him. My joy turned into tears. It was some time after dark before we got into our camp for the night.

Sunday, July 28. We started at seven o'clock, traveled fourteen miles, and stopped for the day. After that we were engaged with our usual Sunday duties, from which there was no escape.

Monday, July 29. We are traveling in a southwest direction. The river makes a great bend to the northwest. Sometimes our road runs near it, but often at a distance across the bends.

Tuesday, July 30. To-day we traveled twenty-five miles. This is a long day's drive, as our animals seldom go out of a walk. If they were urged faster, they would soon fall exhausted. This is the condition of all the stock on the road.

Wednesday, July 31. We started at six o'clock, and soon came up with Mr. Clarke's company. The valley is from ten to twenty miles wide here, much of it rough and covered with sage-brush. The river bottoms are narrow, but we are told they widen towards the "sink." A few cottonwoods and low willows grow along the stream. There is no other timber.

Thursday, August 1. We crossed the slough as soon as we started. Then we had a very bad hill to climb, though it was short. William Johnson went hunting. We came to the river, but could not cross it. Took to the bluffs. Found the road good with the exception of two very rough places. Started again at three o'clock, but did not proceed far before our small wagon broke down, and we had to stop. Mr. Cole's party stopped with us, and we rigged a cart out of the wagon. Mr. Clarke's wagon being ahead, they did not hear of our accident. We encamped in the neighborhood of several boiling springs.

Friday, August 2. We were ready to start at six o'clock. We are now traveling on the south side of the Humboldt River, with only Mr. Cole's party in company. We encamped on a salt plain not far from the river. We found a well near by, but it proved to be salty.

The Arkansas train camped near us. We traded pickles and acid with them for tea and sugar.

Saturday, August 3. After a twenty-five-mile drive, we encamped at evening on the bank of the river. Feed is becoming scarcer than ever. Whenever we come to grass that can be mowed, Mr. Frink has the men cut a good supply of it with the scythe, and it is then hauled in the wagon for future use. In this hot, dry air, it cures very quickly, adding but little weight to the load.

Away from the river, the soil is hard and dry, void of any vegetation except sage-brush, which is worthless for any purpose but fuel. When it is dry, it makes a hot fire, from the oil it contains, but burns out very soon. Much of the level land of this valley is barren, from the salt and alkali in it.

Sunday, August 4. This day we remained in camp to recuperate ourselves and animals. Constant travel over rough roads, through suffocating dust, makes a rest welcome whenever we can take it. Mr. Cole, having a broken wagon to mend, must repair it to-day or lose to-morrow.

Monday, August 5.   We started at six o'clock, following a rough, hard road over bluffs. The way along the river is often shut off by the cliffs, forcing us over low, rocky spurs. The heat is sometimes oppressive. The dust is intolerable. Many wear silk handkerchiefs over their faces; others wear goggles. It is a strange-looking army.

Tuesday, August 6.   We found the grass at this place very good, but we could not remain longer. Just as we were starting out, our friends the Carson boys and their party drove up. Their animals had been suffering from want of feed, and were losing strength every day. Their provisions were also running short, and it was yet three hundred and fifty miles to Sutter's Fort, over bad roads. The long, hard journey was not the pleasure trip they had looked for. Some of the company were contrary, and all of them had become, like hundreds of others, much disheartened at the discouraging prospect ahead of them. But we endeavored to put the matter in the best light we could, and rendered them such little assistance as was in our power. We were able, among other things, to contribute from our reduced stock a supply of those two great luxuries on the plains, acid and sugar, which they fully appreciated. And, having found here plenty of good feed for their stock, and seeing that there was no immediate danger of starvation, the spirits of the party were in great degree restored. So we drove off and left them in camp, promising to let them know of our whereabouts in case we got through first.

It was a hard road we traveled to-day, fifteen miles without water. We broke a new road across a dried-up lake, having an incrustation like ice. It was either borax or soda or salt, probably some of each. Then we came to the river and went into our night camp.

Wednesday, August 7. Starting at seven o'clock, we drove over a spur of the rocky hills, a difficult road. We finally came to the south bank of the river, which here had a westerly course. There was neither bridge nor ferry, and the water was too deep to ford. Some people had made a boat of a large wagon bed, which they had turned bottom upward in the river, with an empty keg lashed under each corner to keep it afloat. A long rope was tied to each end and men on opposite banks pulled it back and forth. When they had finished their crossing, they permitted us to use the boat. We piled our provisions, bedding, cooking utensils, hay, and all other stuff, upon it, and after many trips got everything safely over. When I crossed, I sat with my feet in the wash-tub to keep them dry. The horses swam over, and the empty wagons were pulled through the water by means of long ropes attached to the tongues.

A few days before this Mr. Johnson swam over the river, carrying with him the end of a long rope. At the other end was tied a mowing scythe, which he dragged across after landing. Having cut all the grass we needed, he tied it in bundles, which were hauled over to our side. The scythe was returned in the same way, and then Mr. Johnson swam safely back.

After getting everything landed on the north side, we harnessed up, loaded our wagons again, and traveled four or five miles down the river in search of grass.

Finding none, we fed our animals from the hay that had been hauled in the wagon.

Thursday, August 8. Our horses had nothing to eat this morning. A boat was rigged, by means of which Mr. Johnson crossed the river and cut hay, which was ferried over the river to feed with. By two o'clock we were ready to start again. Some Hungarians passed us to-day who had eaten nothing for two days. I encouraged them all I could, but the situation looked gloomy to every one of us. There was nothing but sand-hills as far as we could see, without a spear of herbage. We traveled on again for ten miles and about sundown came to the river, where we met the Carson boys crossing from the south side to the north side of the stream. We did not stop but traveled along ten miles further, and at ten o'clock at night came to the first water. Around us was a terrible scene; the earth was strewn with dead horses and cattle.

Those whose duty it was to stand guard last night, went to sleep through excessive fatigue, and the horses got to the wagon containing our provisions, and ate all the beans and dried fruit. The animals had had nothing to eat except a short allowance of the hay we had hauled with us.

Friday, August 9. We started at six o'clock and traveled eight miles, to a place where we watered for the last time, there being no water after that for twelve miles. At the end of that distance, we came to a spring in a deep ravine, where we found many of our former traveling companions. It was a pleasant meeting in that desert place. We exchanged congratulations and experiences, each narrating the hardships they had met. Then, for a time, we traveled on together.

One of the Carson's mules gave out to-day. Mr. Frink let them have one of our horses in its place. During the day we passed many dead animals. Just as the sun was going down, we came to a wide tract of marsh land covered with coarse swamp grass, and called the "big meadows" or "Humboldt meadows." Finding no good place for our animals, Mr. Frink bought some hay tied up in small bundles, for which he paid twenty cents each.

Saturday, August 10. The horses were taken across a slough for grass. Here we found many more of our old road acquaintances, whom we were glad to meet. Hearing of better grass ahead, we went on for four or five miles. All the way, both sides of the road were thickly settled with campers. They are resting and feeding their stock, lightening their wagons, cutting grass and making hay, and preparing the best they can for crossing the Humboldt Desert – the worst on all the route – now only two or three days' travel ahead.

We encamped near the edge of the marsh, between Bennett's and Hall's passenger trains. It was Mr. Frink's plan to remain here until enough of the coarse grass had been cut and cured into hay to feed our horses across the desert. On the other side, in Carson Valley, we hope to find good grass again.

The reports which came from the desert of the loss of horses, mules, and oxen were very distressing and caused much uneasiness. We did not know but that our own animals might meet the same fate.

The river is the only water to be had, as there are no brooks, springs, or wells in the valley except at the head, where we first came to it. But we had not traveled fifty miles down the stream before we found the water gradually becoming brackish and discolored from the salt and alkali in the soil. The farther we traveled the worse it became. During the last eight or ten days it seems to have been mixed up with everything nauseous, but we do not expect anything better until we get to the Carson River, about seventy-five miles distant, on the other side of the Great Desert.

Sunday, August 11. Mr. Clarke's company came up and camped beside us. Also part of the Mount Morris company, whom we met on Bear River – William Bryant, Mr. Sharp, the two Coffman brothers, and our lady friend, Mrs. Foshee. The Indians had stolen all their horses except two nice ponies. The whole party were now in sad plight, on short rations, with only two horses, and a lady in the company, whom the young men felt it to be their bounden duty to see safely in California. The young men were willing to walk and carry their own provisions if they could find some one who would take Mrs. Foshee to Sacramento, and accept the two horses for pay. For herself, she had no fear, for she felt sure that God would provide her some way to get there safely, for he had already, in a miraculous manner, saved their company from starvation.

We had met them several days previously, near the Humboldt River, and I had gone to their camp, where I found them entirely out of provisions. They had just eaten the last food they had. But Mrs. Foshee was not dismayed, and was pleading with the young men not to despair, to still put their trust in God, for she was sure they would be provided for. And so it actually turned out. They had not traveled far that afternoon when one of the young men came across a young cow tied to some willow bushes, with a card fastened to her horns, on which was written the statement that nothing was the matter with the cow, that she was only footsore and not able to travel fast, and that any one in want of provisions would be at liberty to kill her for food. This being their desperate case, they stopped, killed the animal, cut the meat into small strips to dry, and traveled on with lightened hearts.

The next day they found a sack of flour with a card attached, on which was written permission to anyone in need of food to appropriate it to his own use. As this applied to their own party, they gladly took it with them. Mrs. Foshee's prediction was fulfilled to the letter.

And now here they were at our camp to-day, the young men offering their two horses to any one who would furnish to Mrs. Foshee a safe passage to California.

While we were all talking the matter over, there came into camp the Rev. Mr. Morrow, a Methodist clergyman, to give us notice that he would preach in a tent near by at two o'clock. We had had some previous acquaintance with him, and I suggested to him that here was an opportunity to put in practise the teachings of Jesus Christ, by giving up to Mrs. Foshee his comfortable seat in the passenger carriage he was traveling in. A train to carry passengers across the plains had been fitted out in St. Louis by McPike and Strother, and Mr. Morrow was with them. The situation was fully explained to him. The four young men, all that remained of the Mount Morris company, with whom Mrs. Foshee had set out from home, now offered to the minister to give him their only two remaining horses, by which he could reach California sooner than by the slow passenger train, if he would give his seat in the carriage to Mrs. Foshee. He could take with him either his own supply of provisions, or her share of the dried beef and flour which the young men had found, and she would accept in return what provision he had on hand.

After discussing and considering the matter a little further, Mr. Morrow consented. The exchange was made. And the next morning we all said good-by to Mrs. Foshee, as she sat in her carriage, smiling and happy, ready to continue her journey. At the same time the Rev. Mr. Morrow, riding one of the two horses and leading the other, packed with his clothing, blanket, and provisions, passed out of sight and we saw him no more.

And so the four young men who had given up their ponies, were left to travel the rest of the journey on foot, each with his bundle of flour and dried meat, which had so fortunately been found a few days previously. They were happy to be relieved of their responsibility for the safety and welfare of Mrs. Foshee. They had to leave behind them, when they started out, a complete outfit of new clothing, blankets, and comforts, with all the little articles which their mothers, sisters, and sweethearts had, with so much care, fitted up for them, as, without their horses, they could carry but little save the bare necessities of life. Mr. Bryant, however, carried his pick, with which to dig gold when he got to California.

Monday, August 12. It being Mr. Frink's intention to make enough hay here to last us across the desert, the men have been at work most of the day mowing grass in the wet meadow and spreading it out on the hot sand to dry.

Many people are passing to-day begging for food. The Carson company came up, but only stopped a short time, being anxious to push forward. Mrs. Cook, a traveling acquaintance, reached here in the afternoon. Among the crowds on foot, a negro woman came tramping along through the heat and dust, carrying a cast-iron bake oven on her head, with her provisions and blanket piled on top – all she possessed in the world – bravely pushing on for California.

Tuesday, August 13. The grass that was cut the day before cured rapidly in the hot sun and dry air. In the afternoon it was tied up in small bundles and piled on the wagon. There was a large load of it. We spent the day in making everything ready for the start toward the desert the next morning. The rumors that came back from there were very distressing – animals dying without number, and people suffering from prolonged thirst.

Wednesday, August 14. This was a pleasant morning, and we got an early start. We had gone but a few miles when we came to a man who was just unhitching his two-horse wagon to abandon it, his horses being unable to haul it any further. Mr. Frink gave him $5.00 for it, and left our cart by the roadside, for any one who might want it. We could carry more hay in the wagon, and it was large enough for some of the men to sleep in at night. It lasted us all

the way through to Sacramento, where Mr. Frink
was offered $40.00 for it and sold it.

After this the road turned nearly south, and brought
us opposite to the end or point of the mountains on
our left, on the east side of the river. A broad, sandy
desert opened and extended beyond them to the east
and also to the south, farther than we could see. On
the west, forty miles away, we could distinguish the
long-looked-for California mountains, the Sierra Nevada, lying in a northwest and southeast direction.
They were dark with heavy pine forests. On the plain
was neither tree, shrub, nor blade of grass.

In a few miles we came to where the river, along
which we have been traveling for the last three weeks,
spreads out on the level plain, and forms a broad,
shallow lake. This lake is called the "sink of the
Humboldt." One-half of it sinks into the sand, the
other half rises into the sky. This is the end of the
most miserable river on the face of the earth. The
water of the lake, as well as that of the river for the
last one hundred miles above, is strong with salt and
alkali, and has the color and taste of dirty soap-suds.
It is unfit for the use of either animals or human
beings; but thousands of both have had to drink it
to save life.

We stopped near the margin of the sink, fed our
horses from the grass in the wagon, and took dinner.
The elevation here is three thousand nine hundred
twenty-nine feet, which is two thousand forty-six feet
lower than "Pyramid City," and is the lowest altitude
we have reached since leaving "Chimney Rock," one
thousand two hundred fifty miles distant, on Platte

River. The total distance we have traveled thus far is two thousand one hundred fifty-eight miles.

After lunch we set forward again, and about one o'clock passed a party of emigrants who were burying a man in the sand-hills, a most desolate place.

Intending to travel in the night as much as we could, we drove on until eleven o'clock. Here we came to the last slough, or bayou, that we had to cross, and remained for the night. The water was horrible. The next morning we were to launch out into the dreadful desert, forty miles wide, with neither grass nor water on the way, and our horses ready to drop from fatigue and hunger.

CHAPTER VIII.

Thursday, August 15. We made our final preparations and crossed the muddy slough by ten o'clock in the morning, expecting soon to enter the confines of the desert. I walked most of the way for the next six miles, to relieve the animals as much as possible. About one o'clock P.M. we stopped to rest and to feed the horses. At three o'clock we started again. A few miles further we came to the last of the sloughs or bayous, that connect the river with the sink. Here we filled our five-gallon water bottles, and other vessels, it being our last opportunity of doing so. The men waded into the middle of the slough to fill them, hoping the water there might be better than near the bank. We then drove onward until dark, when we stopped for a short time to refresh ourselves and our weary horses. As night came on, the air grew cool and invigorating, which was an advantage. Our next drive continued until midnight, when we halted again, fed and watered our animals, and took lunch. Then we slept until three o'clock in the morning.

Friday, August 16. It was long before sunrise when we left camp. Our plan was to travel by easy stages, stopping often to feed and rest our horses. The early morning was cool and pleasant. At six o'clock we halted and rested four hours.

We set forward again at ten o'clock and soon began to realize what might be before us. For many weeks we had been accustomed to see property abandoned and animals dead or dying. But those scenes were here doubled and trebled. Horses, mules, and oxen, suffering from heat, thirst, and starvation, staggered along until they fell and died on every rod of the way. Both sides of the road for miles were lined with dead animals and abandoned wagons. Around them were strewed yokes, chains, harness, guns, tools, bedding, clothing, cooking-utensils, and many other articles, in utter confusion. The owners had left everything, except what provisions they could carry on their backs, and hurried on to save themselves.

In many cases the animals were saved by unhitching them and driving them on to the river. After resting, they were taken back to the wagons, which in this way were brought out.

But no one stopped to gaze or to help. The living procession marched steadily onward, giving little heed to the destruction going on, in their own anxiety to reach a place of safety. In fact, the situation was so desperate that, in most cases, no one could help another. Each had all he could do to save himself and his animals.

As we advanced, the scenes became more dreadful. The heat of the day increased, and the road became heavy with deep sand. The dead animals seemed to become at every step of the way more numerous. They lay so thick on the ground that the carcasses, if placed together, would have reached across many miles of that desert. The stench arising was continuous and terrible.

The fault lay, in many cases, with the emigrants themselves. They acted injudiciously. Their fears caused them to drive too fast, in order to get over quickly. Their animals were too weak to be urged in this way. If the people generally had cut grass and made hay at the "big meadows" above the "sink," as Mr. Frink did, and hauled it with them into the desert, and brought a few gallons of water for each animal, traveling slowly and resting often, much of the stock and property that was lost could have been saved, and much distress and suffering avoided.

Towards noon we came to a carriage by the side of the road in which sat our friend Mrs. Foshee. The horses having become exhausted, had been unharnessed and led forward to the river. She was awaiting their return with her usual composure.

A few miles beyond we met a wagon drawn by strong, fresh horses, loaded with barrels of pure, sweet water for sale. It had been hauled from a newly discovered spring, four or five miles southeast of the road. Mr. Frink bought a gallon of it, for which he paid $1.00. After the nauseous stuff of the Humboldt "sink," this spring water was more than an ordinary luxury.

Traveling slowly onward, we came to a halt at one o'clock and rested several hours, sending Mr. Rose, during the meantime, to water the horses at the spring. When he returned, which was about four o'clock, we resumed our journey. Before night we came to the wagons of the Carson boys, standing idly by the road. They told us that they had taken their mules to the spring, and having given them water, were returning to the wagons. On the way back the mules, unwilling to leave the water, became stubborn, refused to travel, pulled away from the men, ran off into the desert, and never were seen again. Part of their company, when we came up, had already gone on to the Carson River to buy more animals to bring the wagons out.

It was eleven o'clock at night when we reached the river. We had been thirty-seven hours on that frightful desert. But we came through all well and without loss of animals or property. We were completely tired out, but having eaten nothing since four o'clock, we had to get supper before going to bed.

Saturday, August 17. The Carson River comes close to the south edge of the desert. This stream was named after the famous hunter and explorer, Kit Carson, the guide of Fremont. Its source is one hundred and seventy miles southwest, among the snows and granite of the Sierra Nevada. Its water was clear, cool, and pure, free from salt or alkali, as different from the Humboldt soap-suds is from night.

We were informed that the Carson Valley was a beautiful region, abounding in rich pastures, and that our road would follow up the valley for one hundred miles or more, gradually approaching the California Mountains on our right to where the river issued from Carson Cañon. There it would enter the cañon to cross the mountains to Sutter's Fort, only one hun-

dred miles further. Our hopes revived on hearing
we were so near the end of our journey. We knew but
little of what was ahead of us.

By the side of the river, where we came to it, was a
collection of dirty tents and cloth shanties called "Ragtown." California traders had brought supplies here
to sell to the emigrants. Beef was sold at twenty-five
cents per pound, bacon $1.00, and flour $2.00 per pound.
We bought some beefsteak for breakfast, our first fresh
meat since trading with the Goose Creek Indians for
antelope ham, on the 19th of July.

It was at this point that we reached, in our southward journeying, the latitude of our old home in
Indiana, thirty-nine degrees and thirty minutes north.
The altitude is the same as that of the "sink." But
from here the road begins to ascend, at first with
gentle inclination, but afterwards more rapidly till we
reached the highest point on our journey, the crest of
the Snow Mountains.

After breakfast we traveled six miles up the Carson
River in search of feed for the animals. We were compelled to camp where the grass was very poor, but, fortunately, enough of the hay remained that had been
cut at the Humboldt meadows, to feed the horses that
night.

Sunday, August 18. We remained in camp near the
river all day, resting after the severe toil of crossing
the desert. The valley is about twenty miles wide.
On the east side is a low range of hills. The California
Mountains, on the west, are the grandest we have seen.
The sides are covered with pine forests. Above them
are the white snow beds. We expect to strike the foot
of the mountains soon and follow it along to the Car-

son Cañon, the gateway through which the road runs
to cross the Sierras.

We are disappointed not to find the rich pastures
that we heard about. Thousands of animals have fed
them off. Mr. Frink has had the men cut grass
wherever we can find it, to take with us. But for this,
our stock would often fare badly. Much of the slope
between the mountains and the river is covered with
sage-brush.

Monday, August 19. We started on our journey very
much disheartened, our horses having had but little to
eat and being in sad condition. Myself and Robert
picked every spear of grass growing between the
clumps of bushes, and tied it up in small bunches, to
try to keep up the strength and courage of the animals.
After traveling three miles we stopped to water the
horses, the road here leaving the river, which ran
through an impassable cañon. When we had traveled
four or five miles beyond the cañon, we became con-
vinced that there must be grass on the river, as we had
not seen any wagon tracks leading that way. So Mr.
Frink sent Aaron Rose and one of Mr. Cole's men to
prospect, while we kept on at a snail's pace; for the
animals were so weak they could hardly walk. We
soon saw Aaron's signal, and driving out to the side of
the road, we unhitched the horses and sent them to
the river. To our great joy, the men had found a fine
meadow untouched, there never having been an animal in it.

Mr. Frink and I remained with the large wagon by
the roadside all day, the men having taken the small
wagon with them to the meadow to fill it with grass.
The men came up with a big load by sundown, at

which time I had supper ready. It was a campful of happy people, to know that our half-starved animals had had so good a feed. At dark we were ready to start on a long night journey across another desert. There was a bright moon shining and we traveled steadily on. We did not find any water until we reached the river again, at three o'clock the next morning. I walked most of the way over the rough and dusty road.

Tuesday, August 20. This morning we traveled up the Carson River bottom, about ten miles, and at noon dined alone. Usually we have plenty of company. The road runs nearly parallel with the mountains on our right, gradually getting nearer. The emigrants are a woe-begone, sorry-looking crowd. The men, with long hair and matted beards, in soiled and ragged clothes, covered with alkali dust, have a half-savage appearance. There are but few women; among these thousands of men, we have not seen more than ten or twelve.

The horses, cattle, and mules are getting gaunt, thin, and weak, almost ready to drop in their tracks, as hundreds of them have already done. The hoofs of many cattle wear out, so they can no longer travel, and are left to starve. The once clean, white wagon tops are soiled and tattered, and grimy with two thousand miles of gray dust. Many wagon beds have been cut off short to lighten them, or sawed in two to make carts. The spokes of the wagons left behind have been cut out to make pack-saddles. The rickety wheels are often braced up with sticks, the hubs wound with wet rags to keep the spokes in, the tires bound with wire, or wedged with chips of wood, to hold them from dropping off. They

go creaking along the dusty roads, seeming ready to
fall to pieces, drawn by weary beasts hardly able to
travel, making up a beggardly-looking caravan, such as
never was seen before. The great, splendid trains of
fifteen, twenty, or thirty wagons have shrunk to three,
four, or at most half a dozen, with three-fourths of
their animals missing. Their former owners now trudge
along on foot, packing on their backs the scant provisions left, with maybe a blanket, or leading skele-
ton horses that stagger under their light burdens. One
of the "passenger trains" left most of its carriages by
the side of the road, the passengers having to finish
their journey on foot.

One only hope sustains all these unhappy pilgrims,
that they will be able to get into California alive, where
they can take a rest, and where the gold which they
feel sure of finding will repay them for all their hardships and suffering.

Wednesday, August 21.   Our road to-day continued to
follow southward up the Carson. Part of the way was
very rough, over volcanic beds of lava. The low hills
push down near the river, leaving only a narrow passage for the wagons. We have seen no Indians for
several weeks. There are no signs of game, though
some of the emigrants have killed sage-hens, and it
is said there are deer in the mountains. The sage-hens
resemble prairie-chickens, though considerably larger.
We never tire of looking at the great mountains that
we are soon to climb over. They are so close now that
the thick forests hide from view the snow fields
above them.

Thursday, August 22.   Our horse Mark mired down

this morning and had to be dug out. This detained us for some time. We traveled eight miles in the forenoon, and then stopped to rest and feed the horses, as we have fifteen miles of desert road ahead. The roads have been very rough to-day. Mr. Frink had a short interview with some Californians who have come over to this side to prospect for gold. They are looking for a hidden lake in the mountains called "Gold Lake," where the gold is said to exist in great quantities.

The men cut plenty of grass to take with us, and we made everything ready to start early in the morning, to cross another of the many Carson deserts. But these are small as compared with the "Humboldt desert."

Friday, August 23. At sunrise we were ready to start. After traveling several hours, we stopped in the middle of the desert for dinner. Here we met several gold-hunters. Two of them had already found gold. The largest piece was thought to weigh $4.00.

(I have been over this part of the road since 1850. The gold these people had found is where "Gold Hill" is situated, near Virginia City, Nevada.)

In four miles we came to the river. Four miles beyond that place we encamped for the night by ourselves, our traveling companions, Mr. Cole and his party, having gone on further. While we were at supper, two men came up afoot, each leading a mule. After picketing the animals, they sat down on the ground near us. They told us they had no provisions left, but having had their dinner to-day, they felt quite satisfied. They had started from Ohio with a good outfit, but the Indians had stolen their animals, and they had to leave their wagons and nearly everything else. We happened to have two biscuits left, and I handed one to each of them as I would to children. Our stock of provisions was low and we were living on short rations; but their condition was so much worse than our own that we resolved to give them their breakfast in the morning.

Saturday, August 24. We started at six o'clock and in four miles came into what was called the "Carson meadows." During the forenoon we crossed two beautiful streams running from the snow-covered mountains now close at hand on our right. One of the gentlemen to whom we gave breakfast this morning, Mr. Russell, applied to have Mr. Frink bring him through to California, offering his mule for pay. As we were coming soon to where we could buy meat and flour, Mr. Frink consented to take him. The other man, having some money, went on by himself. We overtook Mr. Cole's party, who had decided to remain in camp for a while. We now met many gold-hunters, "prospectors," as they are called. The trading posts became more frequent. Finding at one place some fresh beef just brought over the mountains from California, we bought five pounds, for which we paid $1.25.

Sunday, August 25. For several days we have been traveling along the foot of the Sierra Nevada, in a southerly direction. We drove ten miles to-day, and encamped near a meadow, in order to cut grass to take with us going over the mountains. There is no time for rest, even on Sunday.

Monday, August 26. We remained at our camp all the morning, waiting for our hay to dry in the hot sun, and tying it up in bundles ready for use on the mountains. This delayed us until three o'clock, when we started on our way. At a trading post we bought two pounds of rice for one dollar and a half. At night we had got within ten miles of the Carson Cañon, and encamped on a beautiful ice-cold rivulet that ran out of the mountains and across our road. There are hot rivulets, too, which burn the mouths of unsuspecting drinkers. The great forests of immense trees come down the steep side of the mountains to the edge of the road.

Tuesday, August 27. We rose early this morning, fully prepared to expect a hard day's travel. After tugging over a heavy, sandy road for ten miles, we came, about eleven o'clock, to the mouth of the famous Carson Cañon, where the road turns abruptly to the right, to enter it. This is a great, rocky gorge opening into the granite mountain, out of which rushes the west branch of Carson River, foaming, dashing, and tumbling over the huge rocks that have fallen into it from the high cliffs. It was six miles through this cañon over these rocks. The road, if it can be called a road, lay along the river, once or twice crossing it. The river was nothing but a chain of wild cascades. The road was but a track over and among piles of huge rocks. The teams were sometimes taken off and the wagons pried up and raised by levers, to get them over impassable places.

At noon we stopped in the cañon and took our lunch. Here we met some emigrants, among whom was a lady who had lost or left her husband behind. Their horses had been stolen by the Indians, and he went after them, but never returned. The mother, with seven children, had been brought thus far by strangers, and upon them she depended to get through to California.

In the afternoon we resumed our scrambling over

the rocks and boulders that constituted the road, and continued until sundown, when, to our great relief, we had gotten out of the granite jaws of the mountain and had come to an open, level, beautiful valley, sprinkled over with trees. This is known as Hope Valley, which we thought an appropriate name. We went a mile further and camped in sight of the snow-covered mountains now near at hand. The night was very cold. There was heavy frost in the morning, and ice was formed in the water bucket. In preparation for a still colder climate, we got out our winter clothing to wear.

We are now in the state of Califonia. The line dividing it from Utah territory runs across the Carson Cañon, which we came through this morning. But we have the high Sierras to cross before we get to where they are taking out the gold.

Hope Valley is two thousand three hundred eighteen miles from Martinsville.

CHAPTER IX.

Wednesday, August 28. It was seven o'clock before we started. About a mile before reaching the foot of the "one-mile mountain," we stopped for lunch. The horse Mark got mired down again in a marsh, and we had a good deal of trouble in getting him dug out. At three o'clock in the afternoon we started up the mountain with the small wagon. We first put on four horses, then six. After getting that up, we went back for the large wagon. Most of the load was packed on the horses' backs. But still we could not get the large wagon up the steep road. At last we tied the wagon securely on a large, flat, slippery rock, and left Aaron

Rose and William Johnson to sleep in it. Then we packed all the baggage we could on five horses, and harnessed the remaining horses to the small wagon. As it was now dark, we lit the lantern. I led four of the horses. Robert Parker had one, with a camp kettle and some provisions.

I went ahead with the lantern. Mr. Frink drove the wagon. The going down the mountain appeared to be only step by step, over shelving rocks. I tried to keep in front of Mr. Frink, to guide the wagon after the lantern. In this way we finally got to camp, one mile down from the top of the mountain, at ten o'clock at night. Here the mountain was lighted up with many burning trees. We found that one of our horses had been left behind. Mr. Frink went back with the lantern and found him half a mile back. We had crackers and tea for supper, and went to bed between twelve and one o'clock in the morning.

Fortunately, we here met a Mr. Hutton, from Illinois, who loaned us a tent for the night, – a style of shelter we now slept in for the first time on our journey.

Thursday, August 29. Mr. Frink got up by daylight to go back for the big wagon. He took Mr. Russell and Robert with him, leaving me by myself at the camp. When he reached the place, he rigged up some kind of a machine, and drew up the wagon by hand. They all returned to the camp by ten o'clock, by which time I had breakfast ready for them. Then they started off to hunt feed for the hungry horses, leaving me again at the camp.

Mr. Frink found good grass not very far away, and sent Mr. Russell back to camp for some bags, intending to fill them with grass for our horses on the next big

mountain. When he was returning to where he had
left Mr. Frink, he got lost, and in his wanderings came
upon the body of a dead man with a whip in his hand;
and he was so much frightened, he did not stop to examine him, or find out who he might be.

While I was in camp, there came along a man who
had lost everything. He had one pint of corn meal
left. He was without shoes, and his feet were tied up in
rags. I made a dish of gruel, into which I put a little
butter, with some other nourishing things. I encouraged him to keep up his spirits and try to go forward.
By the time the men came in with the horses, I had
dinner ready; and by half past four o'clock we were
ready to be off. Just as we were about starting, the
Carsons came along with some Cincinnati people and
their wagon.

We all went on together about four miles to Red
Lake, which lies in a valley between the two summits.
After we had encamped, the man to whom I had given
the gruel came again to the wagon, having nothing to
eat and no other place of shelter. I went to a trading
post near by, and begged some meat for him. We
remained at Red Lake that night.

Friday, August 30. It is five months this morning
since we left home. We are now about to climb the
main ridge of the snowy mountains, called the Sierra
Nevada. From the base to the top the distance is five
miles.

The snow is from ten to fifteen feet deep. We had
been advised to start early in the morning, while the
snow was frozen hard, before the sun would melt it.
We had four horses harnessed to the big wagon, and
two horses to the small wagon. The Carsons had two

wagons, with four horses to each, having bought more horses at Ragtown, after losing their mules on the desert. Mr. Russell had his mules, but no wagon.

After traveling one mile from the edge of the lake, we came to the foot of the mountain. It was very steep and high, and looked impassable.

The road turned to the left and went up slanting, which was an advantage. But it was a hard struggle for the weak horses. Though the wagons were nearly empty, we had to stop often and let the animals rest.

After great toil, we had climbed by noon to the steepest part of the road, where it seemed impossible to go any further. Here the road turned directly south, and the sun at noon could shine right into it. The snow in the road was melted down to the ground, leaving the bare rocks to travel over. The snow walls on each side of this passage were twelve or fifteen feet high. From the foot of this steep place to the top was half or three-quarters of a mile.

We halted here and took our lunch, and fed to the tired horses the last of the hay that Mr. Frink had provided for them. So many teams were ahead of us, and climbing so slowly, that we could not start again till two o'clock. We first took everything we could out of the wagons, in order to lighten them, and packed them on Mr. Russell's mules. Then Mr. Frink unharnessed the two horses from the small wagon, and hitched them with the four horses on the large wagon. Then he tied long ropes to the tongue, and strung them out in front. Four or five men put these ropes over their shoulders and pulled with the horses. Others lifted at the wheels, and when the horses stopped, they held the wheels to keep the wagon from rolling back.

Robert and I went ahead leading the pack mules. We
found it all we could do to get up this steep place. We
had to stop often and take breath. The air was getting lighter at every step, and the climbing was hard
work.

At last Robert and I got to the top with the mules
and their burdens. I was utterly exhausted. I took a
buffalo robe from the packs and wrapped myself in it,
and lay down by the side of the road on top of the
mountain and went to sleep. I told Robert to keep
watch over me and the mules.

After a long time Mr. Frink with the men and
the six horses got to the top with the large wagon.
Then they unhitched the horses and took them down
to the foot of the steep place, and brought up the small
wagon. The Carsons doubled their teams the same
way, and Mr. Frink helped them get their wagons to
the top. By five o'clock, after nine or ten hours of
hard toil, struggle, and scramble, we were all safe on
top of the main ridge of the Sierra Nevada. Thanks
that the worst is now over.

We were above where all vegetation grew. When I
awoke from my nap, my voice was gone. When Mr.
Frink reached the top, he was almost worn out. He
was more fatigued than at any other time during the
journey. We had to go a mile further to encamp.
There was some bare ground on the south side, but between the rocks there was plenty of snow. I gathered
some of the snow for use in cooking supper. The
horses were taken down a cañon a short distance, where
was found plenty of good bunch-grass.

It was not far from this place that Col. John C. Fremont and his party of explorers crossed, in February,

1844, six years and six months before we did. He gave the height where he crossed as nine thousand three hundred thirty-eight feet above the sea, which is nearly two thousand feet higher than the summit of the South Pass, which we had crossed on the twenty-fourth day of June, and eleven hundred eight feet higher than the Bear River Range, which we had crossed on the Fourth of July.

During the night I was seized with a severe chill, the result of over-fatigue, from which I was only relieved by having some rocks heated in the fire, which served to restore warmth. Thus passed our first day and night on the Sierra Nevada.

Saturday, August 31. The men on guard with the horses had a frosty night of it, and came in early to breakfast. Some wild onions, or "leeks," had been found, which, at dinner, we enjoyed very much. These were the first vegetables we had tasted since receiving the lettuce and onions from Captain Grant at Fort Hall, seven weeks before.

This was another hard day. We had expected an easier road down the mountains after crossing the main ridge, but were disappointed. Our road to-day was very rough, up and down mountains all the way.

To make matters worse, our white horse gave out today, he having fallen and hurt himself while he were coming up the one-mile mountain. He was a favorite horse, and we gave fifty cents a pound for flour to mix in water for him to drink, thinking it would strengthen him; but we only managed to get him as far as Tragedy Springs, where we had to leave him for the night. It was two miles further before we could find a camping-place, and the next morning, when Mr. Frink sent Russell back for him, he found the faithful animal dead.

These springs were named from a tragical affair occuring in 1849, in which two men, intoxicated, got into a fight with each other, in which one of them was killed.

Sunday, September 1. We are still in the midst of rough mountains. They are covered with heavy forests of pine and fir. Many of the trees are of great size and very tall. Much of the time we are traveling in the shade. We have got below the snow fields, but not beyond the frost at night. In the sunshine at midday it is very warm. The dust is as deep as it was on the hot plains, and there is no wind to blow it away. It settles thick on everything along the road. The road is rough and the hills are often steep and rocky.

Before noon we came to a notice on a tree by the side of the road, saying that the Carson boys had turned off here to find feed, and inviting us to follow. We did so, and in a short distance came to a fine meadow. This style of telegraph was in general use on the plains. Notes were often seen stuck in a split rod planted by the side of the road, where every one could see them. By this means news was conveyed to friends coming up behind.

We remained here all day. The men cut as much grass as we could well carry. We never knew when feed might be scarce. We had kept up this plan for three hundred miles down the Humboldt and one hundred miles up the Carson. By this means every animal came through, except the one lost by accident.

To-day we reached the region of oak timber. We

had seen nothing but willows, cottonwoods, and pines for so long that the oaks seemed like old friends. Near our camp some black oak trees had been cut down, the leaves of which our horses ate greedily.

Before night the Carsons left us and drove on a few miles further to Leak Springs.

Monday, September 2. This morning we started early. There was no change for the better in the roads. The dust was very annoying. The only pleasant thing was the forest we were passing through.

An amusing incident occurred which might have proved serious but only produced a little fun. Robert had picked up a pair of Spanish spurs, and of course had put them on. He then attempted to ride our smartest mule, but had no sooner got on than he stuck his spurs into his sides, and then Billy sent him flying. I thought for a moment he must be seriously hurt, though I couldn't help laughing, he looked so ridiculous flying over the mule's head. We heard no more of Spanish spurs.

We got to Leak Springs early in the forenoon. Here a small stream of water leaked or trickled out from the rocks, but it was so full of mineral that it was not fit for man or beast. There was a trading post here, kept by a California trader, who had supplies to sell to the emigrants. His fresh beef hanging on a hook, not being protected, seemed likely to be eaten up by yellow jackets, which swarmed upon it like bees.

We met here the barefooted man to whom I had given the gruel at Red Lake. He knew our wagon from the name on the side. They had taken him in here until he recruited. He told us the most distressing tale. He had left Red Lake by a cut-off through the mountains, only a pathway, and he was very weak from having so little to eat. He said he found himself at what he called a cave, by the side of the mountain, where the side of the mountain was rock, straight up and down. He was so weak he could not climb, so he wandered around trying to find a place where he could get over; and in his travels he found five dead men, and several others that were, like himself, looking for a place to climb the mountains, and all weak for want of food. He finally got out with some of the others, and, by hearing cow-bells, he had got assistance to a place where he was taken care of by the relief committee, sent out from Sacramento to assist suffering emigrants.

We bought flour at this place at thirty-seven cents per pound. From this time on to the end of our journey, trading posts were more frequent and prices more moderate. They generally kept a small supply of what the emigrants needed most, – beef, flour, bacon, beans, cheese, rice, ship-bread, dried herring, etc., etc.

Tuesday, September 3. This day we reached Dusty Ridge, which was well named. The dust was over our shoe-tops. Mr. Russell was very sick to-night, with symptoms like those of the cholera. In the morning, however, he was much improved and able to continue on the journey.

Wednesday, September 4. At noon we arrived at Pleasant Valley, where we stopped for lunch. Afterwards we concluded to remain all night. There were two or three miners here, but the diggings did not seem to be very rich.

We prospected a little for gold, through curiosity, but found none.

Thursday, September 5. Early this morning we reached Ringgold, which was the first regular mining-camp we came to. Here was another trading post. We bought a supply of potatoes at forty cents per pound. By this time we had found that in California all vegetables, fruits, and grain were sold by the pound, instead of the bushel, as at home.

They inquired of us of we had any flat-irons to sell. I had the very article, had brought them across the plains with remonstrance, and now thought there was a chance to make something, freight-money at least. But when I asked the man five dollars apiece, he only laughed at me, saying, "I guess you have learned all about California prices." So there was no trade and the laugh turned on me. We were afterwards informed that flat-irons were plentier than cobble-stones in San Francisco, having been shipped from the eastern cities in great quantities.

We drove twenty-five miles to-day, and stopped for the night at a place where a shingle-mill had been set up, to make shingles from the pine timber. It is now a railroad station and called Shingle Springs. It is thirty-eight miles from Sacramento.

Friday, September 6. The roads to-day and yesterday are much improved. We are getting out of the high mountains, and descending into the Sacramento Valley. Our drive to-day was twenty-five miles, and brought us to the Rio de los Americanos, or American River, about fifteen miles above Sacramento, where we encamped for the night. The Carsons came up and

joined us and also encamped here. Our journey is
rapidly drawing to an end.

Saturday, September 7. This is our last day on the
plains. We started early and at twelve o'clock passed
Sutter's Fort, two miles east of the city. We stopped
a few moments to examine the place which had become
famous as the home of Captain Sutter, the owner of the
mill where the first lump of gold was found, and the
owner of the land on which Sacramento City was
built. He was no longer living here, having moved to
his ranch on Feather River, called Hock Farm, thirty
miles from the city. The fort was deserted and going
to decay, its walls and buildings being constructed
of large bricks dried in the sun, and called by the
Mexicans, adobes.

Being anxious to finish our journey and encamp for
the night, we soon drove on; we did not enter the city,
but turned southward to a place called Sutterville, on
the east bank of the Sacramento River, three miles
south of the city, and here made our last camp.

We had now traveled two thousand four hundred
eighteen miles, to a point just one degree south of
our starting-place, and four and a half degrees south
of our northernmost camp at Fort Hall. The road we
followed diverged three hundred miles from a direct
line.

During the last eight days of the journey, we had
descended, in traveling ninety miles, from a height of
nine thousand three hundred thirty-eight feet, to within thirty feet of the tide-level of the Pacific Ocean.

We had left home just five months and seven days
before. Our friends the Carsons came into camp with
us. They had crossed the Missouri River with us on

the fourteenth of May, at Bullard's Ferry, ten miles below Council Bluffs, but after that were separated from us for weeks and months at a time. They were strongly of the opinion that Mr. Frink would never get through, because he brought his wife with him. Yet here we are, all together once more, safe at the end of our long and eventful journey.

CHAPTER X.

Sunday, September 8. This morning a row-boat came up the river from San Francisco, containing five men, who stopped at the river bank to cook their breakfast. They told us they had come around Cape Horn, and narrated some of their privations on the long voyage. For many weeks they were on short rations, having only three crackers each, and a small supply of water, daily. For a time there was a fair prospect of their starving to death. After hearing their dismal stories, we concluded that our overland journey was, in comparison, but a pleasure excursion.

Monday, September 9. This was a memorable day in more respects than one; for, though we were not informed of it at the time, it was on this day that the bill was passed in Congress admitting California as a state into the Union. It was not until a month later that the news reached us by steamer from New York by way of the Isthmus of Panama, which at that time was the only means of communication with the rest of the United States.

To-day also witnessed the final breaking up of our party of gold-seekers, and the forming of new plans for its different members. The Carson brothers, who had joined us at the Missouri River, and whose camp was now near our own, removed their animals and wagons into the city, expecting to find there better opportunities of disposing of them, preparatory to setting out for the gold mines.

Mr. Aaron Rose, who came with us from Martinsville, and Mr. William Johnson, who, with his horse, accompanied us from Green River, bade us good-by and started off with high hopes for the rich mines of Yuba River, a large tributary of the Rio de los Plumas,* which flows into the Sacramento about twenty-five miles north of that city.

Our friend Mrs. Foshee, whom we last saw sitting in her stranded carriage in the middle of the Humboldt desert, was not deserted by her usual good fortune. Her party in the passenger train came through in good time and without incident; and soon after reaching Sacramento, she secured an engagement in a private family residing near our camp, at a salary of $100.00 per month.

Saturday, September 14.   To-day Mr. Frink made a visit to the city of Sacramento to inquire for letters, as we had not heard from home since we left Martinsville. He found $5.00 worth of letters, the postage being forty cents on each. At the same time he bought some provisions, among them an onion, for which, alone he paid a dollar.

---

*Note [From original publication]: The principal eastern branch of the Sacramento River was named by the earliest Spanish explorers, "El Rio de los Plumas," – The River of Plumes – from the countless flocks of waterfowl that frequented its marshes. This name continued to be generally known and used by the American population throughout the Sacramento Valley, for many years after the discovery of gold, though gradually displaced at length, to great extent, by the prosaic name, "Feather River." Plumas County takes its name from the river, which rises within its boundaries.

In the afternoon I went with Mr. Frink to the Methodist parsonage in the city, where we met the Rev. Mr. Penn, who came out in 1849. I inquired of him concerning the condition and prospects of the Baptist Church, and he informed me that the Rev. O. C. Wheeler, of New York City, was then in the city, having recently arrived from San Francisco to organize a Baptist Church in Sacramento. He politely offered to accompany me to where Mr. Wheeler was stopping, at the house of Judge Willis, who was then the first presiding judge of the court of sessions. I went with him, and we found there with Judge Willis the Rev. O. C. Wheeler and Rev. J. W. Capen. We were hospitably received and pleasantly entertained. After Mr. Penn had taken his leave, the other gentleman offered to see me to the camp of our friends, the Carson brothers, on L Street, where I had made an appointment to meet Mr. Frink.

I learned from the ministers that on the next day, Sunday, September 15, they were to meet at the court-house, on the corner of I and Sixth Streets, to organize a Baptist Church. I left my letter to be handed in to the organization, and on the next day Mr. Frink and myself went up to the court-house and heard the Rev. O. C. Wheeler preach. After church we were all invited to dine at the house of Judge Willis, as there were to be further services in the afternoon. Mr. Frink thought it would not be prudent for him to stay away so long a time from our camp, but insisted that I should remain for the afternoon services. So I staid, and we were pleasantly entertained at Judge Willis' house. His family had not yet arrived in California, and the two clergymen, Revs. Wheeler and Capen, and a lawyer from Stockton, made up the rest of the company. Being the only lady present, I was invited to preside at the dinner table. The dinner was a good one, cooked by a Virginia negro woman.

In the afternoon we attended services at the courthouse once more. After church we returned to Judge Willis' house again, where I rejoined Mr. Frink, and we went back to camp. This was my first entire day in Sacramento.

Judge Willis' house still stands there, on the south side of H Street, between Sixth and Seventh. It was a very nice-looking place to me, after living out-of-doors for more than five months.

Saturday, September 21. We remained in our Sutterville camp till Mr. Frink rented a house in town, opposite to where the Golden Eagle Hotel now stands. The house had been brought from Baltimore and was used for a time as a retail store. There was one large room below and one above, with stairs on the outside. Nothing was finished but the sidings and floor. I could put my hand through the cracks between the boards. We paid $175.00 for the first month's rent. There was a counter in the room, but we had no furniture. Mr. Frink bought $18.00 worth of lumber, from which he made a dining table, and benches to serve as chairs. He put up a tent in the rear for a kitchen, and paid $50.00 for the kitchen stove. He put a sign over the door, "Frink's Hotel," and we were ready for business.

Our first customers were two men, who, seeing there was a woman in the house, came in and asked for breakfast, which I quickly made ready for them, setting it on the counter, as the table and benches were not yet finished. I had only the tin cups and tin plates we had crossed the plains with, but the men were delighted to stand up and eat their breakfast, for which they willingly paid $1.00 each. This was our beginning in business in California.

During the first month Mr. Frink sold the horses, wagons, and harness, which enabled us to buy such articles of furniture as could be found for sale, which, however, were very scarce. He paid $10.00 for four old chairs. Table ware was more plentiful. After a few weeks a vessel arrived from New York with a variety of goods. Mr. Frink bought a dozen new chairs, which we regarded as a luxury.

By the end of the first month, October 20, we had cleared $200.00. One week later the cholera broke out. All who could do so left for the mountains. Our business fell off and became very light. Through illness Mr. Frink had become very feeble, being barely able to attend to marketing and the financial department. Then Robert fell sick, and finally myself also, though I continued able to give directions to a boy we employed at $75.00 per month.

To show the fatal character of the cholera, one evening a stranger called to stop for the night. He informed us he had been working on a ranch but was now on his way to the mines. After paying his bill in the morning, he asked for pen, ink, and paper, and sat down to write. Mr. Frink being called away, returned about two hours after, and found the man very sick. The man had but just returned from seeing a doctor and now desired Mr. Frink to call the doctor again, which he did. The doctor staid with him till he died, which was about midnight, he having been sick but a few hours.

We then found that the stranger had written over three sheets of paper; but there was no name of person or place by which he or his friends could be identified.

This was a gloomy time. Every day wagons passed by loaded with empty coffins, going out to gather up the unknown dead from the hay-yards and vacant lots, to bury them, without the presence or knowledge of friends or relatives.

One day, while Mr. Frink was at the cemetery, there were six men digging graves. They pointed to a box, saying that the man in the coffin was working with them the day before. The epidemic raged about one month, in which time it carried off at least one thousand persons.

Saturday, November 30. Business having deserted K Street, where we were, we rented a house on J Street between Sixth and Seventh Streets, very similar to the K Street house, except that the stairs were on the inside. For this we paid $300.00 per month in advance, taking a lease for one year, to continue the hotel business. Soon after moving in we rented one-third of the front as far back as the stairway – about twenty feet – for a clothing store, for $100.00 per month. Then Mr. Frink bought three cows for $275.00. The milk was worth $2.00 per gallon, but instead of selling it, we used it all in the hotel, placing most of it on the table for our customers. Finding this good policy, Mr. Frink bought more cows, till we had thirteen in all. All the milk was used on the table. This was a great attraction to men, many of whom had not tasted milk for one or two years. No other hotel in the city set it free on the table for their guests to drink. People would come from distant parts of the city to get meals on account of the fresh milk.

Business now increased rapidly. We had no difficulty in paying the high rent.

Soon after locating on J Street our customers began leaving their gold-dust with us for safe keeping, until sometimes there would be as much as eight or ten thousand dollars worth at one time. The only place we had to store it was between the mattresses on which we slept. One morning it was reported that a store in the next block had been robbed during the night. After breakfast Mr. Frink informed his depositors that he would not keep their gold-dust any longer, and that he intended to deposit his own gold-dust in a bank that very day, which he did.

In May, 1851, Mr. Frink purchased an established dairy of twelve cows, with two horses and wagon, a lot of chickens, turkeys, milk cans, and a possessory claim to sixty acres of land under fence, with a cabin, for $2,250.00. We now had a dairy of twenty-five cows, the milk of which was sold in the city, producing a profit of $40.00 a day, after supplying the hotel.

In August, 1851, we sold out the hotel, and purchased another dairy of twenty-five cows, making in all fifty head. Mr. Aaron Rose, who crossed the plains with us, was employed to sell the milk and collect the money, at $150.00 per month. The milkers were paid from $75.00 to $80.00 per month.

We had by this time given the land of gold a fair trial. We had come here as gold-seekers only, not as settlers. But after a year's residence in the delightful valley of the Sacramento, we had satisfied ourselves that no pleasanter land for a home could be found, though we should roam the wide world over. We gave up our plan of further travels. We had traversed the continent, from the far east to the farthest west, and were now on the verge of its broadest ocean. But we had no wish to tempt the perils of the great deep. The future of California seemed to us full of promise, and here we resolved to rest from our pilgrimage.

With this plan in view, Mr. Frink, in October, 1851, secured by purchase two large lots on the corner of M and Eighth Streets, as the location for our new home. The ready-built cottage which started when we did from Martinsville, on its long voyage around Cape Horn, and which had safely arrived at Sacramento, was put together and completely set up inside of a week from the commencement of the work. On the fifteenth day of the same month we moved into it and thus established our first permanent home in California, after an absence of nearly twenty months from our far-away former home in Indiana.

As the years passed on the mushroom city of tents and rough board houses grew, in defiance of fires and floods, to be the capital of the state, and one of its most prosperous, beautiful, and wealthy cities. The modest White River cottage gave way to a larger and more permanent residence. The grounds grew more attractive each year, with the luxuriant shrubbery and flowers that belong to California. The vine and the fig tree gave their welcome shade to temper the summer warmth, while comparatively little protection, in so genial a climate was needed against even the coldest months of the winter. The progress of time only confirmed us more strongly in our choice of a home, and we never had occasion to regret the prolonged hardships of the toilsome journey that had its happy ending for us in this fair land of California.

Mrs. Margaret A. Frink
Oakland, California

ADDENDA.

WHAT BECAME OF OUR TRAVELING COMPANIONS

Mr. Aaron Rose, after meeting with fair success in mining, returned to Sacramento, and became connected with the dairy business. At the end of two years, having a strong desire to see his parents, he went back to Martinsville, carrying with him about $3,000.00 in gold-dust. There he still resides.

Mr. William Johnson returned with Mr. Rose, and is now living at his old home in Morgan County.

Mr. Avery, who left our party on the Sweetwater River to finish the journey on foot, proved to be so good a traveler that he arrived at Sacramento two weeks in advance of us. But he was disappointed in California, became homesick, and, at the end of the first month, took passage on the *Panama* steamer for home.

The Carson brothers were quite successful in mining, but at length concluded to try something else. Locating in San Francisco, when a great deal of building was being done, they actively resumed their former trade as brick masons and plasterers, in which they succeeded well, and which they continued to follow for several years, finally returning to their old home in Cincinnati.

Mrs. Foshee, the favorite of fortune, was married,

early in the year 1852, to a business man of Sacramento, Captain Edward Smith, and continued to reside there until her death, in 1892. Their son, Mr. Edward Smith, has for many years been secretary of the State Agricultural Society, and resides at the capital. Their daughter also resides in Sacramento.

Our friend Mr. Cole, with his daughter Patience, came through safely a little later than our own party. He settled on a farm in the beautiful Ione Valley, and was joined in a few months by his wife and the remaining children, who came out by steamer. The daughter who accompanied him across the plains, married a Mr. Pardee, a substantial farmer residing near her father's home, thirty miles east of Sacramento.

Mr. William Bryant, one of the young men who befriended Mrs. Foshee at the Humboldt Meadows, by surrendering their ponies in exchange for a seat in the carriage for her, brought his pick through on his shoulders and engaged at once in mining at Salmon Falls, in El Dorado County. Many years after, I met him at Calistoga, in Napa County, where he was residing with his family. He became a minister of the gospel, and is now pastor of the Methodist Church in the city of Salinas, in Monterey County, where he resides.

Robert Parker, the plucky eleven-year-old boy who was determined to cross the plains with us, having reached man's estate, started out on his own account, and, having experienced his share of the vicissitudes of fortune common to life in California, settled in business in Sacramento, where he now resides with his wife and three children.

Mr. Thomas Wand, the Kentucky gentleman whose

acquaintance and friendship we formed near the Ice Springs on the Sweetwater River, settled in Sacramento, where he became a prominent and prosperous merchant, and later a member of the California Legislature. He afterwards removed to San Francisco, and there established a large mercantile business, though he made his residence in Oakland, on the east side of the Bay of San Francisco, where he built a beautiful home. He died several years ago.

Ledyard Frink

Diary from Missouri to California, 1850

❦ Sarah Davis

INTRODUCTION

In the introduction to the first volume of this set, it was pointed out that some of the items would be "mis-spelled, mis-punctuated, or mis-capitalized." Sarah Davis' diary is all of these — in spades. We have tried to be faithful in transcribing her diary, so we kept her language intact from beginning to end.

The original handwritten diary is in the Beinecke Rare Book and Manuscript Library of Yale University. We are grateful to the library and to its curator, George Miles, for the efforts with which the original was photocopied and sent to us. Curator Miles also compared our transcription with the original in several doubtful places. We appreciate their gracious permission to use it here.

Sarah Davis was born into a Quaker family on May 1. 1826, on a farm in Preble County, Ohio. Her parents were Amos and Sarah Green. It was on July 4, 1844, that the 18-year-old girl was married to a young man with the remarkable name, Zeno Philosopher Davis. The wedding took place at "Young's Prairie," in Cass County, Michigan. Zeno was the son of Quakers, Elihu and Lovy Davis. He was 26 at the time of the wedding, and already an accomplished blacksmith and gunsmith.

It was on March 5, 1849, that Zeno left his young pregnant wife in Young's Prairie, and started for Missouri anticipating a journey to the west coast as soon as the new mother could travel. The baby was born on August 9, a girl, named Cleora Adelaide. As soon as they could travel, the mother and daughter accompanied by Zeno's brother, Alexander (nicknamed "Alex" or "Alec" in the diary), left for Missouri. The family remained in St. Joseph, Missouri, and did not start over the trail until the spring of 1850. They did not know whether they were going to Oregon or California until late in the journey. It was when they were camped on the banks of the Weber River as they left Salt Lake City that Sarah wrote in her diary on August 22, 1850, "we lay here half the day and concluded to go to california." The first diary entry was on May 21 on the Platte River of Missouri. Three months later, almost to the day, they made their final decision as to destination.

We have not tried to identify all the names mentioned by Sarah before the time of this decision. She almost never gives anything but the surname, and the task of identifying them, not knowing the given name or initials and not being certain of their destination, is complicated.

After the August 22 date, however, their traveling partners were headed for California too, and we have tried to identify these even though the information given by Sarah is meager.

Is it possible to be illiterate and yet to be literary? Sarah Davis may mis-spell, mis-punctuate, and mis-capitalize, yet sometimes she expresses herself in an intriguing and unexpected manner. Her most memorable diary entry in this respect is that of Sunday, July 28, on the banks of the Little Sandy River, not far from the Continental Divide in present Wyoming:

we went on to little sandy distance of twelve miles and their stoped for the day and to grase our catle   we had to drive them five miles to grase and whilst the men ware gone with the catle this large train come in one mile of us and camped   their a rose a quarel with them and what quareling   I never heard the like   they were whiping a man for whiping his wife   he had whiped her every day since he joined the company and now they thought it was time for them to whip him and they caught him and striped him and took the ox gad to him and whiped him tremendous she screamed and hollerd for him till one might have hare him for three miles

Based on the above quote, it is fascinating to note that there is a reference in the D. A. R. summary of Sarah Davis' life in the California State Library in Sacramento, by Minerva Lester Power, Sarah's granddaughter, to the effect that Sarah became the "corresponding Sect'y of 'Woman's Suffrage Society' (which met at Library Hall, Nev. City, 1871)."

And that is where the Davis family settled, in Nevada City, California, east of Sacramento. There, they were active in the life of the community. Zeno Davis advertised his smithy in the Nevada *Journal*. And Sarah participated in women's organizations.

It was in Nevada City that they died, Zeno on June 17, 1902, at age 84, and Sarah on December 5, 1906, at age 79. Their children were Cleora Adelaide, as aforementioned, and Elbridge Allen, who was born in Nevada City on November 25, 1852.

As an "Epilogue" after Mrs. Davis' diary we have added the words of a speech given by Cleora Adelaide (Davis) Lester, as reported in the Nevada City *Morning Union* on October 21, 1924. The daughter, who traveled the California Trail as an infant, shared what might be called the family memories of the overland experience. One matter of special interest is the way she corrects her mother's English usage and punctuation in the quote from the diary covering the last four entries. This tendency was prevalent at the hands of children and grandchildren who did not wish to expose the shortcomings of their ancestors' spelling, punctuation, and capitalization.

THE DIARY OF SARAH DAVIS

may 21 [Tuesday]   we camped on the plat river and
also lost our cattle   I have bin viewing the plat river
and I think it is beautiful so I think I will write a
litle on the subject   their is plenty of birds to warble
their beautiful notes and sound beautiful   ducks and
their young are accasionaly seen and a few geese   I
saw a snake that some one had kiled that was five feet
long and as large as [?]

may 22   we camped on the black snake hills in bu-
canan county in one mile of St Joseph and a pleasenter
place I never saw building [?]   I never saw the like
and the droves of Catle and mules and the prarie was
beautiful   tounge canot tell the after [?] role of the
beautiful green as fair as the eye can see   a more
beautiful sight I never saw

may 23   we traveled through st Joseph and then
through the missouri bottom

may 24   we camped on the bluffs 6 miles from st
joseph and staid a half a day and cooked and washed
and then started on and then we had a vary bad time
with the Indians   one of them was drunk and he
ordered us of the land and we told him we would
not go and he then got down from his pony and said
we should   we also told him if he did not go home
we would whip him and then he got in a rage and
said whip whip whip god dam you puchall puchall
and wanted us to leave and he then wanted some money
just one picaune [1] and quarter of a dollar and then
Edwin told him to leave again and he would not and

---

[1] A picayune was any small coin of little value.

then they led his pony to take the road and then he
left we also parted with [?] that returns [?] to the
plains this morning one of the best fellows in the
world I believe

may 25 we camped on the plains a half a piece from
the place we [were] at befoer with five or six wagons
in company the next day we started in and traveled
fourteen miles to musketo crik and then we had a
plesent time for we got in company with a mr Right
a cosin of Sarah Ann and he had ten wagons and fifty
men

may 26 [Sunday] we traveled all day and past the
Indian station of five or six houses and one store and
a large farm ad then we campt on the planes near a
small crick whare they say their is no wood or water
for thirty miles

may 27
may 28 we crost wolf river

may 29 we crost nimaha [Nemaha] river and camped
on a creek

may 30 we crost creek to whare their had bin a man
robed and six had to be killed it is about one hundred miles from st joseph their is some butifull timber their I think on the green we stoped on the
plains to take over whare their is no wood no water
no birds of any kind to be seen it is prairie as far
as the eye can see

may 31 we crost the blue river whare their was a
man dro[w]ned and one died and to turned back to
go home we then left our company and find another
company and we all went a half mile from the river

and then camped for the night we then started on the next morning and then we went till noon and then we stoped for the next night

June [1] we crost the quiet creek and then we past nine graves that day and past through phesents prarie as we have past it also I think

June 2 [Sunday] we camped on the prarie a very plesent place

June 3 we crost the big sandy and then had a tremenduous thunder sower it rained till every thing was wet as they could be and still continued to rain till next day

june 4 we started on the next morning and it still continued to rain and traveled on for eight miles and then camped for the night

june 5 we staid on the little blue for one day and washed and dried our close and baked bread and then the next morning we start on

june 6 we traveled on for the day and nothing hapened of any importance

june 7 we camped on the blue and I saw one of the largest wolfs I ever saw in my life it was a gray wolf

june 8 we camped on the litle blue and had a tremenduous thunder Shawer in the evening I saw six antelope that day and one buffalo

june 9 [Sunday] we camped on plains in a butiful place whare their was about fifty wagons in camp and then we left the blue river and came in sight of nebriska

june 10 we stoped to noon and let the catle feed and

then to of our men got mad and went on   one was
captain reed and the other was mr donnald   we told
them to find a good campen plac and a gain we come
on that evning but seing that they would not join then
they decided to come back to the camp on that eavening so we all camped for the night   traveled eighteen
miles that day   I saw one sand lizard that day   we
passed at fourt carney three hundred and thirty five
miles and it seemed good to see a house again

june 11   we left fort carney and traveled on   we
traveled on the bottom of the river   at fort carney
thare was some men in encampment that sold liquor
to the soldiers and they were fiend and to of them
taken to the forte and confined and the rest of their
liquor turned out of the casque

june 12   we come in company with the cincinnatti
train and road with them   we traveled about ten
miles   I also saw a butiful flowr that Sarah found
it seamed to be a specia of prickley pare   they was
beautiful as any flower I ever saw   I also saw prickley pare   they grow plenty here   we are now twenty
six miles from the forte and encamped on the plum
creek one mile from ro[a]d on water and the musketoes were so bad they had like to eat us up

june 13   we nooned on the nebriska whare we had
plentey of water   we traveled for eighteen miles that
day and camped on the plat river   I saw twelve graves
to day   it semed like a grave yard almost to me   I
think we travel vary well   we travel about ten miles
farther   we past thirteen graves

june 14   we travel right in the bottom of the plat
we have past six graves to day   we past twe[l]ve

more and one grave that they had not put the body in yet we had a plesent campen ground last night no musetoes a tal and plenty of wood

june 15 we have now past a high ridge of blufs and come to ash holler and now we noon we past seven graves to day we camped on the plat after travling eighteen miles and then [?] we had a fine super that night and the next morning mr Right come and eat brackfast with us

june 16 sunday we traveled next morning ten miles before noon and one of our company killed an antelop and we now have plenty of fresh meat on hand we got to good spring on plat all of our casque canteens full of water of the best kind we past five or six wagons a goin back they were home sick besids being sick for they were sick

june 17 monday we started on and traveled ten miles and then nooned and the men all went in a swimen and I sow and wash we then started on and traveled seven more miles and got to a good spring and then camped for the night lots of fuel was their their was three large white wolfs atacked a cow and calf they then surrounded the cow and would have killed her but whilst they ware eating their kill a mr crous shot one and he droped down and he thought he was dead but he rose again and run of I saw thirten graves to day

june 18 tues we came on and camped on the bank just above the forde

june 19 we went on and crost the river it was one mile wide we crost at waddells forde and no one got drowned at all I believe we got a cross and camped on the river

june 20 we washed and baked bread and had a tremenduous thunder shower and I sopose their ware a hundred wagons past us our men saw to bare and one white wolf I believe that is all that past that day

june 21 we traveld a bout ten miles I believe we camped on the river for the last time it was the south fork and now we leave it in tirely we only past three graves in all I believe I saw too large white wolfs

june 22 saturday we started on and traveled ten miles and stoped to noon mr jenson and mr meadow had a butiful chase after a wolf this morning they run it down and then shot at it and mist it and mr meadow he broke his gun over its head It fell down and then rose again and it run of and they did not kill it

june 23 [Sunday] we camped in ash holler fifteen miles from whare we campe before and their was a tremenduous thunder sawer one role after nother till it killed a horse that was onley one rod from our wagon that night Sarah was taken sick we had no super

june 24 we camped on the north fork of the plat river and sarah was very sick their was one woman died in the camp of the colera and was buried the next morning when I went to Sarah she was no beter and I soon saw she would die and she did die before noon [2] o how lonely I felt to think I was all the

---

[2] We never learn the surname of the other Sarah; nor do we learn what ultimately happened to the two motherless children.

woman in company and too [sm]all babes left in my care   it seams to me as if I would be hapy if I only had one woman with me

june 25   we came on and camped on the north plat river within a few rods of fifty sue indians   we sup-osed they ware robers for they had a great many horses of the inglish kind and their was a few french with them

june 26   we coome in sight of chimney rock and camped buy court house rock   it looked like a court house   we went on and camped in five miles of chimney rock   we had a plesent camp ground

june 27 thursday   we started on and traveled ten miles and stoped to noon in sight of scots bluffs whare their was plenty of grass for the catle   we traveled twenty miles and encamped in sight of scots bluffs right on the plat river and I washed some that eve-ning   we had plenty of wolfs to visit us that night they ware all through the camp

june 28   we nooned near scots bluffs and traveled eighteen miles and then crost the bluffs   we crost the bluffs near an Indian viledge   they war siouse indians and some french men among them   they had a store and a blacksmith s[h]op   their ware plenty of them   they war expecting a fight every night from the crow Indians   they insisted on our stain with them that night but we did not like to so we went on three miles and camped.

june 29   we traveled twelve miles and stoped to noon we made a fire and got a cup of tea for diner   I tell you that was good on the planes   we crost too

creeks this morning I saw a mountain Sheepe horne
this morning it beats all horns I ever saw it was
five inches through and fifteen Inches long

june 30 [Sunday] we come to larimy fork and then
we crost it it is the swiftest river I ever saw but
not vary wide when we crost it we went a half mile
and camped

july 1 [Monday] we camped near fourte lairimy
and there washed we staid till july 2 and was[h]ed
and then we went on to fourte lairimy and past it
six miles we then staid one day and was[h]ed and
baked again a[n]d july 3 we laid on plat

july 4 [Thursday] we camped near to 1 of the best
springs I ever saw but lital gras for our catle we
are now in the rockey mountains and it is rockey
mountains for certain is some of the largest rocks
I ever saw their are some large pine trees here and
some cedar trees and plenty of lime stone we started
on the next and left mr janson behind hear as one of
his men was sick

july 5 friday we went to and past too handsome
creeks one was biter creek it had some butifull
fish in it we then past dead timber creek and nooned
near the bluffs we now had to pass seven miles with
no timber or water we then into timber but no water
but in a litle while we had plenty of water their came
a tremenduous thunder sawer and came rushing down
the hills in great fountains like the waves from the
lake they came in too feete high

july saturday 6 we started on and traveled eight
miles and then nooned we crost biter spring to day

and horse creek   we had no grass for our catle to day
noon and hardly any to night   we camped on a dry
creek

july 7   sunday   we started on and traveled eight
miles   we stoped to noon on lebonte river [LaBonte
Creek] whare we had no grass for our catle   we
then went on and camped on a branch of lebonte river
five miles farther on whare their was toads with horns
and tails   their was a man died their last night and
was baried next morning   I had almost forgoten that
they kiled too buffalow and what a supper   we had
plenty

july 8 monday   we traveled a bout eight miles and
stoped to noon   we then went on to a leeperle river
[LaPrele Creek] and camped for the night   it was
vary colde water and Clear   we lost one of our cows

july 9 tuesday   we started on and traveled to box elder
creek and stoped to noon   whilst we ware their their
hapend to come a long antelop a bounding like a deer
only a great deal more   we traveld on to fous bois
creek [La Fourche Boisée] and stoped for the night

july 10   we stoped at fous bois river a butifull stream
the water was clear as cristal and it had plenty of
fish in it   we spent one day their a washing and baking   those that could be spared went a hunting and
to of them killed a buffalo and too others killed a
black tailed deer   we had a plesent time of it their

july 11   friday   we started on and traveled fourteen
miles   we then camped on deer creek one of butiful
creeks I ever saw   plenty of fish in it and it is as
clear as cristal and as cold as ice   their is a spring
here that is much colder as you can think   we have

a butifull camping place   plenty of wood and water
and a good shade   I saw too large buffalo to day
and the men after them was same   [Evidently she
means they were the "same" as last night.]

july 12 [Friday]   deer creek   we still lay here a
herding our catle and Zeno went on this morning
before breakefast and [killed] a antelope and returned before noon   the rest [of] the men killed
nothing of any concequence   o yes mr Mclelen killed
a buffalo and to grouse   we still lay here at deer
creek   we lay here three days recruiting our catle
they act so that they ware perfectly crazy

july 15 [Monday]   we started on and traveled on to
the plat whare their was a grove of timber   it was
coten wood and their no[o]ned   Mr sochen and Edwin went out to git some of his buffalo   went in the
morning and did not return till we nooned on the
plat and when they returned they had killed a nother
and brought in some meat with them and then all
traveled twelve miles

july 16   we camped on the plat river and then we
started on and to a litle creek within one mile of the
forde and nooned their   we went on and crosst ferry
and camped just a crost river   we then left river

july 17   we are now crosing a desert   we come to
a minerall lake and spring then we [came] to low
land hily charged with alcholie   we then came to
a spring and water our catle and got some super and
then traveled all night   our catle ware nearly worne
out not having any grass since we left the plat nearly
fifty miles

july 18   we camped on coten wood creek and staid

all day to feed our catle they not having any thing
to eat for the last seventy miles of any consequence
we staied all day their

july 19 we started on and traveled to independance
rock and their s[t]oped to noon their is the most
names on it I ever saw in my life the rock is completly covered with names as far as I can see and a
great many serched out to put theirs their mr Estus
brought me some curents from top of it their is
plenty of them here we have now arived at the
sweete river water [*sic*]

july 20 we camped on the sweete water river and
to men staid with us I say they staid with our company have plenty of good water here

july 21 sunday we staid on the swete water and
the men drove our catle to grass in the mountain five
miles from here and a mr Steele who was with them
killed a bull Elk but he brought none of it in we
found plenty of goosbury her of the best kind I ever
saw in my life I think the sweete water is a butifull
stream it is clear and rapid their is no large fish
in it as we have found yet I expect their is plenty
but the[y] being busy had no time

july 22 monday morning we started on and traveled
six miles and stoped to noon having traveled through
heavy sand all the way we have now past biter coten
wood a dismal looking place it is we had vary sandy
rodes all the afternoon

july 23 we camped on the sweet water and vary
good rodes all day we crost the river four times
and traveled thirteen miles we past through [a]

mountain whare the rock was three hundred feete
high on both sides of us and the river past betweene
them I saw three buffalo to day

july 24 we camped on the sweete water and drove
our catle three miles to grass we have a butifull
campin place here and vary plesent eavening and
morning the catle are now coming and must q[u]it
riting we travel to pass through sixteen miles of
desert to day we have now got through the desert
and crost the sweete water and now we camp here
their is not much grass here for our catle

july 25 we traveled twenty miles to day we have
crost too small creeks and past the twin mounts and
too alcholie lakes and sevrel rockey ridges we can
see the rockey mountains which is coverd with snow
and they look whit[e] litle I think we have now
crost strubery [strawberry] creek and camped for
the night

july 26 we camped on sweete water for the last
time just oposite of the snow mountain and it was
vary colde we past twin mountains they are vary
high we have had plenty of snow to eat [*sic*] here
on the sweete water we nooned on the swete water
to day we have traveled nine teen miles to day
and now we are at the south pass

july 27 we are now in the south pass past the pacific springs and stoped to noon we now stop to
campe on the dry sandy distance from pacific five
miles it rains considerable and it is vary colde almost cold and enuf to realize to think on

july 27 we traveled nine teen miles and then we

stoped on the swete water for the last time   we stoped
near a train of twenty wagons traders a goin to salt
lake   nothing more transpired of any consequence

july 28 [Sunday]   we went on to little sandy distance of twelve miles and their stoped for the day
and to grase our catle   we had to drive them five miles
to grase and whilst the men ware gone with the catle
this large train come in one mile of us and camped
their a rose a quarel with them and what quareling   I never heard the like   they were whiping a
man for whiping his wife   he had whiped her every
day since he joined the company and now they thought
it was time for them to whip him and they caught
him and striped him and took the ox gad to him and
whiped him tremenduous   she screamed and hollerd
for him till one might have hare him for three miles
the little sandy is vary mudy and bout forty feete
wide with swift current

July 29   we started on and traveled a bout twelve
miles   we then crosst big sandy   it is hundred feet
wide with swift curent and vary muday   we then
parted with som [of] our company there   mr crouses
and one mr mire and mr hunter and mr jonson and
harter and three mr Estus s and mr Wilams and mr
heiple and burg some of the best men I ever got
acquanted with   I think they went to california and
us go to oregon   we parted about noon   we then
on to big sandy and then camped for the night in
a butifull place

july 30   we encamped on the big sandy and some
of our men washed and some of them baked   we
baked and fixed for the desert of thirty five miles

we start to night for the desert   one of our men lost
one [of] his oxen with this alcolie and six chicks
is sick   mr stell lost one of his cous yesterday   we
have now eat diner and are all most ready to start
this is butiful place to camp

july 31   traveled all night and come to green river
a distance of thirty five miles   we then crost the river
and camped for the night   we drove our catle five
miles to grass   their is plenty of fish in this river
their is a fery here   this river is clear and swift
curent   the river is thirty rods wide   I saw six snake
Indians here   they cary a white feather with them
a sign of pease   they look fright full

august 1 [Thursday]   we left green river and crost
over the mountain a distance of thirteen miles   we
then come on to a branch of greene river   a butiful
stream it is   we camped on it and we past some
Indians snake Indians

august 2   we no[w] are in sight of an indian town
we then come on eight miles and in betwene too more
mountains within an Indian camp   their was to
m[o]re camps in sight

august 3   we then started on and traveled ten miles
to good grass   was good grass to for it [was] ne high
to a man   we then came to hams fork of greene river
a beautifull stream   it runs vary swift and is clear
as cristal   it is a bout three rods wide and has plent[y]
of trout in it   here is an Indian town   they swarmed
around us   it is the snake tribe of Indians who in
habit these snowe mounutains   they lo[o]k fright full

august 4 [Sunday]   we lay buy all day here to rest

our catle and wash and bake our men took off one
of their wagons covers and sowed them to gether and
used it for a sane they had lots of funn here they
caught about too thousan fish with big litle and all
to gether their is goosebarys here and seatilsey [sal-
sify?] here and some butiful roses and pine in abundance we had plenty of wilows for wood

august 5 we then started on our catle bein all fresh
we then comence to clime the mountains I saw
where we had to go before starting as I had the sick
head ache vary bad I saw nothin all the four noon
In the after noon a more butifull sight I never
saw the whole mountain was covered with f[l]owers
of evrry description you could t[h]ink of we past
through a fur grove of timber it was butiful and
a grove of qaken aspen

august 6 we camped on the mountain side a butifull stream runing beneath it the curent swift and
clear it was mudy buy name we then crost over
mountains for six miles and then we come in bare
river botom and their we had a runaway our catle
run and the leader fell down and that stoped them
nothing got broke we then went on to bare river
and nooned the Indians s[w]armed a round

august 7 we camped on thomas s fork of bare river
we then parted with the rest of our company and
turned rounde to go to salt lake evrybody we past
they a[s]ked are you turned back my what is the
mater why cant you go on we then come on ten
miles and stoped to noon on bare river their was one
Indian come to us for his diner we then went on

for five or six miles and stoped to camp we camped
all a lone it seamed vary lonely

august 8 we then went in the fourte briger road
for ten miles and stoped to camp we past to of the
best Springs I ever saw in my life

august 9 we started on to salt lake we went back
five miles on the road and have not come to the road
yet we went on a bout seven miles farther whare
we stoped to camp and yet we are not in sight of the
road the boys killed four ducks which made us a
handsome mess for breckfast

august 10 we started on and traveled some eight
miles we then stoped to noon and Zeno and Alick
went to look for the road I am vary lonely and
wish we could find the road we lay buy the rest
of the day and not founde the road yet

august 11 [Sunday] we lay buy all day and nothing
transpired of any consequence I think it a long time

august 21 [12] we still lay here and no hopes of
giting a way about four o clock Elick and Edwin
came back and they had found the road & how
I rejoiced to think they had found the road they
brought home aleven ducks with them and we had
fine mes of them mr mclan and mr burten they
went a hunting to day and they killed eleven more
ducks we had a plenty of them

august 13 we started on up the river to find the road
and past through plenty of grass nee high we stoped
to grase in a butiful place and Zeno killed a goose
it was younge and beter meat I never eat in my

life we then went on and I think we traveled fifteen miles that day we ware scarcely out of sight of antelope all day

august 14 we still go on but not founde the road yet we think it is fifteen miles farther we past some of the handsomest grass I ever saw in my life we have now arrived at a place whare some one has camped it seams like home here we have a fare view of the wasatch mountains they are completely covered with snow it is a butifull sight in the morning when the sun shines on it

august 15 we have now arived at the road and we travel vary fast we have traveled ten miles and stoped to noon on yellow creek not hand some at all their has come up her[e] a man who wants to go with us to salt lake he is sick with the mountain fever and wants to ride in the wagon Elick has took him in we have now arived at eco creek a distance of twenty miles we have plenty of grass and good water

august 16 it is a vary bright clear morning we now start vary early havin nothin to hinder us we have now traveled six teen miles and stoped to noon on eco creek we are oposite of a rock one thousand feete high we then went on to weber river and forded it and went one mile to camp whare their now a good spring and plenty of grass weber river is a butifull stream about too rods wide and swift curent and clear

august 17 we started on in the morning and come to a warm salt spring we then pas severel spring

branches before comin to canion creek we come to
canion creek then and crost it eleven times we
nooned on canion creek whare their was now one of
the best springs I ever saw in my life we then went
on some five or six miles and drove one mile up a
canion in the mountain it looks fright full here
the valey is full of rocks of the largest kind

august 18 [Sunday] we started on and traveled fiv-
teen miles down hill all the way we then come to
a large train some fifty men in it we stoped to noon
it commenced to rain and it rained vary hard and
haled some when it q[u]it raining we went on we
had a vary harde time to get up on the mountain and
still harder to get down when we got down we felt
thankefull to think we ware safe we camped on
browns creek

august 19 their our catle run a way we thought
their was no yuse in gardin them and all went to
bed and the wolfs came and drove them of and killed
one of the best cows we thought they had him
stolen from us in the morning the men took of for
them and found them a bout five miles off we then
set out for the salt lake valey and Elicks wagon
turned over in the mud but still we reached the valey

august 02 [20] we past through the city of the great
salt lake it is a plesent place here and seams to be
improving with great rapidity It seams to have a
great deal of vegitation to sell and some rain here
we crost the weber river and stoped it [is] a very
swift curent and bout too rods wide

august 21 we lay here

august 22   we lay here half the day and concluded
to go to california

august 23   we traveled fifteen miles and past plenty
of salt   the lake is as salt as brine let it be made
as strong as it can be   the road is good here and
plenty of good water   we then come to a nother
mormen setelment whare they was building a mill
a saw mill   we then went about a mile to the good
springs caled bentons mill springs   one was salt and
the other not   we then camped being vary tired

august 24   we started on and come to salt works of
the mormons   we then went on to miles and s[t]oped
to noon whare their was a salt spring   we then went
and came to a cane break or grass   grain rather
thick   this is caled willow creek a good spring of
fresh water   we stoped here to put up grass for our
catle a cross the desert   their is plenty of the best
kind here for people that is a crossin the desert
went twenty miles to day

august 25 [Sunday]   we traveled twenty miles   we
past more than twenty salt springs   the water loocked
clear and as if it was the best water ever drinked
the one whare we nooned plased me the best   the
water a bout five feet deep and boiled up in evry
direction   the place it boiled up and spouts as large
as a man head and I think of beads   their thaught
of all colors and s[h]apes   the rivers run in every
direction

august 26   this morning it is raining   it seams so
plesent to see it rain as we have not seen it rane
since we came in the valey before   we now noon
near a salt spring   we then went on to elbow spring

fresh water   it is vary good to   we then [went] on twelve miles farther to the mountain and found a spring   it is rather brackish but good water we traveled nineteen miles to day

august 27 we lay buy all day fixen for the desert we start in the morning   our catle wer[e] drove to miles to grass   the mountains here are vary high and some cedars growin on them and are vary rockey

august 28   we are not started yet   have formed a new acquaintance with mrs crouch [3] this morning   I think we will travel to gether to california gold digins

august 28   we left the springs and started over the mountain and first thing we done to help us along was to turn over Elicks wagon   were about one hour loading but had nothing broke   we then [went] on and had rufest road we have had atall   the distance over the mountain was five miles and it took us till night   we had to duble teams twice coming over and then it was vary harde drawing for the catle team yoke

august 29 this day it was vary hot and seams to me as if every thing will perish   we traveled all night of the twenty eight and all night of the 29   buy this time I have got use to it a litle   we have now got all most a crost the desert   it apears to me as if this has bin a nother great salt lake and I am all most

---

[3] The Robert Crouch family was from Illinois. He was trained as a medical doctor. "The gold of California had more charms for him though than the healing art, and in 1850, he, with others, started out on the long journey across the plains to the Pacific." L. L. Palmer, *History of Napa and Lake Counties, California* (San Francisco, 1881), p. 432. They settled in Napa. This is an example of how the county "picture books" emphasized the male side of life. We never learn in its pages the wife's name.

ready to believe it is the grounde is white with
salt all over   plenty of it   we are now in sight of a
mountain

august 30   we rived at land and water about eight
o clock this morning   we are a cross the great horn
valley   the men are all tired nearly to death as well
as the catle   the men are all a sleepe and the catle
are a resting themselves   we [lost] no catle nor horses
we got through safe and are thankfull   the Indians
swarm around us and are vary saucy   it is easy to
day   I think their was no one perished on the desert

august 31   we left the desert spring with the intention
of goin ten miles to grass and water and when we got
their it was fifteen miles to grass and water   we had
a harde days travle   some of our catle gave out   they
droped down in the desert   also remain with mrs
Slater [4] from chigago today   we traveled twenty five
miles today and then found no grass   the men hunted
round to finde grass and found it one mile

september 1 [Sunday]   since ten this morning is vary
colde but the air crisp and clear   we are here right
in a large canion barely enuf of rume for the wagons
to pass each other and varey ruff roads and we starte
on in a few minets   we have now started on and
found grass in to miles and stoped to grase our catle
we have a vary dusty roads   we have now traveled
twelve miles

september 2   we lay buy all day in whites spring

4 Was this the wife of Nelson Slater, the publisher of an early imprint
of California literature, a book on *The Fruits of Mormonism?* The book
came out in 1851, published in Coloma, Calif. See footnote 20 to "The
Journal of Lucena Parsons" below, entry for June 11, 1851. We do not
know the wife's name.

and washed and grased our catle we founde plenty
of grass here

september 3 we started on and traveled eighteen
miles to grass and water we found plenty of water
here and some grass to day we have had good roads
not vary dusty but some we now take over the mountains to the humbolt river

september 4 we left wind springs in large bogs and
crost over the mountains we had vary dusty going
all day we traveled a bout eighteen miles and came
to water and grass we have now come to a nother
chane of mountains and no humbolt yet we camped
here for the night we have good water here it is
vary cold

september 5 we travel some fifteen miles and got
to a good camp ground plenty of good grass and
water cold as ice a butifull creek comin right from
the mountain it roars like a cataract and springs all
round in evry direction and catle are giten fat on this
grass I was vary sick all night here with a pane in
my breast their was three wagons come up last night
with us I belive here the mountain is all covered
with snow

september 6 we have past over some mountains to
day for it is continualy mountain after mountain
now we have come in sight of a valey it is some
distance to it we have now come to it is ten miles
a cross it to a butifull creek comin in from the mountains it is clear as cristal and cold as ice we have
traveled eighteen miles to day plenty grass of the
best kind for catle

september 7 we past over some of the handsomest
land I ever saw in my life the land was completly
covered with a thick coat of grass it looks like a
perfect meadow we past some five or six boiling
springs the smoke arose from them great fire we
past more than twenty springs of the best kind we
traveled twenty miles to day and traveled vary late
we camped in a butiful place a stream on each side

september 8 sunday a butifull morning the sun
shines bright and clear as cristal we have past the
most butifull sight I ever saw in my life a perfect
meadow with ten thousand springs in it a gushing
right from the mountain clear and cold some of
them large anuff to cary any mill in operation We
have traveled twenty miles to day and stoped at foure
o clock

september 9 we traveled twenty five miles to day
we come to clarks river it is about foure feete
wide and three fete deepe to day the dust was so
bad that it was almost Imposible to travel we have
passt over one humbolt mountain and now come to
another their is plenty of ceder her[e] with some
white pine and pich pine it looks vary corse to me
and their is a curious fence which the Indians have [?]

september 10 mr crouch had all of his team stolen
buy the Indians and their is truly left helpless we
lost one horse and mr porter one and mr Croomley [5]
one the Indian tracks are all over here we think
their was a bout thirty here we traveled about twenty
five miles to git here we got in vary late it was

---

[5] A James Crumsley, who arrived in San Francisco in 1850, is listed in
Samuel Colville, *San Francisco Directory*, 1 (San Francisco, 1856).

dark the Indians had a good time we ware all tired and ware hungry and went to giten super they call this clarks river

september 11 we traveled fifteen miles in a butiful valey all day the grass is like a perfect meadow the catle is giten fat here we have still a vary dusty road it all most sufocates us their is plenty of Indian sign here all the time we still keep in the valey all the time and dont no but we all ways will for their seams to be no hopes of giten out of here we have now come to a sink of this creek intirely crust over have founde a well

september 12 we traveled seventeen miles to day we have past one of the most butifull springs it came right out of the bank and even in the valey it was vary dusty all day to day we have now come in sight of a little creek and the most butifull grass I ever saw the water is clear and runs sweet the stream is covered with willows and they look lovely

september 13 we traveled all day and only made seventeen miles we past some of the handsomest grass I ever saw in my life we came to a nother creek we traveled down it all the afternoon and at night we came to a canion which turned to the west we have bin traveling north for to or three days this stream gits larger here their is plenty of fish in it but we have not caught any

september 14 we have traveled in this canion all day and onley come ten miles we have traveled in the creek half the time I believe or more and some of the banks ware vary steepe the water is vary clear   we found plenty of good wood here and grass in a bundance and some fissh [several unclear words] got out of the canion and camped

september 15 [Sunday]   this day we traveled seventeen miles   this morning we came in sight of the northern road and some teams come up with us this morning we met a vary large train comin from the golde digins   they ware mormns comin to salt lake   we have now come to the humbolte river and the water is believed[?] and warme here and vary clear

september 16   monday   we traveled twenty miles to day over ruff and rockey roads and come to the river again   this travel was vary dusty and harde on the catle   one of them droped down in the yoke suficated with dust   we have now over taken a great many people and almost evry one out of provisions of any kind   we solde almost fifty dolars worth of bakin [baking? bacon?] last night

september 17   this day we traveled seventeen miles and come to the river again   the Indians are vary thick   they have killed to men to day and took their amunition and horses and left them for the buzards they devour them like we would sweete cake   we have to have set a strong guarde all the time or we would be killed and may be we will be killed yet we dont no

september 18   this day is vary clear and bright   we have traveled twenty miles and to day noon we thought we ware all again to be devoured with Indians   they surrounded us   we thought their was too or three hundred   we coulde not tell exactly how many their was but we could see them skulken every whare in the grass   mr hanaway[?] shot one or suposed he did

september 19   this morning is vary clear and bright this day we have traveled seventeen miles   to day noon we had the best grass I ever saw   it looked like a perfect wheete field   we then went on a litle ways and come to the river   their we found a man that had bin killed buy the Indians and his heart taken out   he was buried yesterday and their lay a dead Indian   it apears he was alone and the Indians came upon him and he shot one an then they shot him he was found with four arows shot in his breast and the Indian found shot under the arm

september 20   saturday   this day we traveled twenty miles and crost the river at noon   we founde good campin grounde to   we camped on the oposite side of the river from the other wagons   we had plenty of good grass here   we had vary dusty roads to day it was salaratus dust   their is plenty of salaratus here and plenty of lie to

september 21   this day it is vary colde and cloudy and some rain ocasionaly   we have traveled twenty miles to day   we founde an advertisemnt to be carfull or the Indians woulde kill us   their is plenty of them here   we have plenty of good grass to day for the catle   we have now arived at camp   it is marshey grounde here with here and their a bead [bed?] of salaratus and a pond of alekelie   butifull green grass for the catle

september 22 [Sunday]   we have traveled twenty miles to day and have vary good roads all except some sandy roads we had   we have now stoped to

noon and I founde some of the handsomest flowers
here I ever saw In my life their is plenty of ducks
and sage hens here we have had some of them and
they are vary good now we have arived at camp
grounde it seams plesent to stop plenty of grass

september 23 monday this day we traveled twenty
miles and founde good grass and good camp grounde
we coulde here the Indians a talking on the other
side of river but we could not see them at all but
coulde here them here we had some sage hen and
thought they ware a great rarity it is vary colde
and it has been vary dusty all day we have past
to or thre greaves to day

september 24 tuesday this day we only traveled
ten miles the road being sandy and vary dusty and
it was vary harde drawing all day

september 25 this day we traveled fifteen miles and
had vary good roads all day we had no dust at
all we camped in a low place on the river their
is a nother train camped closet by last night and
the Indians thought they have a good c[h]ance to
s[t]eal from them as they come about tehn o'clock
last night and they shot at them and they run

september 26 this day we onley traveled seven miles
and stoped to git grass for the desert we are in a
vary lonely place the hills betwene us and the river
is vary steepe and bad a wagon just a broke here
their is an encampment of robers

september 27 this day we traveled fourteen miles
the roads beeing vary dusty all day we founde a
good camp to night their is a wagon here that be-

longed to a nother train it seams they had a fight
with the indians seven days ago their is plenty of
good grass here camp ducks in a bundance here
the river here day in sloughs we are now in the
vicinity of the [Humboldt] sink I believe Elick
killed a [unclear word] hen and solde it all out

september 28 we traveled forteen miles to day and
did not a camp till to night we did not have vary
good camp grounde for I believe their are more than
fifty dead horse here but their is plenty of grass here
and water and plenty of good wood this eavening
we can see smoke in every direction some are Indians
and some are emigrants we can see a plenty of fires
this day it is vary dusty all day

september 29 [Sunday] we have did eight miles in
the morning we met a man that told us their was
plenty of flour ahead and meate and coffe we went
on then a bout three miles and their we met a train
just come in with plenty of provisions here we saw
some of the digers they look frightfull and some of
their wigwams their was five I think some of them
come out to the road and they were stark necked

september 30 this day all struck the mane desert
and now we leave the humbolt in tirely we traveled
all night and past the day we stoped to rest a half
our to a time the roads were so bad it is a sight
to see the distruction of property here

october 1 this day we traveled all day and all night
we come to the boiling spring it is the greatest
curiosity I ever saw in my life it will boil one yarde
high to a time this morning we are at salmon trout
river a bout seven o clock

october 2 we lay buy here all day and I washed
october 3 we crost over the river and went to the
trading post and stoped we lay buy all day

october 4 we traveled twelve miles
october [5] we traveled twelve miles
october 6 [Sunday] we lay buy all day and fixed
for packing

october 7 we started on this morning and traveled
twelve miles to the river we had vary ruff roads all
day we have now come in sight of timber and now
we have reached the Firre we camped for the night
here is plenty of timber to be got for fires and plenty
of good water and some grass for the catle

october 8 this day we crost the river twice and then
we come in to the timber it is plenty we now leave
salmon trout river and take over the mountain we
have now come over the mountain to a valey whare
their is grass for the catle and now we stop to feede
we have traveled seven miles their is a small creek
running here which answers for our use and for the
catle we have now a vary heavy snow storm the
mountain is white in the snow and it is vary cold
here I a most froze and the children the men seam
to stand it vary well

october 9 we traveled fifteen miles we have past
some of the handsomest pine trees I ever saw in my
life some of them five feete through and since we
had vary handsome road all day through some pleasant valeys of grass and a handsome creeke runing
through the valey plenty of grass to for the catle
all a rounde

october 10 this day we traveled onley about seven
miles   at aleven o clock when we stoped to noon
we founde good grass here and plenty of water and
wood   we came to cross the sumit and stop here till
morning   their is plenty of good timber here and
pitch pine   it is vary colde here and I am giting
vary tired of my journey   the mountains is covered
with snow

october 11   we have traveled eight miles to day   we
crost siere nevade mountains   it was vary steepe
we had to duble teams to git up and then had rain
harde time   we founde plenty of snow here and
plenty timbre and plenty rock   a litle more to me
like we have got over and found a botom covered with
grass and we founde a butifull creek here

october 12   this day we traveled sixteen miles and
come to yuba river   it is cro[w]ded with stones of
all sizes and sorts from a hens ague [egg] to the size
of a wagon   the water is clear and good   it is about
six feete wide   we have had the ruffest roads I ever
saw in my life   some places were soled rock and it
was butifull to see it   we past over mountains of all
sizes and sorts   we past some handsome timber to day

october 13 [Sunday]   this day we traveled onley
twelve miles and had vary ruff roads all day   we
past one trading post to day   we hurry past toord
[toward] these lakes to day   we also past one cedar
tree which masured tenn feete and I think might
have been   team catle taken off   we now come to
some grass for the catle and camp

october 14   this day we lay buy   all frost all day

and now we have started on we come to a hill
which is a mile up and a mile down and now we
stop grasse our catle and now it is raining frost and
snowing on the mounain   their is plenty wood here
for fires plenty of oak

october 15 we traveled twelve miles and had vary
good roads all day

october 16 we lay buy all day in bear valey to
grase our catle

october 17 we landed in siera nevady city and it
is a city to   his makes five months since we left home

october 18   we got under shelter with mr potinger
he had a house partly finished it is a sight to see
the miners here

october 19 [saturday]   we lay in mr potengers for the
[End of Journal.]

EPILOGUE:

The following is the text of a speech given by Cleora
Adelaide (Davis) Lester as reported by the Nevada City
Morning Union on October 21, 1924:

My Friends:

While I am not a native daughter, I am going to
hazard the statement that I came to California before
any member of Laurel Parlor was born, and I have
raised a native daughter and a native son.

I am prompted to say these few words to you as a
matter of interest in the early history of Nevada City,
mingled with the desire on my part to ascertain the
correctness of what I believe to be a fact, and that
it that I am easily the pioneer resident of Nevada
City, and in addition have lived in this city continu-

ously more years than any other person now living
or dead. It may surprise you when I state to you
that I arrived in Nevada City October 17, 1850, and
that I crossed the plains in an ox-team and arrived
here 74 years ago yesterday. But I might add that
I was carried in the arms of my Mother, Mrs. Z. P.
Davis. My Mother, Mrs. Davis, kept a diary while
crossing the plains, which I have kept all these years,
and it teems with interesting facts and incidents as
stirring as those presented in the "Covered Wagon,"
but I was too young on that eventful journey to
remember any of them.

My father, Zeno P. Davis, started for California
March 5, 1849, leaving his young wife, who was
about to become a mother, at Young's Prairie, Cass
County, Michigan. He reached St. Joseph, Missouri,
April 3, 1849. The baby (myself) was born August
9th of that year, and when three weeks old, in company with my mother, we started West and joined
my father at St. Joseph, Missouri, where the family
remained over the winter, owing to the severity of
the cholera which was raging on the western plains.

According to the diary kept by my Mother, they
camped on the Platte River [Missouri] May 21,
1850, and I find these entries on the last page of
the diary:

> October 16, 1850. We lay by all day in Bear Valley to
> graze our cattle.
> October 17, 1850. We landed in Siera, Nevady City (note
> spelling) and it is a city too. This makes five months since
> we left home.
> October 18, 1850. We got under shelter with Mr. Pot-
> tenger. He had a house partly finished. It is a sight to see the
> miners here.

October 19, 1850. Zeno bought Mr. Pottenger's house and
I feel that I never want anything more for now I have a chair
and a table and a roof over my head.

This house of Mr. Pottenger's was in reality a half
finished cabin, one of the few roofs in this town, all
other habitations being tents. The cabin stood on the
corner of Spring and Pine Streets, now vacant, and
the property owned by Mr. Smoke.

My father, Z. P. Davis, pre-empted the property
on the corner of Spring and Pine Streets, including
the lot where the Baptist Church stood, now owned
by E. T. R. Powell, and the property where I now
reside. I have with me the original pre-emption notice
stating that the land was to be taken up for building
purposes, which was recorded Sepember 23, 1853,
in Book B of Preemption Notices on Page 27, Records of Nevada County, Wm. S. Patterson, Recorder.

Of course, all these records were destroyed in the
fire of 1856 and therefore I have one of the very
few original pre-emption claims made on any lot in
Nevada City that was recorded and preserved, and
here I have resided ever since and here I expect to
end life's journey. But I hope to be present at many
more of your future gatherings of pioneers which
Laurel Parlor No. 6 of the Native Daughters of the
Golden West have so successfully arranged for the
purpose of bringing together the pioneers of this
community.

The Mormon Trail, 1850

❧ Sophia Lois Goodridge

INTRODUCTION

It was on April 8, 1850, that Benjamin and Penelope Goodridge left their Lunenburg, Massachusetts home, a short distance northwest of Boston, and started for the Mormon Canaan, Salt Lake City, with their six daughters, ranging from 14 to 25 years in age and their youngest child, George Albert, age 11. The first part of the journey was made in the usual way by stagecoach, steamboat, and fragmentary railroad episodes. They met their fellow Mormons in Kanesville, Iowa, and it became a covered wagon trip from then on. The wagon journey is the part of their westering experience that was told by Sophia, the next-to-oldest daughter, who was 24 years old, in the following diary. (The family pronounces her name Sofe-EYE-uh, with strong accent on the long "I" of the middle syllable.) Another relative who traveled with them was "Aunt Hattie," her mother's sister, whose married name was Harriet Dodge.

Sophia mentions one of the captains several times, Leonard Wilford Hardy, a farmer also from Massachusetts, but gives no hint of any special feelings about him; however, soon after their arrival in Salt Lake City, they were married on November 28. He was 45 years of age. He already had one wife, whom he had married in September, 1826. She was Elizabeth Goodridge, widow of Barnard Goodridge of Georgetown, Massachusetts. In the years following two of Sophia's sisters became the third and fourth wives of Leonard Hardy: Esther on August 20, 1854, and Harriet Ann on March 28, 1858. There would be 18 children by the four wives. Sophia was the mother of nine of them. If today there is a large Hardy Family Association of America, it is understandable.

The Goodridge family was deeply involved in music. Sophia wrote in her diary on June 8, "Had two violins in our ten [*sic.*]; had some music and dancing." She herself played the melodeon, and brought one out with her on the long journey. She was also a gifted singer, one of the earliest members of the Tabernacle Choir. In Massachusetts she had studied with the famous Boston music teacher, Lowell Mason. He imbued her with a love of sacred music. Mason had written the music for several of the best-known hymns, including "Nearer My God to Thee," and "My Faith Looks Up to Thee." The favorite Mormon song, "The Glorious Light of Truth," is said to have been composed for Sophia by William Clayton after hearing her sing.

In Utah, Sophia grew flax and wove linen out of it to make clothing. She also processed wool from the raw product into clothing. She learned the tailoring trade and made clothes for the entire family. It is also surprising to discover that somewhere she learned to diagnose diseases, and the doctors of Utah often consulted her in this capacity. One of her daughters, Martha, wrote of her, "She had a pretty good knowledge of chemistry and was a great reader. She had read many of Shakespeare's plays and had seen all of them but one. She read all kinds of books, enjoyed a good detective story . . ." It was also known that she knew the Bible and the Book of Mormon so well she could quote them extensively.

Sophia Goodridge Hardy was in poor health the last ten years of her life and died on November 3, 1903, at the age of 77, surrounded by her family.

Because of the great number of persons named by Sophia in her diary, we think it too complicated to clutter the pages of such a short document with a host of footnotes. Therefore, we have prepared a "Dramatis Personae" in which they are listed and identified insofar as it has been possible. In addition, there is also a bibliography. Some of the persons with common names among the Mormons such as Smith, Snow, Johnson, Howard, and others, as indicated in the 1850 Federal Census, remain unidentified. Incidentally, the 1850 census was taken in 1851 in Utah (Deseret) and so includes the 1850 overlanders.

The typescript from which this diary was copied is in the Utah State Historical Society in Salt Lake City. However, it was given to them by Hardy Jenkinson of Magna, Utah, and he has graciously given us permission to use it. We have inquired of several of the Hardy clan as to the whereabouts of the original, yet so far it has not been found. Two of them have been especially helpful, Aretta Hansen of Salt Lake City, and Gayle H. Anderson of Golden, Colorado.

DRAMATIS PERSONAE

Capt. Andrus, who found "a new route to the pass, was Milo Andrus, who was just returning from a mission to England. (Bitton, *Guide*, p. 11.)

Brother Atwood, according to the *Wilford Woodruff* biography, p. 341, was one of the wagon captains named Miner Atwood. The 1860 Federal Census of Salt Lake City lists him as Miner G. Attwood, a laborer from Connecticut.

Brother Badlam evidently had one of the early large-wheeled wooden speedometers attached to one wagon wheel. He was Alexander Badlam, a New Englander from Massachusetts.

Brother Blazerd, who was taken sick on June 27, was John Hopwood Blazzard, an Englishman and wagon maker, listed thus in the Federal Census of Salt Lake City, 1860.

Mr. Burns, whose child died of cholera on July 16, was Enoch B.
Burns, a Canadian. He became an Ogden settler, eventually
moving to Arizona. (Bitton, *Guide,* p. 50.)

Brother Burrows was David B. Burrows, who, with his wife, Sarah,
had emigrated from County Down, Ireland. Early Church Information Card Index.

Brother Crosby, whom, according to Sophia, they met with "seven
other missionaries on their way to England," was Jesse Went-
worth Crosby. In his own journal, Crosby listed eight persons
by name who accompanied him on the English mission. (Crosby,
"History and Journal," p. 185.)

Brother Currier was identified by Wilford Woodruff as James
Currier, one of the captains. (*Wilford Woodruff,* p. 341.)

Mrs. Delin, who "gave birth to a daughter" on the night of October
14th, is so far unidentified. There were Delins who came several
years later from Sweden. This could also be a misspelling of
Dallen or Dolin or Dolan, all of whom have representatives in
the 1860 Federal Census of Utah.

Brother Emmet, who "killed an Antelope" on July 20, would nat-
urally be thought of as James Emmett, a rather free spirit of
several cross-country migrations. However, Dale L. Morgan
proved this man to be in California at the time of the 1850
migration. The Emmet here was Moses Simpson Emmet, son
of James. He was a Kentuckian, who, with his wife, Catherine,
and James Emmet's deserted wife, Phoebe, was on his way to
Salt Lake City. (Morgan, "Reminiscences of James Holt," pp.
164-65.)

Phebia Foss, who jumped to safety out of Brother Woodruff's
carriage when the horse became frightened and ran away, was
Phoebe C. Foss, daughter of Calvin and Sara B. Foss. She was
the great-niece of Wilford Woodruff. (*Wilford Woodruff,* p.
341.)

George Gardner was captain of the ten to which the Goodridges
belonged. He was the brother of Penelope, Sophia's mother, and
had been the first of the family converted to Mormonism. "Goodridge-Goodrich Family Story," p. 253.)

Brother Gibson, who tipped his wagon over on October 5th, was
an Englishman from Yorkshire. It was Gibson's daughter, Mary

Ann Gibson Green, who died on June 27. ("Graves Along the Trail," p. 429.) See next item.

Sister Green, who "died of cholera" on June 27, was Mary Ann Gibson Green, daughter of the Gibsons, see above, who had emigrated from Yorkshire, England. She was 32 years old, the wife of Thomas Green, who took the top boards of his wagon box to make a coffin for his wife. She was buried right alongside the trail. Three days later Jane Green, the 18-year-old daughter, died, and on July 1 Joseph Green, age 19 months, passed on, "making three out of one family that have died within five days." ("Graves Along the Trail," pp. 429-30.)

Brother Hall, who was "dead with the cholera" on July 1st, was Joseph Hall, one of the captains. (*Wilford Woodruff*, p. 341.)

Brother Hanks was Ephraim Knowlton Hanks, a Mormon leader on the way back over the trail to aid later wagon companies at the behest of Brigham Young. (*Biographical Encylopedia*, II, pp. 765-66.)

Samuel B. Hardy was the brother of Leonard W. Hardy, both of them New Englanders, born in Bradford, Massachusetts. He was listed in the 1860 Federal Census of Utah as a farmer.

Brother Hawood or Haywood, was Joseph L. Heywood, who married another young woman who kept a journal of the 1850 journey, Martha Spence. Their story is ably told in Martha's own words by Juanita Brooks in her 1978 book, *Not by Bread Alone*.

Edward Hunter was the leader of another company to Salt Lake City in 1850. It was the last to reach the destination as they had a large shipment of freight from England. Hunter handled many of the financial aspects of the western migration. His work would lead to the Perpetual Emigration Fund. (Arrington, *The Mormon Experience*, p. 130.) Hunter later became Presiding Bishop of the Church. (Bancroft, *Utah*, p. 774.)

Brother Hyde was met by the party on October 4th. This was the dynamic Mormon Apostle, Orson Hyde, who was taking eastward the Fourth General Epistle of the Church, which had been promulgated in September. ("Fourth General Epistle – Sept. 1850," *Our Pioneer Heritage*, pp. 419-28.)

Lucy Johnson "took sick this afternoon and died at 12 o'clock," on July 4th. This is a correction of the date given as July 9 in

Wilford Woodruff, p. 341. Jesse W. Crosby indicated in his "History and Journal" that there were two Johnson families with the 1850 migration: Captain Thomas Johnson and Captain Aaron Johnson (p. 191). So far, Lucy Johnson is not associated with either of these families or any other Johnsons.

John and Sara Kay were musicians from England. He was also an expert metal worker. (Stout, *Diary,* p. 728.)

Brother Moffet "was chosen Captain of the remaining 20 wagons." This was Armstead Moffet, a blacksmith, who, with his large family, would become key settlers in the Ogden area. (Federal Census, 1860.)

Capt. Petty "was chosen Captain over a hundred." This man is identified as Robert Petty in *Wilford Woodruff,* p. 341. Robert C. Petty later became a well-known Utah lawyer. There are numerous references to him in the Stout *Diary.* He became a partner with Stout in the herding business (Stout, p. 507.)

William Ridge was struck and killed by lightning on July 15. Wilford Woodruff says that "On the 15th, . . . a severe thunder storm arose and Brother Ridge, from Staffordshire, England, and his oxen were killed by lightning." (*Wilford Woodruff,* p. 341.)

Brother Rawson was Horace S. Rawson, a chairmaker from New York, who, with his family, became pioneer settlers of the Ogden area. In 1856, he married Eliza Jane Cheney, a young woman among the 1850 overlanders. (Bitton, *Guide,* p. 287; Federal Census, 1860.)

Brother Smoot was Abraham O. Smoot, a prominent early Mormon leader. He would become the mayor both of Salt Lake City and of Provo and would prosper in business and banking. (Bitton, *Guide,* p. 328.)

Brother Stratton was met coming with Brother Ephraim Hanks (see above) on August 24 with a letter from Brigham Young. This was Joseph A. Stratton, who also met the Heywood party a week later on August 30. (*Not by Bread Alone,* p. 21.)

The "Mr. Wallace," who saw a sleeping bear on August 6, and did not disturb him," is so far unidentified. Perhaps he was not a Mormon as she designates Mormon men as "Brother."

Joseph Webb "tipped his wagon over" on October 3rd. Again,

because she does not designate him as "Brother," he may have been one of the rough and ready non-Mormon teamsters.

Brother Whipple was made Captain over the Second Fifty on June 18. This was Nelson Wheeler Whipple, who traveled to Salt Lake City in 1850. There is a typescript of his "Autobiography" in the Utah Historical Society Library. There is a biography of him in *Biographical Encyclopedia*, III, p. 561. (Bitton, *Guide*, p. 377.)

Brother Woodruff was the Mormon Apostle who would later become the Fourth President of the Church in 1889. He presided over the dissolution of polygamy. (*Dictionary of American Biography*, XX, pp. 498-99; William Mulder and A. Russell Mortensen, *Among the Mormons*, pp. 415-17.)

Brother Wooley, who camped with the party on August 30, was Edwin Dilworth Woolley. He was a member of the Pioneers, the overland group in 1847. He later was a member of the Utah Territorial Legislature. He became the superintendent of Brigham Young's private business. (Stout, *Diary*, p. 299.)

THE DIARY OF SOPHIA LOIS GOODRIDGE

June 7, 1850 [Friday] We started from Kanesville [Iowa] at 1:00 P.M. – rode 10 miles camped at Margreta Creek, a very beautiful shady spot. We heard the wolves howl in the night for the first time. Our horses were frightened.

June 8. Traveled 7 miles. We enjoyed ourselves very much at the last two places we camped. Had two violins in our ten; had some music and dancing. Good feed and water for the cattle. We stopped at this place until June 14.

June 14 [Friday]. Went 3 miles; camped at a place called Bethlehem. Had a pleasant time – some music and dancing.

June 18. We traveled 6 miles today; camped at a creek – good feed and water. Our company was organized today. Capt. Perry was chosen Captain over a hundred. Leonard W. Hardy Captain over the first fifty; brother Whipple over the second fifty. George Gardner Captain over ten. Our company all well.

June 19. Did not travel. Did our washing.

June 20. Still in camp. Did our ironing and picked some gooseberries on the banks of the creek.

June 21. Traveled 4 miles. Camped on the banks of a creek.

June 22. Went 4 miles. Crossed a creek.

June 23 [Sunday]. Traveled 4 miles. Raining.

June 24. Went 2 miles. Still raining. Camped by the side of a creek.

June 25. Crossed the creek this morning. Passed 5 graves. They died the 15th of June. They all had grave tablets made of wood rudely hewn, and the name engraved with a knife. A verse was written on the grave of M. Dona, which was very touching. We crossed three more creeks today without accident. Went ten miles and camped at Weeping Water Creek.

June 26. We traveled ten miles today. Passed three graves. No names on them. Came up with a Government Company. One man sick with cholera. Died and was buried in the forenoon. In the afternoon, passed three more graves, no names, died June 22nd. One of our company took sick with the cholera. Camped at Salt Creek.

June 27. Sister Green died of cholera this morning. Brother Blazerd taken sick. Crossed the creek and

went on to the bluff and camped for the night. The
first fifty caught up with us today. They are on the
other side of the creek. One man sick with the cholera
among them.

June 28. We started about noon and traveled six
miles and camped on the open prairie without wood
or water. Found water about one-half mile from camp.
Passed the grave of a child.

June 29. Our company all in good spirits this morning and I feel grateful of my Heavenly Father for his
kindness in preserving our lives and health this far and
that he has preserved us from accidents and dangers of
all kinds. We traveled eight miles and camped on the
open prairie without wood or water, except what we
brought with us. There is nothing to see but one bound-
less sea of grass, waving like the waves of the sea, and
now and then a tree. We had a very heavy thundershower this morning.

June 30 [Sunday]. Jane Green died of cholera this
morning. She was 18 years old. Our first fifty came up
with us this morning. They had buried Brother Smith
this morning. The rest of the camp all well. We went
four miles and camped where there was wood and
water. We killed a rattlesnake.

July 1 [Monday]. Joseph Green died this morning,
age 19 months, making three out of one family that
have died within five days. Came up with our first fifty.
Found Brother Hall dead wih cholera. Our camp
afflicted and distressed. We felt like humbling ourselves before the Lord and pray that he might turn
from us the sickness and distress. We therefore met
together, the speakers exhorting us to be diligent in

our devotions and united. A vote was taken to that effect. They then called upon the Lord in prayer, that He would bless and preserve us on our journey to the valley. We then started on our journey rejoicing. We met the mail from the Valley. Brother Crosby and seven other missionaries on their way to England. We were very glad to see them. They brought cheering news from Salt Lake which caused us to rejoice. We traveled six miles and camped on the prairie.

July 2. Very warm and pleasant. We traveled 16 miles – all level plain.

July 3. We traveled about 15 miles; camped on the bluffs on the north side of the Platte River. Plenty of wood and water. Our first fifty camped about a mile from us. Samuel Hardy buried his youngest child today.

July 4. Stopped to wash. Lucy Johnson took sick this afternoon and died at 12 o'clock.

July 5. Went 12 miles. Stopped at Clear Creek.

July 6. Traveled 16 miles.

July 7. [Sunday]. Camped for the day. Sister Snow died this morning, making five that have died in our division since we started.

July 8. We traveled 16 miles and camped on the Platte River. Good camping grounds – our two companies together – all well.

July 9. Had a heavy thunderstorm last night. This morning cool and cloudy. Brother Woodruff baptised 12 persons – Father, Mary Jane, and George among the number. We traveled 17 miles and camped on the Platte River.

July 10. Cool and pleasant. We traveled 15 miles. Camped on the bank of the Platte River. Heavy showers.

July 11. Heavy showers. Very warm and sultry. Sister Huntington, of the first division, died of fever. The road was very wet and hard to travel. We went 10 miles and camped on the Platte.

July 12. Had a heavy rain last night. The river rose two feet. One horse drowned. Traveled about 10 miles and camped on the open plain. Heavy thundershowers. The cattle wandered away – found them all again.

July 13. Weather cool and clear. Went 10 miles. Camped on the Platte.

July 14. Sunday. Camped for the day. Both divisions camped together. Held a meeting in the afternoon. Brothers Whipple, Hardy, and Woodruff were the speakers. We felt very much encouraged by what was said.

July 15. We traveled seven miles. Came to Fort Childs, formerly Fort Carney. A thundershower came up and William Ridge was struck by lightning and instantly killed. Three of his cattle were killed at the same time, and one of his children slightly injured. A number of people felt the shock. We went two miles farther and camped.

July 16. A child of Mr. Burns died of cholera this morning. The weather is clear and cool. Very muddy. Traveled about eight miles and camped on the prairie. Used buffalo chips for fuel.

July 17. Traveled 14 miles. Saw an Antelope. Did not kill any.

July 18. Went 18 miles and camped on Plum Creek. We passed a number of groves of trees. We saw some animals, probably buffalos. Weather good. The roads good. The camp in good health.

July 19. This morning clear and beautiful. We traveled 16 miles and camped on the open plain without wood or water.

July 20. Traveled 14 miles. The weather cloudy. Brother Emmet killed an Antelope. It was distributed among the camp. We found it very good eating. We camped on the bank of the river – a beautiful place. The bluffs begin to look higher and more rough and rugged.

July 21. Sunday. We did not travel today according to council. We held meetings in the forenoon and afternoon and received some excellent instructions which cheered us on our journey.

July 22. We started this morning in good spirits. David Cook shot a sage hen. We saw some antelope and some wolves. Did not kill any. We passed Brother Woodruff's company about noon. Brother Petty was sick – had buried one of his children the day before. We traveled about 16 miles. Camped on the Platte. Grand place for bathing. Brother Woodruff's company caught up with us tonight.

July 23. Traveled 14 miles and camped near the Platte river. Brother Emmet killed an antelope. We had a steak from it – very good. Brother Woodruff's company camped with us tonight.

July 24. We laid over today to do some repairing.

July 25. We traveled about eight miles and camped.

We passed near a number of herds of buffalo. Our division killed one and brought it into camp. The first division killed two. The feed for cattle scarcer. We saw quite a number of buffalo dead on the ground. We made a rule *not* to kill more than we needed to eat.

July 26. It is very warm today. We traveled about eight miles and camped on the Platte South Fork. Our folks killed a buffalo and brought it into camp.

July 27. Cloudy. Saw two big white wolves. Passed a number of herds of buffalo. Went about four miles and camped. Our wagon wheels were very musical. We had to stop and burn coal. Our men cut wood and started a coal pit in the afternoon. Part of our company stopped at the last camping on account of the excellent hunting. There was no wood there but cedar which they thought would not make as good coal as the willow. We found this place grand for wood and water. It is situated on the South Fork of the Platte River. There is quite a large island covered with groves of cottonwood and willow and excellent feed for our cattle.

July 28. Sunday. Did not travel. Had a meeting in the forenoon. Had a heavy shower which we needed very much. It tightened our wagon wheels and saved our men the trouble of taking off the tires and re-setting them. Brother Woodruff is sick today – worn out with fatigue and care.

July 29. Traveled about 17 miles and came near a small creek about two miles from the Platte. Saw a herd of buffalo.

July 30. We traveled about 10 miles when a stampede started in the first division. There were three wagons smashed. It was caused by a runaway horse. The first division stopped to fix up their wagons. A number of wagon tongues were broken. Brother Woodruff's beautiful buggy horse had his leg broken. The buffalo bellowed all night and we expected they would be down among us before morning but fortunately they kept back among the bluffs. Their bellowing sounded like distant thunder. Brother Leonard Hardy is quite sick with cholera.

July 31 [?] and came to the crossing of the South Fork of the Platte River. Our wagons all crossed in safety before dark. Camped on the bank of the river. It is about ¼ mile wide.

Aug. 1 [Thursday]. We ascended the bluffs this morning and came upon an extensive plain or rolling prairie. Had some very steep bluffs to descend. It seemed impossible for such heavy loaded teams to descend in safety, but we all reached Ash Hollow in safety. We traveled 18 miles and camped on the North Fork of the Platte.

Aug. 2. We washed today. Ash Hollow is a beautiful place. Bluffs on both sides of the Hollow which appears to have been the bed of a river once, which opens onto the North Fork of the Platte. Brother Woodruff's company joined us tonight with the exception of six wagons which were left, two broken down, and it became too dark to drive down the steep hills. Brother Hardy's health very poor.

Aug. 3. Remained in Ash Hollow to fix up our wagons.

Aug. 4. Sunday. Had a meeting this afternoon. Brother Woodruff made a proposition – that he stop with his ten baggage wagons and let the first and second divisions, or as many as wished, go on ahead. He felt he had so much care on his shoulders. Brother Whipple said he would take the burden of the ten baggage wagons on "his" shoulders. Brother Gardner, the blacksmith, worked all day and had a number of men to help him repair the wagons, but did not get all done.

Aug. 5. Brother Hardy is better this morning and started out with 16 of his division to go ahead. Brother Whipple started with part of his division and went four miles in search of feed for our cattle which was very scarce. The land on the north side of the river is prairie, while on the south side is high towering bluffs which look like fortifications in many places.

Aug. 6. Brother Hardy started off this morning feeling very much better. Mr. Wallace saw a bear. He was asleep. He did not disturb him.

Aug. 7. Brother Woodruff came up with us this forenoon. He had a meeting this afternoon. Had a new organization – Brothers Whipple, Gardner, Goodridge, and Rawson were transferred into Brother Woodruff's division making 24 wagons in that division. Brother Moffet was chosen Captain of the remaining 20 wagons.

Aug. 8. Very warm. Started out about 8 o'clock, the second division taking the lead. We had a very hard road today – sandy and steep hills to climb. We traveled about 12 miles and camped on the Platte River. Feed rather short.

Aug. 9. Had heavy showers last night – very sharp

lightning and loud thunder. The wolves killed a calf belonging to Brother Whipple. We traveled about 15 miles. Camped on the bank of the Platte.

Aug. 10. Saw some antelope this morning and some wolves. We traveled about 15 miles and camped on the Platte. Found good feed.

Aug. 11. Sunday. We did not travel. Held a meeting this afternoon. We had an excellent discourse by Brother Whipple on the difference between Jews and the Gentiles. Brother Woodruff and Gardner gave us excellent instructions. This evening we saw the prairie on fire.

Aug. 12. We started on our journey at 4 o'clock. All well. We passed a high bluff called the Exchange on account of its resemblance to a large building. Passed Clear Creek, a small stream of very clear water. It comes from the bluffs and flows into the Platte River. We traveled 18 miles. Had very good roads. We met some Government trains from Fort Larimie. They said our first division was about 15 miles ahead of us. Killed two rattlesnakes.

Aug. 13. Started about 8 o'clock. Traveled 16 miles. Camped about 3 o'clock on the Platte. A heavy rain started just before we stopped. We passed Chimney Rock. This is a notable curiosity. It is 834 yards around the base and 200 feet high. The main shaft 100 feet in diameter. It appears to be formed of clay and sand of two colors – gray and white. It also has the appearance of cement between the two columns. It is supposed by some to be the work of the Nephites.

Aug. 14. It is a clear beautiful morning. We made

an early start and went about 19 miles. We saw some Indians for the first time since we started. Their wigwams were spread along the road. They were Sioux. They looked very neat and clean for Indians. The men came out on horses to look at us. The Squaws with their papooses stood along the road and tried to sell us some moccasins. One of the men wanted to trade a horse for a white woman. We passed Scotts Bluff on the right. We leave the river here and strike into the bluffs. We found chokeberries and wild plums not quite ripe. We camped on the open prairie. There is a beautiful cold spring here.

Aug. 15. We did not start until late this morning. We had a long meeting to settle some little difficulties between some members of the company, not worth mentioning. We crossed Horse Creek and camped about half a mile farther on. This creek is several rods wide, about a foot deep and very muddy. The water after standing awhile, becomes perfectly clear and very good to drink. A very heavy shower came up just after we camped. We traveled 12 miles.

Aug. 16. We started at 7 o'clock and traveled 15 miles, over rolling prairies and sandy bluffs, and camped on the Platte River.

Aug. 17. We traveled about 10 miles. We passed by a good many traders and Indians. Some of them had the small pox. The feed is very poor.

Aug. 18. Sunday. On account of the feed being so poor, we thought it best to travel. Went about 12 miles. Passed Fort Laramie. We camped on the Platte. We found Captain Hardy's train about ¼ mile from us. We had not seen them for two weeks.

They were all well. Mrs. Bird had a still born child Saturday morning.

Aug. 19.   Cold and stormy all day. Did not travel.

Aug. 20.   We traveled about 2½ miles. The feed was so good we thought it best to let our animals feed up and rest. A company of "Shian" Indians came along in the afternoon and camped beside us. They had been out on a buffalo hunt and were returning to Fort Laramie to sell their skins. They looked very neat for Indians. They came down to see us and were very friendly. We traded some with them. Brother Woodruff lost an ax last night. He had to go back to the Fort for more, which delayed us some.

Aug. 21.   We started about 2 P.M. and traveled about 4 miles. We had a very bad hill to go down. Brother Woodruff's carriage horse became frightened and ran away. Phebia Foss was in the carriage but jumped out. The horse ran until he got tangled up in the brush but there was no damage done. We camped on the Platte.

Aug. 22.   Started early, traveled about 21 miles over a very uneven road. We passed through a band of "Shian" Indians. They were camped on the bank of a beautiful clear creek. There were several hundred of them. We crossed another creek and camped.

Aug. 23.   We started early and traveled 25 miles. We crossed three creeks. One of them was about 3 rods wide and a foot and a half deep. The roads very uneven – dangerous in some plaes and in others nice and smooth. Camped on the Platte. Cool and pleasant. There were some buffalo on the bank where we camped.

Aug. 24. We are in the midst of the Black Hills. They look black at a distance but when you get near them, they are green and covered with stragling pines. We traveled 8½ miles and camped for the day. We met Brothers Stratton and Hanks from Salt Lake. They had been sent out to meet us and cheer us on our way. They brought us some potatoes which tasted *so* good. They will tell us where to find good camping places. We held a meeting in the afternoon. Brother Stratton read a letter from Pres. Brigham Young. It was truly cheering to hear from our friends in the valley and know that they had not forgotten us. It caused us to rejoice and feel like starting anew on our journey. We camped on the Platte.

Aug. 25 [Sunday]. We took a vote last night to travel today on account of the delay we had the forepart of the week. We traveled 19½ miles Labont Crossing. This is a beautiful river about 2 rods wide and a foot deep – clear and cool. The road was rough. Our first and second division left this place this morning. Brother Hardy lost an ox and his horses were giving out. We found some cherries. Camped on the Labont River.

Aug. 26. We traveled 18 miles. Came up with our two first divisions. They were all well but Brother Hardy, who is still suffering from cholera. Only three families came up; Brothers Gardner, Goodridge, and Rawson. The rest of our division camped about a mile and a half.

Aug. 27. Our division that stayed back lost about half their cattle last night. We have got to stop and hunt them. The first and second division went ahead. Brothers Stratton and Hanks killed a buffalo today and brought it into camp. They saw a grizzly bear.

Aug. 28.   No cattle found yet. We cannot travel today. We went out this morning and picked 14 quarts of cherries.

Aug. 29.   Part of the cattle found last night. They are out hunting the rest today. It is very sandy here. The last day we traveled about three miles through it. We saw some mountain sheep on the hills.

Aug. 30.   We started this morning before breakfast and went to the place where the remainder of our division were camped on the Laprelle Creek. Our company killed two buffalo today. The rest of the cattle were found all but three. Brother Smoot passed us today. Brothers Hawood and Wooley camped with us tonight. They had had but one death in their company and had got along remarkably well.

Aug. 31.   We started this morning about 10 o'clock. We crossed Boxelder Creek. Brother Badlam has got his road meter going today. We traveled 14 miles and camped on the Platte.

Sept. 1 [Sunday].   Started at 10. Crossed Deer Creek. Traveled about 13½ miles. Passed Brother Smoot's company. Had strong winds and some rain.

Sept. 2.   Started at 10. Crossed Crooked Muddy Creek and camped on the Platte. Traveled about 13 miles. We picked 33 quarts of buffalo berries. They taste very much like currants and are red. They have one seed in them and make very good sauce and pies.

Sept. 3.   Started at 8 and came to the Platte crossing. We stopped two hours to rest and feed our cattle and then crossed the river. The scenery along the Platte River is very grand. A long and high mountain chain extends southwest. We have followed it for three days and have not come to the end of it yet. We crossed the North Fork of the Platte without any accidents. We traveled about 9½ miles and camped on the Platte. Saw a grizzley bear.

Sept. 5. We planned an early start but our cattle got mixed up with Smoot's on account of our herdsmen not attending to their duty. George caught some fish, bass and suckers. We traveled 14 miles and camped by a beautiful clear spring. We passed quite a number of dead cattle, perhaps 25, caused by a poisoned spring of water which we passed today. The country here is not quite so rocky and barren as it has been the last few days. We came through a place called Rock Avenue. It is about a quarter of a mile long and lined with rocks on each side.

Sept. 6. We traveled 16 miles and camped on Greesewood Creek, a beautiful place of good feed. The weather is very pleasant. We camped with Brother Smoot's company. Brother Stratton started. They took a beautiful wild horse with them that they had captured.

Sept. 7. Traveled 8 miles today. Passed a saleratus lake. Camped at the foot of Independence Rock. This evening we had a dance on the banks of the Sweetwater. The whole company participated. We had a good time.

Sept. 8 [Sunday]. I have just climbed Independence Rock and the view is beautiful. The Sweetwater flows southeast at the foot of the rock and winds around at the foot of the mountains. The Saleratus Lake is seen in the northeast, the Devil's Gate is in the west, while mountains are to be seen on all sides. We crossed the Sweetwater and traveled until we came to the Devil's Gate. We stopped and ate lunch. The rocks are perpendicular, 400 feet high and in one place, the gap between them is only 2 feet wide. The Sweetwater flows through the gap. Some of us crossed it on foot just for the novelty of it. We traveled 15 miles and camped on the Sweetwater.

Sept. 9. We crossed the Sweetwater twice. The road is very sandy and heavy. We passed many high bluffs and rocky hills. We camped on the Sweetwater opposite a high sandy bluff. We went 12 miles.

Sept. 10. We traveled eight miles over a heavy sandy road. Crossed the Sweetwater and camped. We were detained in the morning until nearly noon on account of Brother Woodruff's teamsters. One of them was fired and the other two left. They were rough, obsene men, did not belong to the church and were stealing the supplies.

Sept. 11. We started early. Crossed the Sweetwater three times. Camped at Ice Springs. Traveled eight miles. Windy and dusty – many rocky hills. The Ice Springs are a great curiosity. About one or two feet below the surface of the ground, any quantity of ice can be found. It is not good to use. It has a bad smell. The ground is soft and marshy above it. Very little feed here.

Sept. 12. We started early this morning. We passed

a very fine saleratus lake. We gathered what we wanted. It was very white and clean. We crossed the Sweetwater. Good feed. We found ice in our pails this morning.

Sept. 13. We started at noon and went eight miles and camped on the Sweetwater. Plenty of good feed. Some of our cattle gave out last night, so our Captain thought it best that we rest part of the day.

Sept. 14. We started at 9 and traveled about two miles and came to a new route to the pass, made by Capt. Andrus. We took it and went 11½ miles and lost three miles by doing it. We found it rough, stony, and uneven. We traveled 13 miles and camped on Quakenasp Creek. We met several head of cattle and one wagon for Haywood and Wooley.

Sept. 15. [Sunday]. Traveled four miles and camped on the Sweetwater. Started a coal pit and held a meeting. Four wagons came up from Hunter's company.

Sept. 16. We crossed the Sweetwater for the last time. We traveled 15 miles and camped at Pacific Springs. We met Captain Hardy in search of his horses. They had been lost two days and two horses belonging to another man.

Sept. 17. We stopped to do some repairing this morning. We let Capt. Hardy have a yoke of oxen so he could travel on. We started about noon. Just as we were starting, five Indians came up. One could speak English. They said they had found two horses. Brothers Woodruff and Atwood went with them to their camp. They took a few articles to give them in case they were not willing to give the horses up. Aunt

Hattie sent a blanket shawl. We wait the results. We crossed two creeks. Traveled 13 miles and camped on Bitter Creek.

Sept. 19. We have heard nothing from Brothers Woodruff and Atwood and we feel somewhat alarmed at their long absence. We sent two messengers back to Captain Wooley's camp to see if they had heard from them and if not, to have him join us and send united forces of men after them. They had not been gone more than half an hour, when we saw them returning with Brothers Woodruff and Atwood with one of Brother Hardy's horses and one of Brother Curriers. We were very glad to see them. It seems that the Indians had stolen them and wanted to be paid for returning them. When the brethren got to their camp, they found 300 warriors and about 1,000 horses. They were going to war with the Shians. These Indians were Shoshones. They lost one of the horses. He was an ugly wild thing and ran away and took several of the Indians' horses with him. We traveled 11 miles and camped on the Big Sandy River. William nearly shot an antelope.

Sept. 20. We camped last night with Haywood and Wooley's company and our first division. We started out at 10, Captain Hardy moving out first; Brother Wooley next. We traveled 16 miles and camped with Brother Hardy's company on the Big Sandy River.

Sept. 21. Brother Woodruff's ox died last night. Brother Woodruff could not go on. They concluded to let him take Brother Goodridge's oxen which was on one of Brother Hardy's wagons and Brother Hardy take one of Brother Burrows, so as to have all the borrowed animals in this division. We traveled six miles and met Brother Young from the valley. He stated there was no feed on Green River, so we camped on Big Sandy River.

Sept. 22. Sunday. We held a meeting and felt very much instructed by the remarks of the speakers. We made a coal pit. Set some tires and made shoes and nails.

Sept. 23. We traveled nine miles and camped on Green River. George caught a cat fish a foot long.

Sept. 24. Started at 8. Went 19 miles and camped on Ham's Fork. We passed some beautiful scenery on the banks of the river. We met two Brethern from the Valley, stating that the Snake Indians were hostile and had killed some of the brethern; that 400 Indians were in the mountains and we had better be on our guard.

Sept. 25. We started at 10 and traveled 12½ miles and camped on Black Fork.

Sept. 26. Started at 10. Went ten miles and camped on Sunset Creek, a beautiful stream of water two rods wide and two feet deep.

Sept. 27. Started about 10, traveled 8½ miles. Camped on Bridge's [Bridger's] Creek, about a mile from Fort Bridges [Bridger].

Sept. 28. We drove our cattle in order to make an early start. Found after one got started that about 10 cattle were missing. All hands went to search for them and finally concluded that they had gone back. Some of the Brethern mounted horses and finally found them 14 miles to the back trail. Got in with them about dark. We were very glad to see them. We spent the day. Caught some beautiful large trout.

Sept. 29 [Sunday]. We started early and traveled 11 miles and camped on a small creek. We had a very bad hill to descend. Some of the wagons were broken.

Sept. 30. We had to lay over to mend our wagons. Some of the first division went ahead. Some of them complained a good deal at being detained so much.

Oct. 1 [Tuesday]. We started early and went 15 miles. Had a very good road, hilly but even and smooth. One of Brother Woodruff's cows died in the yoke today. We passed the highest summit of the journey today. There is some beautiful scenery in these mountains. We camped in a valley at the foot of the mountain.

Oct. 2. We had rain, thunder, and lightning last night. Cleared up this morning. We traveled six miles. Had a very steep hill to climb, had to double teams. We camped on Bear River. We caught a glimpse of our first division climbing the mountains ahead of us.

Oct. 3. We picked 12 quarts of haw berries. We intend to make vinegar of them. We traveled six miles and camped on a small creek. Joseph Webb tipped his wagon over, which prevented us from going any farther today. Our road winds along at the foot of the mountains, very wild and picturesque. Camped on Yellow Creek.

Oct. 4. It was very cold last night, froze the water in our buckets quarter of an inch thick, but it has been a beautiful day. We met Brother Hyde on way to the States. He brought good news from Salt Lake. We traveled 10 miles.

Oct. 5. Started early, traveled 18 miles. Camped on Echo Creek. Brother Hunter came up and camped with us. We had to cross the creek a number of times and some places it was bad and we had to fix the roads. Brother Gibson tipped over without doing any damage.

Oct. 6 [Sunday]. We traveled eight miles and camped on the Reed Fork of the Weber. Our road very rough and bad on account of having to cross the creek so many times.

Oct. 7. We laid over to rest our cattle. Caught some trout.

Oct. 8. We traveled 12 miles and camped on a small creek at the foot of a mountain. We met a relief team from the Valley. We were rejoiced to see them.

Oct. 9. We had a snow storm. Were obliged to lay over.

Oct. 10. The mountains are covered with snow. It melted partly as it fell in the valley. We traveled 7½ miles. We had to make our fires with damp wood which made it very bad. Brother Woodruff's wagon tipped over – no damage. We crossed the creek seven times.

Oct. 11. We traveled three miles and camped at the foot of the mountains. We had dinner and then started for the top. The second division being ahead, we found the road very bad, but we made out to get to the top. We made seven miles and camped on top of the mountain.

Oct. 12. We took our teams and went down the mountain and helped the others up. We traveled down the other side of the mountain about nine miles and camped at the foot of another mountain.

Oct. 13 [Sunday]. We traveled and camped at the mouth of the canyon.

Oct. 14. Mrs. Delin had a daughter born last night. Brother Woodruff came up with us this morning and we all drove into the Valley of Salt Lake and camped in the Fort. It was rather a dreary home coming. It was very dry and dusty and the wind was blowing the dust in clouds. Only a few little log and adobe houses to be seen, fenced in with willow and rail fences. A few shade trees and fruit trees to be seen here and there. I thought at first, have I got to spend the rest of my days in this dreary looking place? But soon felt all right about it and love my mountain home. We stayed in the Fort for a few days and then Father moved his wagons up to Brother Wilford Woodruff's lot, caticorner from the Temple block. On the southeast corner of the Temple Block was a large bowery covered with brush where the Saints held their meetings and amusements. It was here that John Kay, Sara Kay, and Sophia and Esther Goodridge, and Clara Hardy sang the Resurrection Day, the first time it was sung in public.

BIBLIOGRAPHY

Arrington, Leonard J., and Davis Bitton. *The Mormon Experience.* New York: 1979.

Bancroft, Hubert Howe. *History of Utah.* San Francisco: 1890.

Bitton, Davis. *Guide to Mormon Diaries & Autobiographies.* Provo, Utah: 1977.

Brooks, Juanita, ed. *Not by Bread Alone: The Journal of Martha Spence Heywood, 1850-1856*. Salt Lake City: 1978.
————. *On the Mormon Frontier: The Diary of Hosea Stout, 1844-1861*. 2 vols. Salt Lake City: 1964.
Carter, Kate B., comp. "Goodridge-Goodrich Family Story." *Our Pioneer Heritage* (Jan., 1972): 253-304.
Cleland, Robert Glass, and Juanita Brooks, eds. *A Mormon Chronicle: The Diaries of John D. Lee, 1848-1876*. San Marino, Calif: 1955.
Cowley, Matthias F. *Wilford Woodruff*. Salt Lake City: 1909.
Crosby, Jesse W. "The History and Journal of the Life and Travels of Jesse W. Crosby." *Annals of Wyoming*, II (July, 1939): 167-219.
"Early Church Information Card Index." Microfilm, Salem, Oreg. Stake Lby., Church of Jesus Christ of Latter-Day Saints.
Forest, Hazel Hardy. "History of Sophia Lois Goodridge (Hardy)." Typescript.
"The General Epistles." *Our Pioneer Heritage*, 17 (1974): 385-532.
Goodridge, Penelope R. "Copy of a Diary Written by Penelope R. Goodridge in the Latter Years of Her Life." Mimeographed copy provided by Mrs. Aretha Hansen, Salt Lake City, Utah.
"Graves Along the Trail." *Our Pioneer Heritage*, 16 (1973): 421-76.
"History of Leonard Wilford Hardy." Typescript.
Jensen, Andrew. *Latter-Day Saint Biographical Encyclopedia*. 4 vols. Salt Lake City: 1901.
Morgan, Dale, ed. "The Mormon Ferry on the North Platte: The Journal of William A. Empey, May 7-Aug. 4, 1847." *Annals of Wyoming* (July-Oct., 1949): 111-67.
————. "Reminiscences of James Holt." *Utah Hist. Qtly.* (Jan, April, 1955): 1-33, 151-79.
Mulder, William, and A. Russell Mortensen. *Among the Mormons: Historic Accounts by Contemporary Observers*. New York, 1958.
United States Census, 1850 and 1860.
Young, Kimball. "Wilford Woodruff." *Dictionary of American Biography*, 20. (New York, 1936): 498-99.

An Overland Honeymoon ❦ Lucena Parsons

INTRODUCTION

It was on April 7, 1850, that Lucena Parsons wrote in her diary, "Oh, how long this day has been to me not seeing any one but strangers & no meeting place within 5 miles that we could attend. They say Sunday has not got here yet. . ."

Here was a young woman going beyond any horizon she had ever dreamed of — even beyond Sunday — all the way to California.

Her maiden name was Pfuffer. She and George Washington Parsons had been married on March 18, 1850, and the next day, Tuesday, March 19, she made the first entry in her diary. Lucena had been a school teacher in Rock County, Wisconsin, with Janesville as the center of activities. George, her new husband, was a farmer from Walnut Grove, Henry County, Illinois, right on the way to the Far West, not far from the Rock Island, Illinois — Davenport, Iowa crossing of the Mississippi. They spent March 23 in Henry County at "Glenns." Was Glenn a brother or some other relative, or just a friend? We don't know. Lucena was not writing her diary for readers 130 years hence, but for herself.

In other ways Lucena Parsons stays just out of reach of our probing historical sensor: For instance, we do not know her date or place of birth directly. We learn the date of her birth through her official death notice. The Oakland Public Health Office has supplied us with the "Mortuary Record" of "Parsons, Lucena, white, female, 83 years. 10 mo. 19 days" old. There is no birth date actually given. With the date of death on June 23, 1905, some subtraction

is in order. We challenge you to try it. At least we do
know that she was born in the year 1821, probably in early
August. That means that she was 28 when she was married
and started the cross-country journey in the late spring of
1850, and thus she was 30 when she arrived in California
a year later. Census records indicate that her husband was
several years younger.

Now as to her place of birth. All we learn from official
records is that she was born in New York State. There
is an intriguing reference in her June 25 diary entry made
somewhere along the Platte River on the Great Plains:
"We had a fine place to camp, it pleased so well I call it
Pleasant point & the creek Chrystal creek in memory of
my native home." This would indicate that her "native
home" was likely somewhere in the Catskill Mountains,
now a scenic state park in New York. In the Pine Hill
area there is a Crystal Spring, the water of which is so
clear and clean that it has been bottled and sent south to
New York City. There is also a Pleasant Lake and a
Pleasant View.[1]

It was in Oakland, California, out on San Pablo Road
near the bay, on the way to Berkeley, that George and
Lucena Parsons settled to farm in their new homeland.
He was labelled a "farmer" by the federal census takers.

We go to the same census records to learn about the
children. In the 1860 census there were three children
listed: Ellen, 7 years old; Marget, 4; and Charles, 2. The
1870 census listed the following: Ellen, 17; Mary, 13;
Martha, 10; George Washington, 7. Deaths had inter-
fered in family growth, a common picture of the experiences of many families during the 19th century.

The value of their property was given in the 1860 census
as $2000 in real estate, and $4000 in personal estate. By

---

[1] Alf Evers, *The Catskills from Wilderness to Woodstock* (New York,
1972), *passim.*

1870 those figures had grown to $76,000 real estate and $4000 personal estate.

The death of George Washington Parsons, Sr., was noted by an obituary in the Oakland *Tribune* on August 6, 1882: "George W. Parsons, who received fearful injuries by being thrown from his wagon against a car of an East Berkeley train on Friday afternoon died yesterday between 12 and 1 o'clock from the effect of his injuries." Lucena's own death is noted in the City of Oakland Mortuary Record, already referred to as taking place on June 23, 1905. She died of "Fatty degeneration of the heart."

We are grateful to the Department of Special Collections of the Stanford University Libraries, Stanford, California, for making the Lucena Pfuffer Parsons Journal typescript (M85) available. The typewritten copy was made by "E. and E. Wilbur," and it is labeled as copyrighted. The United States Copyright Office finds no record of such a publication.

The early part of the diary from Janesville, Wisconsin, to the Council Bluffs (Kanesville) crossing of the Missouri River (March 19-June 12, 1850) is not included in this transcription of the journal. We begin our record with the crossing of the river at Martin's Ferry on June 13, 1850.

THE JOURNAL OF LUCENA PARSONS

June 13 [1850]. Last evening Mr Hyde from Kanesville came down & organized us in a company of 50 wagons under the command of Captain Foote & this morning we are repairing as fast as possible to the ferry. We are crossing at Martins ferry 2 miles above Bethlehem. There is as much as both ferries can doe as there are some 700 teams yet to cross. They go in companies of 100 & are divided into companies of 50 & 10 & have captains over each division. All armed with rifles & muskits. Wether very hot.

June 14. To day our company of 50 waggons all got across the river & we are encampt a half mile from it. We shall probably get started in a short time. I had the pleasure of giving the chief of the Otoe tribe a loaf of bread, for which he was very thankful. He is a very fine looking man. He is called by his people the Buffalo chief. This aft we had a shower & it is still very warm.

June 15. The women are washing & baking to start Monday. It takes a great deal of fixing to get started where there is so much order observed. Each captain looks to his own division.

June 16. To day it is very hot & sultry & there are some complaining of the headache. I have the sick head ache to day. This afternoon we had preaching in front of the camp. There was an Indian chief visited my tent to day. I gave him some dinner & he gave me a knife. This is rare for them to give any thing away.

June 17. We started about noon. We were delayed in wating for some muskits which our captain went back to Kanesville & got. These were distributed among those that were destitute of them. We travelled only 3 miles & encampt on Three Mile creek. We are in 2 companies of 50 waggons. Our chief captains name is Wall, & the captain of our 10 is named Maughn. Very fine men.

June 18. This morning we started about 7 oclock

& travelled only about 4 miles. We were detained by crossing slews. They are very frequent so far. The company being so large it takes some hours to get over. We passt the road this morning that comes in to this 6 miles from the Bethlehem ferry. Saw severall teams on the road. Very warm to day.

June 19. This morning we had a powerfull rain. It commenced to rain just as we all had breakfast ready. We were obliged to lay over till near noon. This afternoon we passt the grave of a man that died the 15th of the dreaded cholera. His name is Warren. We travelled 8 miles & encampt on a small creek. Fine camping ground.

June 20. This morning we were hindered by the first 50. Did not get started till late. Travelled over a beautifull country. Passt 6 graves all made within 5 days & all died of the cholera. We met some waggons on the back trace. They had lost some of their friends with the cholera. This afternoon passt 2 more graves, they seem to be of the same company as the 6 who died. Encampt to night on the Weaving Water creek. Went 18 miles to day. Very warm wether.

June 21. We have been obliged to stop this morning to bury 2 of our company, the first to die with cholera. One man by the name of Brown & a small child. We have severall more sick in the company. We have made 15 miles to day & have been in sight of the Platte river. We encampt to night on the banks of Salt creek. Our company came up with another child dead. They buried it at twilight on the bank of the stream. The wether very hot.

June 22. This morning we have buried 3 more

children who had the cholera, they all belonged to
one family. We went about one mile then crosst Salt
Creek. While crossing it commenced raining very
hard & we had to wate some time. It was noon
before we started. Travelled very late. The worst
time we have had since we left the Missouri. Severall
sick. The wether damp & everything wet with very
little fire in camp.

June 23. Last night visited a very sick boy, son of
the first man that died. This morning started early.
Passt some beautifull country. All it wants to make
it delightfull is a little of the arts of civilization. It
has rained nearly all day. Encampt at 3 oclock on
what I call Mud creek from the nature of the stream,
having made 18 miles. The boy that was sick died
about noon to day on the way coming. These are
hard times for us but harder for the sick. Nothing
for their relief at all it seems. Still it rains. Very hot.

June 24. Last evening there was 3 more died out
of the same family. One was a young lady & there
was another child. The 3 are buried together 2 Spof-
fords & one Brown. Staid here all day & some of the
company did up there washing. It rained by spells
all day. Had a meeting in the afternoon to consider
whether it is best to travel in such larg company or
not. We are to remain as we are a short time longer
& then split if the sickness still continues. Passt 5
graves to day of people who had died in another
company.

June 25. We were again detained some 2 hours this
morning by the first 50 of our company. We have
campt near each other for the last 2 days. The roads

are very muddy as it rains every day. This morning
the mother of the 5 children that have died was
taken sick & died at evening. We had a fine place
to camp, it pleases so well I call it Pleasant point &
the creek Chrystal creek in memory of my native
home. We made 8 miles to day through rain & mud.
We had a dredfull time. It rained hard & some went
to bed without their supper.

June 26. The wether was cool & fine this morning.
Started early & travelled over a fine country. Passt
Black Oak grove in the forenoon. On the left of it
passt 6 graves & it seems very melancholy to pass
so many new graves. The sick in our company are
getting better. Met 5 government waggons, they are
from Fort Carny [Kearny] & are after lumber. We
have not seen an Indian since the first night after
we started from the river. Roads very crooked. Campt
on the prairie without wood or water.

June 27. Started in good season this morning &
travelled about 15 miles. Campt on the great Platte
bottom on a small stream. The timber we find here
is oak, elm, & bay. With such a fine rich soil to
grow on I should think it might grow higher. It is
only found on streams or small rills which we often
find are running from lime rocks. It is very small &
scrubby. Met 2 teams from Salt Lake. They said they
met the first emigrants at the mountain pass.

June 28. We have staid here all day for the purpose
of having a general wash as wood & water are plenty
here. The water is hard & we have found it so most
of the time. We have some very sick in camp to day
& one woman, Mrs. Crandall, was immersed twice

to day. It seemed to do her good. The wether is very hot. Rained last night. Some 13 teams from Woodruffs company passt here this forenoon but the rest are behind, all well too.

June 29. We had the hardest thunder storm last night I have witnessed in some years. Started on this morning & soon came to a very bad road, low marshy land. A little before we stopt at noon there was a woman by the name of Beal died. She was buried on the banks of the Clearwater, a fine stream about 10 miles from where we came on the bottoms. They immersed 3 in this stream for the cholera. Travelled 14 miles & slept on a high spot on the marsh for the night. Met the Salt Lake mail, they said they met 8000 teams when they got to Fort Laramee. Since that they have not kept count. Wether very warm.

June 30. We started this morning & had fine roads some of the way & the rest part very bad. Some hard slews. Travelled 14 miles. We stoped at night on the Platte river, the bottoms are from 8 to 10 miles wide. The river is about ½ mile wide here & runs rapid, the water very rily. I find plenty of wild flowers here, roses in abundance. Mrs. Crandalls daughter died to day. She is of the family who have buried so many. She was buried this evening besides 4 others on the bank of the river. They were some who had died of another company. Wether fine & cool.

July 1 [Monday]. Started early, travelled over a flat low strip of land with the river on the right & high bluffs on the left. The ground is covered with beautifull flowers, it looks like flower gardens. Travelled some 7 miles & came to an Indian town. It contained some 200 wigwams. They are made under ground, laid up with sticks & covered with earth. Some of them are larg & show ingenuity. The inmates have all deserted them & gone on a hunt. There are immense beds of sun flowers in this reagion, they look like ours at home. Passt 8 graves to day. The roads have been good, the wether fine & cool. Made 16 mile.

July 2. We started early & travelled over hills & dales all day. Reached the foot of Grand Island at noon. Here we stopt & buried a girl, daughter of Capt. Coon. She died before reaching this point. Here is a fine camping ground as wood & water are plenty & they are very scurce in some places. Travelled 18 miles in all & encampt near Table point as I shall call it from the nature of the bluffs running near the river. Passt 2 graves. Wether cool & fine.

July 3. Started in good season & travelled 15 miles. First rate roads & fine wether but some appearance of rain in the eve. Stopt at noon as our captain had left a chain behind. We stopt an hour & did not come up with our company that night. We campt without wood & one mile from water but good grass. Passt 6 graves, they most all died between 15 & 28 of June. There seems to be some division in our company. Some of them are so slow & some go too fast. Some sick.

July 4. Started early, travelled about 10 miles. Here we overtook our company & found the Captains ox was gone. We had to stop again & wate for them to go back & look for it. We went to washing as we had a fine chance, plenty of soft water from a slew.

The wether very hot. The boys that went back did
not get back to night. We were in hearing of cannon
at oald Fort Carny & it seemed like home. We are
all on the river bank & in sight of each other.

July 5. This morning the boys returned without
finding the ox & Captain Maughn with some others
have gone to look for it, they dont like to go on
without it & the wether is so hot it is impossible to
go far in a day. This afternoon saw 2 waggons on
the return. They had been as far as Fort Larimee &
were sick & their company went on. This afternoon
the men got back without finding the ox. The Indians
may have it, we hear they are watching us daily but
they are seldom seen. We saw some elk & some deer
but game scurce.

July 6. Started early this morning & travelled about
18 miles over a very poor country, grass light & dry.
Passt 9 graves 5 of them were children. Stopt at noon
on a slew. No good water. To night we are in sight
of Fort Carny. We are all well & our 10 have been
so far.

July 7. Got started about 8 this morning, we have
some lame oxen. Travelled 7 miles & reached Fort
Carny at 11 oclock. It is a pleasant place on the river.
They have 450 soldiers there now, cultivate some
land & have fine gardens. There are some 8 houses
built of wood, they get their timber from as far as
the Missouri river. Overtook 25 government waggons
bound for Larimee loaded with provisions. They have
125 yoke of oxen & carry 60 hundred pounds to a
waggon. Passt 5 graves, one of them an Indian grave.
He was buried in a sitting posture. The tribe here

is the Pawneese. Travelled 9 miles this afternoon
making 16 miles to day. Wether dry & cool.

July 8.   The same thing over & over again, nothing
new. There seems to be a sameness in the make of
the country. It is generally level with high bluffs
on the left & the river on the right. Travelled 16
miles & passt 6 graves. Campt to night with a ten of
Footes. They are sick.

July 9.   Our cattle still lame & we are not able to
go far in a day. Came to Plum creek at noon. Here
we found our company were some 3 miles ahead.
They had buried a boy of Lovells. He fell from the
waggon & broke his leg & died soon after. This is
the second child that has broke a leg and died soon
after. Footes company of 50 is camped on Plum
creek. They have buried 7 & have some more very
sick. Passt them & went on. The lame cattle travelled
10 miles. Passt 7 graves. Fine wether & roads good.

July 10.   Travelled 16 miles to day over a dry country. Passt 13 graves. Found water at noon for the
teams. Came near the river this afternoon then struck
off on the bottoms. Stoped at night without any wood
or water some 2 miles from the river. Rain this
morning.

July 11.   Started early this morning in the hope of
overtaking our company. We travelled about 18 miles
over fine looking country. Passt a good camping place
in the afternoon but too early to stop. We finally had
to camp without wood but we found some buffalo
chips which answer very well to boil tea & coffee.
We see some elk, buffalow, deer & antelope. Passt
18 graves to day, there seems to have a great many

died in June & mostly of cholera. Footes company camped near us to night. We had the most musketoes we have had. They were very very troublesome.

July 12. Last night had a hard storm, very warm this morning. We started out before Footes company & travelled slow on account of sick cattle. We were looking for a place to wate when a little boy of Captain Maughns, 3 years of age, fell from the waggon. The 2 wheels run over his stomach & he died in about an hour. While stoping the other company passt us. This is the first death in our 10. Saw three buffalow feeding on the bottoms. While stoping we found 30 head of sheep some one had left. We brought them on. Travelled 10 miles, found water by diging. Good wood one mile off. The cattle some better. Passt 6 graves. The wether cool & pleasant.

July 13. Started early this morning & overtook the company that passt us yesterday. We have travelled over a pleasant country to day, plenty of timber in sight all the time. Came to Cotton wood creek at 11 oclock. Passt on 3 miles to Ash creek & camped to wash & bake. Here is the best of grass & plenty of ash timber & river water which is soft. Passt 12 graves to day. We expected to have met Captain Wall here but they have gone on. Wether is cool & the health of the emigrants seems to be better. Went 10 mile to day.

July 14. We are obliged to wash & bake to last us about a week as there is no wood for 100 miles ahead. Formerly the emigrants have found flood wood here but there is none this year on acct of the high water this spring. The rain has also injured the buffalow chips. We have a beautifull place here, a fine spring of water & the place where we are is surrounded with trees of oak & ash. There was preaching this afternoon & severall baptized in the branch of the river.

July 15. We are again permitted to renew our journey. We are now in the buffalow reagion as they are seen by the thousands. They have the finest place in the world to live in. The country here is high bluffs & deep ravines in which there is plenty of cedar for them in winter. As far as the eye can reach these bluffs rise one above the other. Travelled 12 miles. Passt 13 graves. Came up with our company in the eve. Glad to see them & they so. They had killed 3 buffalow. There are larg amounts of prickly pears & mushrooms here, these look like the ones in the east.

July 16. We took our places this morning in our company & it seems like home again. We passt 3 graves. Travelled 18 miles over a very sandy country, the road is white sand. Met 3 teams from Fort Laramie. We have seen hundreds of buffalow to day. They seem to care very little about us, they will hardly move for the firing of a gun. There is also plenty of deer, elk, Antelope & wolves of the largest kind. Campt at night on one of the prettiest places imaginable & with plenty of wood. We are on the river bank. Wether fine and cool. Generally camp now in good health.

July 17. Still we are journeying on & in good spirits. We have some fine times with all our troubles. We have made 18 miles to day over a very dry country.

There seems to be plenty of saleratus, salt & larg beds of prickly pear & some smart weed[1] on this these bottoms. We have found fine camping places & plenty of fuel so far. Passt 19 graves, most of them from Missouri, they died in June & all are young men between 20 & 30 years of age. Wether still pleasant.

July 18. This morning the wether is hot, too hot to go far. We only made about 12 miles. Stoped some 2 or 3 hours in the hotest part of the day. The sheep seem nearly done over with the heat. We have passt some 12 graves & I am told there is a burying ground near here of 300 graves. If so it must be a general camping ground for near these I find the most graves. I see some painfull sights where the wolves have taken up the dead & torn their garments in pieces & in some instances the skulls & jaw bones are strewed over the ground. Feed very poor what we find is on the river in low places. Wether dry as yet.

July 19. Started early & pushed on as fast as possible to reach the ford which we learned from a company of men on the back track was 8 miles ahead. Those men had 4 waggons. They had had some trouble & were going back to Missouri. Reached the ford & found 30 waggons on the ground to cross. There was 80 with ours. We had good luck & all got over in half a day & all camped together at night. The feed very poor, not much to be seen but white sand hills. I find dry soda on the bank that I can scrape up. This is the south fork of the Platte. The river is shallow & 1 mile wide.

---

[1] Smartweed would have been any plant whose leaves give off a sharp, stinging material that causes irritation upon touch.

July 20. We found this morning that most of our cattle were gone. They left in search of grass as there is none here. The man that went to look for them returned about 10 oclock with a part of them. A party of horsemen went in search of the others & some of us went to washing as we could not leave here to day. About noon Capt Footes company came up. They all crosst sefely over & campt with us. In the eve the men came back having found all the cattle. Late in the eve we had some rain.

July 21. We again are pursuing our teadious journey. For the first 3 miles it was up hill then we came to a ridge. This extended to Ash hollow & when we came to it we found ourselves on the top of a high hill, precipices & deep ravines. In these ravines & on either side of the bluffs are trees growing in crevises, ash & red cedar. It is the most romantic place we have seen yet. The hollow is some 3 miles long when it widens as it nears the river. In it I found wild grapes, cherries, gooseberries, & pepper mint herbs & good springs of water. Passt some 6 graves. Wether fine.

July 22. Here we stopt to wash & bake & take on wood to last us over the sand hills which are ahead. We are now in a very different looking country from the one we have been in. We are now again on the main stream of the Platte & it is very pleasant in many places. We are now in the Sous [Sioux] & Sian [Cheyenne] country. There are none of them on the road this year. There are 20 graves in & around this hollow. The fork empties in near here.

July 23. We have started again this morn. In good

spirits & hoping to get through to Larimee in 12
days. Left a company of 50 waggons on the ground
to repair a waggon. Passt some fine sights to day
among the hills. The water has washed them in all
forms. Some resemble pulpits & others look like hay-
stacks. All look fine. Travelled 18 miles. Passt 12
graves, one a man of 84 years old. We meet teams
most every day, some on the back track, others for
the government.

July 24. Wether very hot & dry & we can not hurry
much. Passt the Castle rocks this morning, so named
by their appearance. We are travelling near the river
all this week. In some places the food is very poor.
It looks as though there had been either a freeze or
a burn. We passt 13 graves, the graves on this side
of Ash hollow have not been disturbed. We cross
many dry streams, some of them 8 & 10 rods wide.
Made 13 miles. All well.

July 25. We have been travelling in 2 tens, that is
we have 21 waggons, since we left Ash hollow. We
find that small companies get along better where
there is a scurcity of grass. There is no wood. This
afternoon we passt the ancient bluff ruins on the north
side of the river. They look like castles & fortifications
gone to decay. We are some miles off but we could
see them very plain. They are infested with rattlesnakes I am told. Passt 14 graves. Travelled 22 miles.
Crosst a fine creek & camped on the river. Good grass.

July 26. Wether is very hot & dry but we travel
at a good rate. To day came in view of a splendid
looking sight, like a stone castle. Did not go near
it as we learned it was 5 miles off the road. It is 300

feet high & composed of pipe clay. Passt 13 graves. Travelled 20 miles with beautifull country before us. Game not plenty. I find wild locust & worm wood in abundance. Grass very good at the camping places on the river banks.

July 27. Did not start till late on acct appearance of rain. Went 1 mile, it rained, we stoped till afternoon. Started again. Fine cool travelling. Came opposite Chimney Rock which has been sight since yesterday. It has been seen 30 miles off on a clear day. Three of us went to it. I was struck with amazement at the grandeur of the scene. It is large at the base & then runs up some 300 feet, the last 100 feet is nearly square & in the form of a chimney in the top of a round tower. We found thousands of names engraven in every place up & down its sides. There are similar hills in the vicinity. Some look like churches with spires & others like houses. In front is a small lake. Travelled 10 miles. We campt on the river bank.

July 28. We currelled last night opposite the most splendid scenery we have met with on our travels. They are sand hills intermixt with rock or a hard substance resembling rock that rise & tower over the other like splendid mansions with numerous chimneys rising to a great hight. They are called Scotts Bluffs & extend from Chimney Rock to Pony creek, a distance of 30 miles. It rained this morn & we did not start till noon. Went 12 miles, passt 7 graves, campt in a pretty place on the river. No wood but good grass. Wether pleasant & cool this eve.

July 29. Started early this morn & travelled over beautifull country. No grass or water till we came to Trading point. When within 6 miles of the point met 3 mewl teams from Fort Larimee. They told us it was 50 miles to the Fort. It seems like home again to meet so many on the road. We did not look for it in this wild country. I found the skull of a man by the roadside. I took it on & buried it at the point. There is a blacksmiths shop here for the accomodation of emigrants kept by a french man.[2] Here are a number of stick huts & I am told they keep a good assortment of dry goods. We could find no grass till we went severall miles. Here the whole 50 waggons met & campt. The rattlesnakes are very thick here. Good water. Wether fine & cool.

July 30.   Started late this morning on acct of trading camp where cattle & horses are traded. The men have squaws for their wives & when our men were there the women were making mince pies with choke cherries & buffalow meat. Travelled 12 miles & campt on Pony creek. No wood. Saw plenty of Indians to day, they camp with the traders. They seem very harmless, do not beg but want to swap their mocasins for some bread. They say nothing about whiskey. Grass is light & dry except where we camp, there it is good. Passt 5 graves. Soon after we campt had a hard wind & some rain. Part of the company went on. All well.

July 31.   Fine morning. Did not start early on acct of lame cattle. Some of them get gravel in their hoofs & others have sore necks. Roads are very rough in some parts. Came to another trading post this afternoon. They have a house made of bricks dried in the

---

[2] The "french man" was Antoine Robidoux, a well-known trapper. J. S. Holliday, *The World Rushed In* (New York, 1981), p. 166.

sun. They are the couler of clay. Passt 13 graves. Travelled 18 miles & campt on the river. We carry wood with us from one wooding place to another & by using economy we have plenty. The river water is very rily but it will settle.

August 1 [Thursday]. Travelled 15 miles. This brought us to Fort Larimee which we were glad to see as here we crosst the Larimee fork of the Platte. The main river is also near. The Fort is built on the Larimee fork some 1½ miles from the river. We had not trouble in fording it the water being low, though there have been 5 men drowned here this spring in crossing their teams. They were carried down by the current which is very swift even now. We passt a camp of Indians to day that have the small pox. They have it very bad & many of them have died. We saw one squaw dead under a blanket & her papoose wailing round her sick.

August 2. This morn went to the Fort to get some blacksmithing done but could not they have so much work. This is a very pretty place to look at, it is so clean. The Fort is commanded by a Major Anderson,[3] he is a fine man. There are 250 soldiers & some 12 families. They have a saw mill, one publick house, one store. They hold goods high & work is also high. They offer for carpenter work 60 a month & find them, & a woman to cook 20 a month. Flour is 18 per hundred & whiskey 8 per gallon in the emigrants store. They are now building severall fine frame buildings. They say there have 75 thousand pass here this

3 Fort Laramie was commanded at the time by Major Winslow F. Sanderson of the Regiment of Mounted Rifles. Robert A. Murray, *Fort Laramie* (Fort Collins, Colo., 1974), p. 75.

season & some days there were 1500 here. There was some sickness among them & some deaths. There are hundreds of waggons left here which can be bought for a few dollars each from the soldiers. Started about 10 & went 9 miles. Passt 6 graves. Roads very sandy, one bad hill to come down. Campt on river wih rest of the company. Wether dry & very dusty.

August 3. We stoped to let the teams rest here to day & the men went to work & burnt coal to doe their own blacksmithing. They have a bellows & anvill & are now busy preparing to shoe the cattle as their hoofs are wearing out with driving over the gravelly roads. The women are baking, washing, cleaning, & repacking waggons as they do when we stop. We have plenty of good grass & water & are in sight of the Black hills which we expect to begin to ascend soon after leaving here. Had a wind & sprinkling of rain this afternoon & heard distant thunder.

August 4. In front of our camping ground is a high & beautifull rock with many names carved on the front side. I find none but strangers though I have searched for familiar ones. The soldiers are hawling long logs by here. They find timber in the mountains. We are in sight of Larimee peak, a high black hill. Wether very dry & hot.

August 5. Still we are here. The cattle have good feed & the men are shoeing them & setting waggon tyres & getting things ready for a hard road which we expect for the next 100 miles. There has not an Indian been round here though they are plenty round Larimee. They all have fine ponies & larg horses. They will not sell them for money but will trade them

for coffee, sugar, or blankets. There is no wild fruit
on this road except choke cherries & black currants.
These are plenty & doe well to make pie of. Wether
very hot.

August 6.   Started his morn & concluded to take
the river road in preferance to the Black hills on acct
of grass which we hear is not plenty on the hills. In
4½ miles we came to a warm spring, next passt a lime
kiln & then crosst Bitter creek, little water in it. At
noon we crosst Dry Timber creek, good water. Went
16 miles & passt 6 graves. The road has been up &
down hill all day. Campt on a small stream. Poor
grass. We now find plenty of wild sage. Wether very
hot & roads dusty.

August 7.   Started early & have travelled over beautifull country on acct the Black hills. We are among
them & I like them much. They rise very abrupt &
cover the whole country. The reason of their dark
appearance is their being covered with low pines.
There are larg beds of bachelor buttons, marygolds
& china oysters [asters] all along this road. They are
the same appearance as the tame ones in our eastern
gardens. Passt 2 graves. We are now geting into a
healthier climate. It seems a pity to see the amount
of property that is left on this road, waggons & cattle
& various things. Travelled 18 mile. Wether fine.
We have good clear spring water & plenty of wood
& good grass to night.

August 8.   We have travelled some 45 miles without
seeing the river. Came to it again at noon. Here are
beautifull hills. I went to the highest & found beauty
stones of all coulers, some white, some clear as glass.

Went on. It rained a little & we stoped in a fine spot of grass. The road runs in a valley some miles. Here the sage grows some 4 feet high, the stocks 4 or 5 inches through. In the last few days we have seen the heads of larg buffalows killed by the company before us. We also see many Elk horns by the road side. Went 12 miles. Campt on a dry creek. Some springs, good water & no grass. Wether pleasant.

August 9.   Started early to find feed for the cattle. This article is getting scurce in many places. Went 16 miles over a hilly country, saw no graves. Here are many dry creeks on the banks of which are the finest kind of choke cherries, they are black & sweet. There is another kind of berry sour as currents, they are the bulb berries & are plenty on the banks of these creeks whether with or without water. Came to the La Bonte & campt on it.

August 10.   We found a company campt here & got plenty of buffalow meat from them as they had killed 2 larg ones. Started early this morn & travelled 19½ miles over hills & hollows. Some of the rocks looked as though they had lately been piled up in a careless manner. Passt 3 small creeks, mostly dry & came to the La Prela [Prele]. We campt on its banks & had good water.

August 11.   Started early, went 4½ miles & came to Box Elder creek. Near here Capt Maughn lost an ox, it droped down in its yoke & died. This creek runs rapid, very bad to cross. Not much grass here. Went on again 4½ mile & came to Fourche Boise. Here found 2 companies campt. Went up the river 2 miles & found good grass, wood & water. Passt 5

graves. This river is 30 feet wide & 2 deep. Here
the cherries & the black currants are plenty. Here
the men saw a larg bear since we got here. Rained
this afternoon.

August 12. This is a fine cool morning & many of
the women are washing & baking as usual when we
lay over. Some of the men went on a hunt but returned without seeing any game. They went down
in the tall canions of the mountains & found tall pine
trees, some 200 feet high. There are now severall hundred waggons within 30 miles of each other. Feed
very poor. We had a powerfull rain this eve. Camp
all well. Many bever dams across this river. Have
seen some bever.

August 13. This morning we packed up to start
but concluded to stop here another day to doctor
lame oxen. A company of us went up the river some
2 miles & found the finest kind of black & yellow
currants in abundance. We spent the day very pleasant
in rambling over hills & vallies. At the south mountains reared their black heads & on the north the
river glided noiselessly along bringing gladness to
man & beast for on its banks they were fed & in the
stream they quenched their thirst. We returned at
eve laden with plenty of the good things of nature,
thankfull to the river of all the good things of this
wild country & I find comfort though in this wilderness.

August 14. Started early & travelled 4 miles to the
North fork of the Platte. The river is clear & rapid
with a fine growth of timber on the bank. We came
to Deer creek in 5 miles more. Plenty of fish & grass

here. Passt 2 graves. Went 15 miles. Wether pleasant. There have some 10 head of cattle died in our company caused by eating too many choke cherry leaves & the cherries.

August 15. Started late this morn on acct of the slothfullness of some of the company we are with. Left them & came on alone, 8 waggons of us. We feel there is no time to be lost. Came to Muddy creek, then on 5 miles to Crooked Muddy. Went 5 miles more, crosst a dry creek, came to the river & found Capt Wall there. Stopt & staid all night. The whole 100 waggons & another 50 waggons campt near here. It is a fine place. In the evening they all met & had a ball. The grass is the best we have seen since we crosst the north fork.

August 16. Staid here to day as Capt Wall thought it best to stop & recruit our teams. We staid but were not contented. Passt the day in washing & baking. In a whole company of 150 waggons I have no heard of any sickness except a little diarrheea. We do not see any Indians & we are mostly out of the buffalow reagion. Some of the co went on a hunt but killed nothing.

August 17. Started this morning for the upper Platte ferry & ford, it being some 9 miles to it. Came to a green spot of grass at noon & let the teams eat. It commenced raining & thundered hard. It cleared up & we went on again. Crosst the ford without any difficulty & went down the river some 3 miles. Rained before we got to the camping ground. We have had lightning every night for 2 weeks without rain. One of the co lost an ox to night.

August 18. Started late on acct of rain, went 9 miles over a new & hilly road & came to the Mineral creek which comes from a mineral spring up on the oald road. We are on the river to find wood, grass & water as there is none on the bluffs road at this time of year. Campt on river, it still rains & the wether is very cold, the wind in the north. On the opposite bank are high mountains that look red. There is supposed to be Iron ore & coal beds in abundance in this region. Saw 10 Californians on the return. One of them came to our camp. The news very good from there.

August 19. Still detained here on acct of rain. It rained incessantly all last night & this morning. It looks very gloomy. When it stops for a few moments the mountains seem to smoke. There are campt near us the 10 Californians. They have been there one year, made a fortune & glad to get back home. They say some 200 miles this side of there they found men without food eating their horses & mewls. One young man rather than eat his horse plunged in the river & drowned himself. There are also with the Californians men from Fort Larimee in search of deserters this season. Still rains & as cold as winter.

August 20. It cleared up & we started about 10 oclock. Found very bad roads the first 6 miles. We then came to the oald road again & found this better. Went 2 mile & came to the Rocky avenue where there are high rocks on both sides of the road. It is beautifull. In 2 miles came to a mineral springs & swamps. These are very poisonous & many have lost nearly all their teams by letting them drink the water & eat the grass. In 4 miles more found good water &

surrounded with willow. Went 4 miles more & campt on a slew. Some grass, no wood, but wild sage which is a good substitute for wood. Some water here. Passt 1 grave to day. Wether pleasant but cold. We have seen many dead oxen & some horses to day.

August 21. This morn found our cattle all gone. The men went back & found them on Willow creek. Started late, only travelled 6 miles. Came to Greese wood creek. On the bank is a kind of a shrub something like cedar or low hemlock & the whole covered with thorns. This is the greese wood. Campt in a pleasant place, no wood, poor grass, but plenty of sage & good water. Passt 1 grave & many carcasses.

August 22. We have been in sight of the Sweet Water mountains since Tuesday. This morn 2 of the men went on a hunt & returned about 10 having killed a fine buffalow. We were detained till afternoon to secure the meat. Started, left the main road & followed the creek down for grass. Came to Sweet Water river, campt on it & jerked our meat. Passt 2 graves. We have had 2 nights of snow & frost.

August 23. Started early & are now to the Saleratus ponds. The ground is covered with a thin coat like frost for miles around on both sides of the river. We went to severall ponds & found the late rains had injured the saleratus, having covered it with water. The men had to go in & cut it up with spades in some of the ponds. These lumps look like ice & when it is dry on the banks it looks like snow banks. In a dry time it can be obtained very easy & very nice it is, one half the strength of the common saleratus. Went 6 miles & came to Independence rock. This rock in

shape looks at a distance like a steamboat. There are
many names on it both painted & chiselled, many done
on July 4, 1850, this year. It is very larg & high composed of gray granite. The river is within 4 rods of
it. Went on 5 miles & passt 5 graves. Campt on the
river. Wether cold & pleasant.

August 24.   We are stoping to day to have a hunt.
The grass not very good & dry cedar to burn by
going up in the canion for it. Two miles back passt
the Devils gate. This is where the river passes through
perpendicular rocks 400 feet high forming a gateway
from one valley to another. These mountains look
very singular, they seem to set up edgewise & are
all cracked apart. They are hard granite. Two grisly
bears were seen on top of these hills. There have been
many killed by the emigrants, some of them weighing
from 7 to 15 hundred pounds. There are no buffalow
here. The reason of the river being called the Sweet
Water is on acct of the saleratus in it. We are now
among the Sweet Water mountains. Clear & pleasant
in the middle of the day but cold at night.

August 25.   Started late & travelled 9 miles. Struck
the river & campt for the night. Good grass. It is a
desolate looking country, not much vegetation but
greese wood & sage. The valley of the river is some
10 or 12 miles wide bounded on each side by high
mountains. The game is sage hens & ducks, deer, elk,
antelope & hare. The flies & bugs look different from
what they did in the east. No Indians on the road since
we crosst the north fork of the Platte. We have been
in the Crow Indian territory. This side of the creek
there are no berries. There are larg flocks of crows,

they have good living this year there being so many carcasses. Wether cool this evening.

August 26. Started early, went 19 miles. Crosst the river twice. Saw 6 graves. Crosst Sage creek & on the bank saw the grave of a young man dug up & his body nearly eat up by wolves. Campt on the river, a fine place & good grass.

August 27. Started early & have some lame cattle which hinders some but we are able to go from 10 to 12 miles. Rained a little & very cold. Passt 2 graves. Forded the Sweet Water 4 times to day. Came to it at night & campt. Very poor feed it being an oald camping ground. The road to day passt through some very romantick places. Cold rain this evening.

August 28. Left early, came to Ice springs at 10 & here let the teams feed. These springs are on a low swampy spot on the right of the road. Ice may be found here at all times by diging 2 feet. There is lime & alkali in abundance here & many cattle have died suddenly by drinking this water. There are 2 alkali lakes near here & more springs. Road very heavy to day, steep bluffs to ascend & descend. We forded the river & campt. Passt 1 grave in a very pretty spot. Many waggons in sight of us. Plenty of willow & some grass, clear water. Travelled 15 miles to day.

August 29. Travelled 8 miles to day over fine country. Forded the river once. The road wound through beautifull vallies & the river moved noiselessly along in its solitude with here & there a grove of willow on its banks. There seems to be plenty of fish in its waters. There are many difficulties to encounter on this road such as sickness, death & a great loss of property. Since we left Fort Larimee we daily pass much abandoned property such as waggons, horses, oxen, cows, chains of the best kind, & stoves, all destroyed. Camped on the river. Found some currants. Wether cold but pleasant.

August 30. To day travelled 17 miles & soon after we started we crosst the river. The reason of fording so often is to avoid the high bluffs. On the top of the highest hill we ascended saw 2 beautiful lakes with plenty of ducks in them. Next came to Quaking Aspen creek & in 2 miles more came to a fine poplar grove on a side hill on the left side of the road. Next came the Sweet Water, crosst it & went on 2 miles to Willow creek, a fine stream. Camped on its banks, plenty of grass, wood & clear water. Passt 2 graves & some beautifull locations, it being a fine country. Wether pleasant. Roads hilly & gravelly.

August 31. After leaving Willow creek we rose a long hill & then had a beautifull road. Went 4½ miles, crosst one branch of the Sweet Water. Went 7 miles more & passt the Twin mounds, 2 pretty mounds near the road. Came to the Sweet Water but did not cross it. We leave the river here & from here to the south pass the road is broad & fine as any turnpike. See snow in the mts & the hollows. Came to Pacific springs & campt. Passt 7 graves to day. We went 17½ miles.

September 1 [Sunday]. Started early & went up the Pacific creek 2 miles. It being Sunday & our teams tired we lay over to rest. The south fork forms a divide between the Atlantic & Pacific Waters, the streams on the east side of the pass run nearly east & on the west side they run s w. This pass, as it is called, is nothing uncommon in appearance. Its altitude is 7085 feet. Here we find alkali on the surface, plenty of it. Poor water, some grass, no wood. Met a company of American soldiers from Oregon on their way to Fort Leavenworth. They all had Spanish mewls. Wether pleasant.

Sept 2. Did not start till 2. The boys went on a hunt & killed several hares & sage hens. The hens are good at this season, late in the fall they taste of sage. There are no buffalow this side of the pass but deer & antelope in abundance. In 2 miles we left the oald road & turned to the left. This is a new road made about 10 days ago to find food & shun the gravelly road. Went 10 mile, crosst the Dry Sandy river. Water in holes brackish & not good. Camped on a low spot, no wood, not much grass. Roads sandy & wind swept.

Sept 4. Started again this morn ourselves & teams much fatigued with travelling so late. Went 8 miles over heavy roads & reached Big Sandy. These rivers are rightly named for look which way you will they are sandy. Reached here at noon. This is a fine stream about 7 rods wide. Water clear & very good. Some willow & grass. Here we found severall companies of merchants taking goods to Salt Lake. They have 40 waggons, severall loads of them stoves. Yesterday the mail going from Fort Bridger to Larimee overtook us. There is a great deal of travel from one fort to another. We are now in the Snake territory of the Indians.

Sept 5. Our company left us this morn & went on. We stopt to wate for a cow as many on this journey are obliged to do or lose many of their cattle. At noon there came up 3 waggons & stopt for the night. Wolves very thick here.

Sept 6. Those wagons went on this morning & left us alone again. Rather lonely for one waggon to stop in this dreary place. Saw no one all day, the emigration mostly going up on the oald road some 3 miles above here. A short distance from here on the river is a natural lime kiln, plenty of lime rock. Wether warm & pleasant.

Sept 7. We went after berries & black currants which are very plenty on the banks of this & nearly all the streams in this reagion. These currants grow as larg as the Inglish cherries at home in the east & are as black as the cherry when ripe. They are sweet & make very good pies. Came home & found the cattle gone. We were in a fine fix so far from help.

Sept 8. The men started at daylight in search of them & found them near where we had left the cow some miles back. They found some one had taken her on so they came back & made preparation to start very early in the morning as there is no use stoping any longer.

Sept 9. Started early, went 8 miles, came to a bend in Big Sandy, did not cross it but left it on the left hand. In 6 miles came to the Green river, the most beautifull stream I ever saw. The water is very green & runs very swift over a smoothe bottom covered with pebbles. Plenty of tall timber on the banks. Crosst over without any trouble, went 5 mile up the stream & campt. Made 19 miles. Passt 3 graves.

Sept 10. With the morning we toiled on again. Travelled 15 miles without wood or water, nothing but dry sandy hills. In the eve came to Black Forks. Camped alone. This stream is some 4 rods wide, clear water & swift current. Plenty of willow & grass. Made 18 miles to day. Wether cold.

Sept 11. Started early & in 3 miles came to Hams Fork, a fine stream & staid here till noon. Made 5½ miles & came to Black Forks a second time. Here we camped in a pretty place with hills on the right & left, all of them green as coperas.

Sept 12. Started on again & in 1½ miles crosst Black Forks. After this we found a rough road for 10 miles & no water. Crosst Black Forks the 3 time but found no place to camp. Went 2 miles & came to Black Forks for the 4 time & campt. It being an oald camping ground we found poor grass. Wether pleasant. Made 15 miles.

Sept 13. Again we were on our way at an early hour. Found some rough roads & a very cold day. By hurrying all day we reached the stream that runs through Bridger & campt 2 miles down the stream. Saw some 200 Indians on horse back riding at full speed. It commenced raining before we reached a camping place. Made 14 mile to day.

Sept 14. This morning we had some rain which hindered us till noon. On the way to Fort Bridger passt 1 grave & crosst 3 rushing creeks. It cleared up but the wether is very cool. We travelled 8½ miles & campt on a small creek this side of Fort Bridger. The Fort is composed of 4 log houses & a small enclosure for horses. I think it is a beautifull spot. There are many Indian huts in sight & the land is very rich.

Sept 15. Left Bridger at noon. Went 6 miles & passt a good spring on the right side of the road. There is some timber here & a little grass, but the country here is hilly & rough. We camped at the foot of a hill on a small creek. Wether clear & cold. Travelled 8 miles.

Sept 16. Started this morning & soon began to decend to lower land by a steep & teadious rout. We then came to Muddy fork, here is some bunch grass & plenty of willow. There is now a fine pleasant valley before us & on the left some beautifull white mountains interspersed with green. I left a flag on the highest one. On the left of the road at the foot of the hill is a coperas [4] spring. We then climbed a high hill, 7315 feet, & half way down this we camped. Good feed but water scurce. Made 10 mile. Wether pleasant.

Sept 17. Started on early & met the U S mail. Here are lots of service berry bushes on the hills. We next passt down a narrow ravine & for nearly 5 miles the road winds among high mounains till we arrive a Sulphur creek at the bottom of the mountain. On the left is a sulphur spring & a little above it is a bed of stone coal. At the foot of the bluffs after

---

[4] One would think that a copperas spring would contain dissolved copper salts. As a matter of fact, the light green dissolved salt is ferrous iron sulphate.

we crosst the creek we found a fine spring of good water. One mile south is an oil or tar spring covering severall rods. Here are many curious places. We left this beautifull spot, went 1¾ miles, crosst here & stoped. Current very strong. Travelled 14 miles.

Sept 18. After leaving Bear river we crosst a small ridge, then we travelled down a nice narrow bottom where is plenty of grass & severall fine springs of water & many small snakes. At the bottom of this valley are some very singular rocks. It appears sublime to me to see these rocks towering one above the other & lifting their majestick heads here in this solitary spot. Oh, beautifull is the hand of nature. I hate to leave these beauties but must on. Camped between 2 high hills. Made 11 miles to day. Wether cool & pleasant.

Sept 19. On our way yesterday we passt the Cache Cave in the hills on the right of the road & not far from it. The mouth is a fine arch some 10 feet in sight & 20 in width. Many a weary traveller has there left their names. It is not very roomy but is pretty inside, the walls being white & smoothe. We crosst Echo creek often while travelling down this canion. Campt one mile from the water & travelled 16 miles to day.

Sept 20. This morning crosst the Red fork of the Weber. I imagine this river takes its name from its coming down among these red hills, for they are all as red as new burned brick. This river is good to cross. Plenty of timber on both sides. As we strike the river there are 2 roads. One is Pratts new pass, but we kept the oald road which turns to the right

& passes up a high ridge & then down to Canion creek. Passt down this & began to ascend the highest mountain. Camped half way up. Made 18 miles.

Sept 21. Started early & had a very steep mountain to climb. We then began to decend & passt down the canion that leads into the valley of Salt Lake. While going down this canion we crosst a small creek many times & passt many teams loaded with merchandise that were stalled for this is the worst road we have found yet. We reached the mouth of the canion about 4 oclock & came to the city of Salt Lake in the evening, it being 5 miles from the canion mouth. Travelled 12 miles. Pleasant wether. All camped. Very tired.

Sept 22. We had a good feast to day, Sunday, on potatoes & green corn & other vegetables & we think we never saw as good before having so long been without. The wether is very hot & dry. Most of the Californians emigrants with us went on to day. We shall stop here till spring. Our cattle are tired & so are we & by stoping we shall all rest.

Sept 23. This morning Capt. Maughn started for Tooele Valley, about 35 miles west of the city & south of the head of Salt Lake. They say they are making settlements there this season to make room for the Mormon emigration. They are also making settlements north & south. What was formerly supposed to be little Salt Lake proves to be a saleratus bed or some thing of the kind.

Sept 24. We left the city this morning & started for Gardners Mills which is about 15 miles up the Jordan. Here my men found employment for a while.

[Gap in the diary from September 25, 1850, through January 28, 1851.]

Jan 29 1851 [Wednesday]. We stopt some 6 weeks in Gardners mills. About the last of October there was a company starting for Williams ranch. We thought we would go with them for by this time we began to learn some thing of the Mormons & thought there was as much comfort on the road for us as living among a set of pirats. We went to the city for the purpose of getting ready to go with them but there came up a snow storm which lasted 2 days. We then gave up the Idea of going & concluded to try & tough it out till spring. We hired a room as good as a common hog pen east & paid 5 dollars per month.

I will now give a description of the situation of the city of Salt Lake. It is located within 3 miles of the mts which enclose the east side of the valley, within 3 miles of the Utah outlet & 22 miles from the great Salt Lake. This valley extends from Bear river north to Utah lake mouth, a distance of 120 miles. The Salt Lake extends from a point a little south west of the city to about 80 miles north, forming the N W boundary of the valley. The valley is surrounded on the west, south & east by high mts. There is a stream of good water comes from the mts east of the city. At the upper part it divides in 2 branches both of which pass through the city to the Utah outlet.

The valley is from 30 to 75 or 80 miles wide. The soil is good in many parts of this country & is well adapted to the raising of wheat but too frosty for corn & beans. On the whole the valley is a good place to live in were it not for the Indians & wolves. They are very troublesome. Cattle & sheep have to be herded here the year round to protect them from the wolves & the California Lion. There is a great deal of wind & dust here in the fall but very little rain. Consequently they have to irrigate their crops about 3 times a year. This is attended with a deal of trouble for they have to ditch for miles. Their wood is getting scurce. What they have comes from the many canions & it is very difficult to get in these in the winter on acct of snow which falls so deep there. There is a great deal of cold wether & frost even in summer & in my heart I wish them no better for a meaner set lives not on this earth than those very people calling themselves Latter day saints. And I am bold to say that an honest person can not live 6 months with them without saying the same. I know many instances where they have cheated men out of a whole winters work merely because they did not belong to their church.

Who could belong to such an unprincipled sect as these Mormons. They live like the brute creation more than like white folks. I know many men who have mothers & their daughters for these so called spiritual wives let the number be what it may. Oald Brigham Young for one. Archibald Gardner for another & Capt Brown for another & many more I could mention but it is too mean to write. These demons marry some girls at 10 years of age. For instance a man will take a mother & her daughters & marry them all at one time & perhaps he has persuaded her to leave a husband with whome she has always lived happy, or be damned. She believes it for perhaps he is one of the heads of the church & in this way many respectable families have been ruined. This I know to be true. What will become of these men the Lord only knows. I have had the opportunity of knowing many of the women that are called spiritual wives & among them all I never saw one that seemed the least bit happy, but on the other hand they are a poor heart broken & deluded lot & are made slaves to the will of these hellish beings who call themselves men. All the preaching & teaching that is heard in this valley is obedience to rulers, & womens rights are trampled under foot. They have not as much liberty as common slaves in the south.

Brigham Young has some 70 women it is said. Heber C Kimball has 50, Doctor Richards 13, Parley Pratt 30 or 40, John Taylor 8, Capt Brown 8, & in fact all the men who have but one are looking out for more. If when they have got them they would use them well it would be better but far from it. They fight & quarrel & the women leave one man & go to another. When a woman wishes to leave she goes to Brigham & gets a divorce & marries another & this is the way things are going all the time.

[Gap in diary.]

Feb 18 [Tuesday]. We have finally started again for California after spending a long dreary winter among the Saints. The road runs north to Bear river. Three miles from the city we came to a hot spring that boils up out of a larg rock. The water is hot enough to boil eggs in 5 minutes. The road runs near Salt Lake. We saw many ducks. Travelled 8 miles & camped.

Feb. 19. Last night it snowed a little & this morning the wether was cold & dreary. At noon passt a settlement called Sessions, a very pretty farming country, high mts on the right & Salt Lake barrons on the left. There is but one waggon & 4 of us, my Coz, D. Wilcox,[5] our friend H Bentz,[6] my husband & myself. Travelled 12 miles & camped alone. Wether cool.

Feb 20. Started on slowly our cattle being weak. Feed poor & roads very rough & muddy. We begin to find better feed the further north we go. There has been more snow south than north this winter. Camped at Nolins to night. Travelled 8 miles. Very cold.

Feb. 21. Started early, the wether more pleasant. We reached the Weber river at evening & we are now 40 miles from the city. Here the Californians meet to organize & go on as soon as spring opens.

[Gap in diary.]

March 31. We stoped here 6 weeks to recruit our cattle & get more teams to go on with. While here we took in a man & his wife by the name of McCoy.[7] They are fine folks. We now have 2 waggons & 5 yoke of cattle & think we can go on if nothing happens.

April 1 [Tuesday]. This morning we packed & started. Crosst the Weber. Browns fort is situated near the Weber river on the north side. We next pass Ogden

---

[5] There is no other identification of "Coz" (Cousin?), than this one as "D. Wilcox."

[6] So far unidentified.

[7] The McCoys are unidentified. It is difficult to identify those who have common surnames without knowing the given name or some other fact.

fort, this is built on the Ogden river. Stoped here all night. Travelled 6 miles. Cold.

April 2. One of our cows went back to Weber so we lay over here for a day.

April 3. Started on this morning with a company bound for California. Travelled some 8 miles. It rained & we camped.

April 4. This morning started on & reached Box Elder river. On the way we passt severall hot & salt springs. From Weber to Box Elder is 20 miles. Here we stop untill a sufficient company comes up.

April 9. To day there has come up a company of 22 waggons. We at once organized & chose a captain by the name of Davis.[8]

April 10. Started this morning for Bear river. Fine roads & the wether pleasant. We had a pleasant view of the surrounding mountains & the Salt Lake. Stoped at noon at a larg spring. Made 12 miles to day. It is good to be on our way at last.

April 11. Reached Bear river at noon & prepared to cross over as soon as possible as the river is on the rise. It is rily & rapid & some 3 feet deep. Crosst over with little trouble. Found the other companies had all gone on some 8 or 10 days. We found a paper warning Californians that the Indians had been troublesome. Made 8 miles. No wood here but willow & grass poor.

April 12. We have decided to stop here to day in hope of more companies coming. We have but 54

---

[8] There are Davises galore. This one is not identified.

men & we think this is a small number as we have
heard that the Indians are getting very bad on this
road, on acct of small companies going on late last
fall. They took one company of 13 men, killed them
all, & carried the women off on the Yellow Stone
river & tried to sell them at Fort Hall.[9]

April 13. No companies appearing we started on.
Had to go 10 miles up the Molad [Malad] river
to cross as it is a bad stream. Not wide but deep,
in some places 6 feet. Met with a company of men
from Fort Hall going to Salt Lake to buy provisions.
Reached the Molad & camped. Sage & grass are
plenty here & there are plenty of sardines in this creek.
The men caught many & they are fine. Wether good.

April 14. Went down the west side of the stream
to the oald road & passt on 2 miles further. Found
a small rivulet coming from the mountains & good
grass. We are now heading the Salt Lake. There is
still snow to be found in the ravines. Travelled 12
miles to day.

April 15. Started early & went on to the Blue springs.
Stoped at noon. Plenty of grass but no water. In the
afternoon saw an Indian on a white horse watching
at the left of the road. Later saw 2 antelopes. One
of the men killed one. The Captain divided it among
the company. Made 12 miles. Wether warm.

April 16. Travelled over a dry sage plain. No feed
or water till we reached Hansells spring, a distance

---

[9] There were many wild Indian tales prevalent along the trail. John D.
Unruh, Jr., quotes Madison Moorman, an overlander, as using the term
"Madame Rumor" to describe the tales. Most of them were not true, or
only partly so. *The Plains Across* (Urbana, Ill., 1979), p. 175 ff.

of 12 miles. This water is better being fresh, but feed is rather light. Saw more Indians to day. This evening is rainy & windy & some thunder.

April 17. Rained this morning. We travelled slowly as the going was not very good. Came to Deep creek, crosst it, the crossing not good because of high banks. Followed it down 6 miles towards the sink. We found good feed & sage for fuel. Rained a little again this afternoon. We saw Indians at a distance. Here we lay over to wash & bake. The company all well. Made 12 miles. Wether cool morning & evening.

April 18. Stayed here all day & did up washing & baking & unpacked our waggons & aired our flour & other things. This necessary to be done often on this journey or the flour is injured by heating. The wether is rather unsettled.

April 19. Left Deep creek this morn, went on 10 miles & came to Pilot springs. There are 2 lone springs in a desert place. We saw 7 Indians on ponies. They wanted powder from us but we did not give them any. Went 2 miles to camp but found no water so had to go back to the springs & pitch for the night. It rained hard.

April 20. Started late, went 3 miles & came to a spring of good water on the left of the road. We then turned to the right & had a long hill to ascend. In 3 miles came to Oregon creek & stoped for dinner. Went on again 9 miles & came to Caplus creek. Found good grass & wood & water. Passt 2 graves to day. It appears the Indians have been very troublesome to the company before us. We found a dog belonging to the Indians. Made 15 miles to day. Some rain & cold wether.

April 21. Started early & turned to the right round a mountain road. Came to the Decassure river at noon & campt for the night as the grass is good. It rained nearly all afternoon. At the right hand of our camp, on the opposite side of the stream is a cave in the rock. I did not go to it because of the wether. Made 7 miles.

April 22. Some of the company crosst the stream this morning while others preferred going round the foot of the high mountain. Both ways are bad as the river has to be crosst twice & a bad crossing. The mountain road is rocky & riddling. At noon one of the company broke a waggon. We stoped near the City [of] rocks [or Cathedral Rocks]. Some rain, wether cold. We made 5 miles.

April 23. Last eve went to the City rocks. They are at the junction of the California & Salt Lake roads.[10] They are white & about 300 ft high running up to a peak. They are composed of a substance resembling salts & are in a state of decomposition. A few more years & then will be leveled with the ground. They look at a distance like a ruined city. Left here this morning & found a rough hilly road. We are now climbing Goose creek mts. Came to the east bank of Goose creek & camped. Saw the bones of a man dug up to day.

---

10 The route they followed from Salt Lake City to join the California Trail was known variously as the Salt Lake Road or Cutoff, or sometimes as the Deep Creek Cutoff. George R. Stewart, *The California Trail* (New York, 1962), p. 205.

April 24. Followed down Goose creek all day. Very pleasant. We stopt at noon in a nice bottom. Went on a few miles, found a good place & camped for the night. Feed good, plenty of water, & willow for fuel. Some very bad roads to day, some miry & bad hills to go over to save crossing Goose river. Made 15 miles. Wether pleasant.

April 25. Left Goose creek about one mile back & came to a small creek in the afternoon. Camped as the feed is middling good. This eve the company voted to lay over here one day. This afternoon saw an Indian who had been killed by the emigrants before because he had killed a mewl. We see writing on bones every day stating the deeds of the Indians. Made 12 miles to day.

April 26. This morning early there were Indians discovered near our cattle. The men ran out with guns & they passt on. We were all busy at washing & baking. About noon a company of 7 Indians rode up & in plain sight drove off 4 head of our cattle. Our men pursued them & the Indians shot back at them. As 2 of the cattle did not run fast enough to suit the savages they shot them & went on. One was a fat cow. The owner later dressed it & sold the beef. Our men followed the Indians till night but without success. They fled to the mountains. Some rain this afternoon. Wether warmer.

April 27. Started on to day much chagrined to think we were obliged to let these savages go unpunished. We found a rocky road all day as it followed up a canion creek, in many places high mts on both sides of the road. These were covered with dark cedars

making a capital place for Indians to run off & secrete
themselves & their plunder. Came to Rock spring
which rises among rocks. Wether warmer. Made 12
miles.

April 28.   It is 4 miles from Rock spring to Mountain spring. the water good but grass poor. We then
went 2 mile over hills & came to an alkali spring
which is very bad for cattle. We have been travelling
on a bottom this afternoon where the Indians not
long ago made an attack on 10 men & killed 2.
Camped on an alkali creek. No feed. Made 14 mile.

April 29.   Started early & in 6 miles came to a small
creek of good water & some good grass. Here we
stoped some 3 hours to let the cattle eat as they were
hungry not having had much for 2 days. We have
passt 15 graves since we started but none made this
year. Those killed by the Indians are buried off the
road. We crosst Warm creek this afternoon, then 8
miles to a spring on the mountain side where we
camped. Made 16 miles.

April 30.   Went on this morn through a canion some
3 miles. We expected to see Indians as it is a good
place for them to hide among the cedars. At noon
came to a very pretty bottom, good grass but no water.
Passt 2 graves. Came to the best creek of water yet
found, the head waters of St Marys river, the river
runs S W. Camped. We have 16 men on guard every
night. Made 12 mile. Wether pleasant.

May 1. [Thursday].   This was a fine May morning,
not a cloud to be seen. Came to some wells at noon,
good water. Soon after we started we discovered there
were 2 Indians following us so we watched them.

The men drove them off to the mountains. Camped early to repair a broken waggon. Crosst a small creek. Poor grass with much saleratus in it. There are high mts on the left covered with snow. Made 16 miles. The wether good.

May 2. Started down stream again. Found much saleratus & some very miry ground. Came to the main stream of St Marys river in the afternoon. Water high. We went one mile below to find a crossing. We made 10 miles. Wether warm.

May 3. This morning we repaired to the river & made 3 ferries to cross with waggon beds & boxes. Carried the things over by hand, then fastened ropes to each waggon & towed them over. Drove the cattle over loose. Had good luck, no accident. Dried & packed the waggons & went on 7 miles. Camped near the river. Passt the grave of a man killed by Indians. Pleasant wether.

May 4. Started as soon as it was daylight to find feed. Went 2 mile & stoped & cooked breakfast & fed the cattle. This is a beautiful place. Here we saw a bone stating that Indians had run off 27 mewls & horses. passt 8 graves. Crosst a stream, very gravelly bottom & not deep. Made 16 miles.

May 5. Pleasant morning & fine roads. Saw 8 Indians armed with rifles on the hills. All on horse back. They took off to the hills. We stoped a few minutes at noon on the bank of the river which is larg & deep at this place & very rily. Wind & dust bad all afternoon. We have some sick oxen. The company all well. Camped & the men shot severall wild geese. Made 18 miles. The willows are beginning to leaf out, the banks are covered with these trees.

May 6. Went on a few miles & came to a canion. Here the road leaves the river again & runs among a chain of hills all day. Came to the river bottom & camped. Wether cold, a west wind. Good feed, clear water, & sage for fuel. Made 20 miles. It is 86 miles from this crossing on St Marys river.

May 8. After going some 8 miles the road left the river & went among more hills. We saw a notice where Brays [11] company had passt along this road the 30 of April. Found no water till near night then we got to some good springs in the canion. Camped here as it was late. Some of our company very much afraid of the Indians. It has been dusty to day & rough roads. Made 15 miles.

May 9. Had high hills to cross this morn but came to the river in 6 miles. Near here one waggon upset but no damage done. At noon we came to a road that crosses the river. We kept the right hand road over the hills again. In the aft we had some rain & snow. It was very cold & windy. Came to a good spot of grass & camped near it, one mile from the river. Made 20 miles.

May 10. This morn was snowey & rainy & very cold. Started about 10 & came to Stony point, the prettiest place I have yet seen. Many rose bushes on the bank, also high willows. We are now 128 miles by the guide

---

[11] John Grandin Bray traveled from Missouri to California and became a prominent businessman and banker in several locales. Daughters of the Revolution of California, *Genealogical Records of the Families of California Pioneers* (San Francisco, 1938), typewritten, copy at the Calif. State Lby., Sacramento, VI, p. 935.

from the crossing of the Marys river to Stony point. We have travelled all day on a sandy plain, plenty of greese wood. Came to the river & then camped. Made 14 mile. Some warmer.

May 11. Rained a little this morn, then cleared up & we started at 9. Passt 3 graves of men killed last season by Indians. The mts on both sides of the river are covered with snow. The bottom is from 15 to 20 miles wide here. We are travelling near the river & crosst one bad slew. Stopt on the river at noon, good grass. We then travelled N W over a saleratus plain, no grass. We turned off our way to camp & found middling food. Made 20 miles. Wether better.

May 12. This morning the company voted to lay over here for to day. Some were dissatisfied & hiched up to go on & could get but 4 waggons to go with them. They gave it up & took their places again in the company. The blame was laid to the Captain. The company came together & chose a new one, a Mr Lewis.[12] All well suited. Stopt here all day. We have some sick cattle owing to alkali. It is very plenty here. Feed poor & wether cold.

May 13. This morning at 3 oclock 2 Indians came creeping up to the mouth of the currell. They were quickly seen by a guard & followed a short distance but they disappeared in the tall sage. All the camp got up but no more was seen of the Indians. We started on at 8 & had fine roads. Crosst a larg saleratus bed; then went round a bend in the river. We found good grass. Made 20 miles. Wether cold but more pleasant.

---

12 Unidentified.

May 14. Started as usual at 8 oclock & travelled N W to head a mountain. Just before we stopt at noon there were 2 men came up with us from a train behind of 14 waggons. In their company they have 35 men & only 2 women. All are well. In our company we have 21 waggons & 77 persons & 140 head of cattle & 17 horses. Crosst on the larg saleratus bed, following a ridge around a slew. Came to the river & camped. The company behind came & camped near us. Made 18 miles. Warmer.

May 15. Started early & found a good road part of the way this forenoon. Stoped at noon & the back company rolled up as we were about to start on again. We found some of our friends among them from Salt Lake City. Mr Comstock [13] brought us a letter from the east, the mail got in to Salt Lake after we left. All well at home. The other company will lay over here to day We went on & in the afternoon found heavy roads with deep sand. We are near the river. Came to a good spot & camped. Made 15 miles. We are over half way down the river. Saw 2 graves.

May 16. Started early. We still find sandy roads winding among the hills. Sometimes it seems as though we were coming to the end of the road. Stoped at noon & 3 waggons remained to come on with the company behind. Found better roads this afternoon. The valley is some 30 miles wide. Came to the river crossing. Here there is a sage plain. Made 18 miles. Some rain & not very good grass.

---

[13] Could this have been Henry Thomas Paige Comstock, who later discovered the Comsock Lode not far west from where they were at the time of this meeting? George D. Lyman, *The Saga of the Comstock Lode* (New York, 1949).

May 17. Started about 8 & at 11 came to a fine spot of grass. We stoped 2 hours & then started again. Passt 5 graves & many dead oxen & horses that died last year. At 4 we passt some good feed but did not stop. Nothing but sage & sand as far as the eye can reach. At 8 we turned down to the river. It was dark when we came to camp & we had a steep bank to decend. Found some grass. Had a hard drive to day but made 25 miles. Some appearance of rain.

May 18. Some rain last night in the valley but snow on the mountains. Cold this morn. Elected Captain Davis again this morn as we have been 2 days without a captain & things go bad when we have none. All things being settled we moved on at 9 & had a long sand hill to go up. We then made the oald road. Saw more dead animals & destroyed property this forenoon. More than we have seen before. Found another long sage plain with many sandy bluffs to cross. Came to the river & camped early. Made 10 miles. Rained a little.

May 19. It rained all night. Cleared up & we started at 10. Our road lay over sand till noon. A little before noon we met a company of factors, 8 in number, from California with the U S mail. We went on & at eve came to the big meadows on the spread of the Humboldt river. We found plenty of grass to day but not first rate. Made 18 miles. The wether pleasant.

May 20. This morning we moved down about 5 miles to make hay for the desert. Rained a little to day. Here we find hundreds of dead animals & lots of stoves & all kinds of iron works where the emigrants lightened their waggons to take on grass & water.

Made 5 miles. We are now some 40 miles from the desert & there will not be much feed till we get over it. Here we have to take on water also as the water below is impure. Plenty of rushes & good grass here. We baked our bread & made the best preparation we could for crossing the far famed & dreaded desert.

May 21. We moved this morn towards the Sink of the river. There seems to be plenty of grass some miles down the spread. We left it & went to the right & drove through some high bushes. We saw 5 Indians. We then came on a saleratus bottom. Not a spring of green for some miles, nothing but sand & alkali. Late in the afternoon came to where the river forms a lake. There is not a spear of grass on it & the water is brackish. Went down a few miles further & came to the last slew. Found some grass. The water is good at this time of the year but very little greese wood. Camped. Made about 18 miles.

May 22. We did intend to go on the desert this afternoon as we are but 2 miles from it, but a man lost a cow & this morning went back to look for it. We moved on 2 miles & camped on the Sink, the most beautifull spot on the rout. We are on a high ridge lying between the lake & the Sink. The surrounding waters & high sandy mts look splendid, and then around the Sink is a beautifull green. Far back on the road we came the level ground is as white as a new scoured floor, the sun is shining out in all its splendour to cheer this solitary spot. In the summer they say there is but little water here & no grass at all. At this place lies a poor dead squaw & her child killed by some one.

May 23. This morn we crosst the last slew & went

some 2 miles & camped. Here are plenty of wild
oats, the cattle like this feed first rate. Stoped till
3 oclock & then stared on the desert. In 12 miles we
crosst little mounds as thick as they could stand.
From these we came to a saleratus bottom which was
very smoothe. In 2 miles we passt many many carcasses
of oxen & horses. I counted over 100 of them. After
we got over the saleratus bed we stoped & eat supper
& milked the cows. We then went on again till 3 in
the morning. We then stoped till it was daylight. Fine
cool morning.

May 24. This morning at 9 we reached the Carson
river. This is a fine swift stream, good water but no
grass where we strike it. The last 10 miles of the desert
is very sandy. It is 40 miles long & it is estimated that
2400 cattle & horses have died on it. The last part of
this desert rout is covered with the reck of waggons
& other property of all kinds. There are some fine
carriages standing in good order for rolling on. We
all got over without losing an animal. Went up the
river 3 miles & found some grass & camped. The men
& cattle are glad of rest. We saw 6 graves, 2 at one
end & 4 at the other end of the desert.

May 25. Some sick cattle this morning. The Captain
thought it best to move on 3 miles. We did so & found
a nice green & camped. Some did up a little washing,
the water is so soft. The feed is middling. We had a
high wind in the afternoon & evening & the wether
cool. The company behind rolled up & passt us.
They had good luck crossing the desert. One mile
from where we left the desert we met a company
of packers coming from California. They started the
10th from Sacramento.

May 26. Started at 7. Left the river in 3 miles &
turned to the right & went over some stony bluffs,
the river in sight some of the way. Found a bad
road it being over stony ridges & many hills. We
came to the river at noon & camped for the night.
The cattle must rest. The grass middling & the banks
covered with lofty cotton wood trees. Snakes very
thick on this river. Made 12 miles. Passt 2 graves.

May 27. Left a big part of our company behind,
some 7 waggons of us starting at 7. Went on a few
miles & found good grass in a very pretty place.
We had a heavy sand road all day. Went over a
flat bottom some 10 miles down the river. We then
rose a bluff, turned to the left round a mountain &
came down to the river again. Camped. Good grass,
wether warm but windy & dusty. Plenty of cotton
wood. Made 26 miles.

May 28. Our company passt us last night. We started
on this morn & went 5 miles to the river. Here we
left it for a short distance & went over a high stony
bluff. Came down on the bottom & found a company
of gold diggers in these hills. They have been here
a week & are making 3 to 5 dollars a day. We all
camped here. Made 6 miles. A windy afternoon.

May 29. There are now 3 companies stoped here to
prospect for gold. All ready some 200 have packed
over from California to prospect. The men from our
company all went to work this morning in a canion
fronting to the East. Most of them returned without
finding any gold. Water is scurce but gold is more
so yet. We find we can not cross over the Sere Nevado
[Sierra Nevada] mountains till June. We heard that

San Francisco nearly burned down this spring, also that times are good there in California. Very high winds this afternoon. We are 25 miles from Carson valley.

May 30. I had a great desire to see the gold diggings so I went out this morning, with my men folks & the rest. The diggings are in a rough rocky canion on the west side of the Carson river. We went up the canion some 3 miles & passt many at work washing gold. They take a pan nearly full of sand & stones & shake it & in the meantime pore off the water & the stones till they get it all pored off but the gold, this sinks below. I washed a little & got a little gold. Wether pleasant.

May 31. This morning the gold fever raged so high that I went again to dig with the rest but got very little gold. Some are doing well in their mines. One man found a lump worth 19 dollars to day. This encouraged others to try their luck. Some make 5 dollars, others more, & some less. Came home tired to night. Still in good spirits. Very windy afternoons here.

June 1 [Sunday]. There are many packers here from California in these mines. They are called the Chalk hill mines.[14] Some are out there working to day but others are resting in their tents & waggons. It is a very poor place to spend a Sabbath. Nothing to see but the river & red mountains towering high above the clouds. At first these were very pleasant to look

---

[14] Later the workings associated with Chalk Mountains or Bluffs would produce wealth from auriferous gravels using the hydraulic method. Erwin G. and Elizabeth K. Gudde, *California Gold Camps* (Berkeley, 1975), p. 66.

upon but a repetition of these sights becomes tiresome. The wether pleasant.

June 2. We again went to the canion to find that bewitching ore that is called gold. We had better luck in finding it to day, my husband & I making 16 dollars in fine dust. I have 2 cows which give a fine mess of milk & milk is 15 to 25 cents per quart & butter from 50 to 75 cents per pound. I sell both & this brings in some money, too. We are all anxious to make all we can after so long & so hard a journey. The company is well.

June 3. This morning there was a general turn out to the mines. Some go up the canion as far as 4 or 5 miles while others go up one or 2 miles. In fact it is alive with diggers from the mouth up. There are some 3 companies of French from California here digging with the rest. Some of the young men from our company have started over the Sere Nevado. They were impatient to get over to where gold is more plentifull. We made 10 dollars to day.

June 4. This morning severall of our company rolled on to Carson valley, 25 miles from here. There is plenty of grass there & clover. The greater part of the emigration this spring are recruiting their teams there. We went to the canion again & did very well, made some 8 dollars to day. It is very hard work to dig & wash sand. The water is failing fast. In July the water is all gone from this place.

June 5. This morning Reese, a merchant from Salt Lake City, came up. He had some 16 waggons, mostly loaded with flour, to supply Carson valley. He stoped near our camp. We went to the canion as usual &

made about 8 dollars again. This is better than doing
nothing as some say we can not cross the mountain
pass till July 15. This is a long time to waste. The
wether pleasant.

June 6. This morning Reese rolled on to Carson
valley & more of our company with him. We went
to the diggings & I found a lump of gold worth 5
dollars & 4 in fine gold. The two of us made some
14 dollars to day. But we are beginning to be tired
of working in the water & the mud & we think of
going on soon. The diggings seem to continue to hold
out good in some places. It rained this afternoon.

June 7. I did not feel well to day & therefore did
but little. This evening there came a man from Carson
valley & said there was a company going to try &
dig through the snow & the prospect was we could
cross the Sere Nevado in a few days. We therefore
made up our minds to go to the valley & recruit our
teams & cut hay to last us over. There are 60 miles
to go without grass at this season, on acct of snow.
The wether pleasant.

June 8. [Sunday]. This is a warm sultry morning
& I hardly know how to spend the day. There is no
place of worship to go to & no new thing to read,
so I spend part of the day in bed & the rest in thinking of home. When awake or asleep I am dreaming
of same. The evening I visited the other company &
found some of them preparing to leave in the morning.

June 9. This morning we bought us a larg milch
cow with the gold we had made here. We paid 55
dollars for her. Then we yoked up & 6 waggons of

us rolled on for Carson valley. We found a very rough rocky road for 10 miles. We then crosst Chalk hill, which is white but not high. Went a few miles further & came to the river & camped. Made 12 miles. It rained & thundered a little.

June 10. Started on again & reached Carson valley in the afternoon. We had a very heavy sandy road over a sage plain till we came to the river again. There are many high mountains covered with snow around this valley & these are covered with the tallest of pine & firs. In some places they run down to the valley. These mountains are of a whitish surface creased here & there with a canion creek coming into the valley. We made 10 miles to day. Wether cool but pleasant.

June 11. We have a fine camping ground with plenty of tall grass which the cattle are eagerly trying to dispatch. They eat a while & then lie down to rest. This morning some of our company went to the station 4 miles away to find what the news is of crossing the pass. While they were there the company returned that had been to make a road & reported the going impossible for 3 weeks at least. They said they nearly froze & that it snowed incessantly. A Mr States [15] is at our camp to get signers to a petition to Congress for redress of wrongs done to the emigrants by the Mormons in Salt Lake last winter. It was unanimously signed by all the company.

---

[15] There were several persons named States who settled in the San Francisco Bay Area and were mentioned in the *Alta California* newspaper of San Francisco. William N. States' death was announced in typical brief fashion by the *Alta* in its Jan. 15, 1875 issue.

June 12. Wether warm & some rain in the afternoon. Mr. Coffin went to the station & picked out a camping place for the company.

June 14. Some of our company are trading their cattle for mewls & preparing to pack over. Wether pleasant but windy.

June 15. This morning some of our company started over, among them my Coz, D Wilcox. They go by way of the George Town cut off when they have crossed the mts. There are packers coming over from California often. Some bring groceries & liquors to sell to the emigrants. They say times are good there this spring.

June 16. Severall waggons left here this morning but we could not find. . . .

[End of the Diary]

Index